● 漢 ● 語 ● 教 ● 學 ● 名 ● 家 ● 講 ● 壇 ●

漢語教與學必備： 教什麼？ 怎麼教？ 繁體
（上）什麼篇：語用與語法走廊

Chinese Essentials:
What and How (Volume One)
What: A Functional and Grammatical Walkthrough
(Traditional Chinese Edition)

■ 傅海燕 著 ■

北京語言大學出版社
BEIJING LANGUAGE AND CULTURE
UNIVERSITY PRESS

（京）新登字157號

圖書在版編目（CIP）數據

漢語教與學必備：教什麼? 怎麼教? 上，什麼篇：
語用與語法走廊/傅海燕著. – 北京：北京語言大學出版社，2007.5
ISBN 978-7-5619-1869-2

Ⅰ.漢…

Ⅱ.傅…

Ⅲ.漢語－對外漢語教學－教學研究

Ⅳ.H195

中國版本圖書館CIP數據核字（2007）第068228號

北美地區售書獨家代理: 美國希望教育基金會
Executive Agency in North America: Hope Education Foundation
www.hope-edu.org Tel:1-800-341-7983

書　　　名：漢語教與學必備：教什麼? 怎麼教? （上）
　　　　　　什麼篇：語用與語法走廊（繁體）
責任印制：汪學發

出版發行：北京語言大學出版社
　　　　　BEIJING LANGUAGE AND CULTURE
　　　　　UNIVERSITY PRESS

社　　址：北京市海淀區學院路15號　　　郵政編碼：100083

網　　址：www.blcup.com

電　　話：發行部 （86-10）82303650/3591/3651
　　　　　海外部 （86-10）82303080
　　　　　編輯部 （86-10）82303647
　　　　　讀者服務部 （86-10）82303653/3908

印　　刷：北京新豐印刷廠

經　　銷：全國新華書店

版　　次：2007年5月第1版　　2007年5月第1次印刷

開　　本：787毫米×1092毫米　　1/16　　　印張：23.25

字　　數：427千字　　　印數：1-3000

書　　號：ISBN 978-7-5619-1869-2/H.07088
　　　　　05500

目 錄
Contents

A. 語音——漢語拼音 Phonetics—Hanyu *Pinyin*   *1*

I

4. 國家/人/語言　Country/People/Language　*73*

7. 行爲與事件　Actions & Events　*118*

8. 愛好/選擇/責任　Hobby/Preference/Obligation　*132*

9. 評議行爲　Evaluating Actions　*143*

13. 叙述與詢問　Telling Stories—Narration and Inquiry *186*

14. 疑問句　Questions *198*

18. 名詞組　Noun Phrases　*238*

19. 度量衡　Measurements　*248*

20. 比較　Comparison　*251*

21. 指路　Asing and Giving Directions　*263*

22. 指令　Giving Instructions（Orders，Directions）　*285*

Haiyan Fu has been teaching Chinese to speakers of other languages at postsecondary institutions since 1982 and teaching high school for the last eight years. She is currently teaching all levels of Mandarin Chinese at Northside College Preparatory High School in Chicago. In 2003, she was selected to appear in the Annenburg Foundation production "Teaching Foreign Languages K-12: Putting the Standards to Practice." Fu is a trainer in the U. S. Department of Education's Teacher-to-Teacher Training Corp; a writer for Chicago Public Schools' Project MAJIC, a U. S. Department of Education-funded effort to develop K-12 curricula for Chinese and Japanese; an AP Chinese textbook reviewer for the College Board, and has been president of the Midwest Chinese Teachers Alliance since 2000. In 2006 she was elected as a board member of Chinese Language Association of Secondary-Elementary Schools.

Fu has a Master's Degree in education from Smith College, and an Ed. D. from the University of Massachusetts at Amherst, specializing in second language acquisition, instructional leadership and curriculum development. She is certified in Chinese, English, ESL, Language Arts and Bilingual Education in the State of Illinois.

傅海燕自 1982 年開始在中國及北美大學從事對外漢語教學。1999 年開始在芝加哥高中教授漢語。2003 年傅老師的課堂教學被選入 Annenburg 基金會與美國外語教學協會委托波士頓電視臺録制的課堂教學示範系列,作爲培訓中小學外語教學師資的樣板。2004 年加入美國教育部資助的芝加哥公立學校漢語日語教學大綱編寫小組。2004 至 2005 年審閱伊州中文教師資格考試框架設計、內容與評分;2005 年開始爲全美大學委員會審閱中文教材。自 2000 年起擔任美國中西部中文教師聯盟主席。2006 年被選爲美國教育部教師對教師培訓計劃的培訓員、美國中小學教師協會理事會理事。

1989 年獲史密斯學院教育碩士,1996 年獲麻州大學教育學院教育博士。主要研究課堂教學教法及課程設計與發展。持有美國伊州初高中的中文、英文、英文爲第二外語、雙語教學及語言藝術等科目執教證書。

致 謝
Acknowledgements

After 26 years of teaching Chinese to non-Chinese language speakers, I have accumulated some classroom experience that I wish to share with other teachers. However, I would never have thought about writing anything down if it was not for the encouragement and support of the following people.

My husband, Kenneth Kocanda, urged me to take on this project and helped to edit the book. Without his continuous support and countless hours of work, this book would not have been possible.

Several people gave me feedback and suggestions. The contribution of these three friends, colleagues, and partners on many projects was instrumental in this particular book. Their generosity in sharing their experiences and opinions as well as the encouragement to make this book a reality is a testimonial to their friendship and professionalism and will always be cherished.

Dr. Yu, Hongwei translated the segment of Questions and Answers and compiled the List of Measure Words and the Usage of "duo."

Jane Lu contributed to the early idea of this book and cooperated with me to begin this project.

Dr. Yvonne Lau, who has worked with me on many projects, and given me suggestions on styles of writing and discussed concrete examples of classroom practice with me.

Special gratitude goes to Golden Yuan for believing in me and giving me technical support to publish this book.

I dedicate this book to all my students and their parents, especially those who granted me permission to use their work in this book.

Acknowledgement of Permission:

Student Work (1999 to 2006 Northside College Preparatory High School)

"What" and "How"
"教什麼" 與 "怎麼教"

In Chinese we call teaching — "教書," which literally means "teaching book." Traditionally, a language teacher comes to class with a textbook and student workbooks. The teacher teaches according to the book and students learn from their books. This kind of practice would be convenient if there were books fit for all classroom situations. The reality is that in the United States, Chinese as a world language in the K-12 classroom is an emerging, fast-growing and ever-changing phenomenon. Students of Chinese language are a very diverse population with regard to age, grade levels, needs, language backgrounds and learning styles. Instructional conditions vary in terms of class size, contact hours, intensity of instruction and the availability of equipment and materials, etc. Professional development for teacher preparation and training is inadequate. There is no teaching material that is one-size-fits-all. An effective classroom teacher must have an effective teaching practice to cope with these challenges. Many teachers have organized teaching and learning materials based on the needs and characteristics of students with the goal of making classroom practice more practical than just "teaching books." This is a good practice. This is true teaching: 教學 vs. 教書. This kind of practice should not be used out of desperation but out of necessity.

　　"Teaching" 譯成中文常常成了 "教書"。按照字面的意思譯成英文 "教書" 就成了 "teaching book"。傳統的教學方式就是老師照本宣科，學生在練習本上做功課。這樣的做法本可方便課堂教學，前提是有一本教科書能滿足所有課堂教學的需求。在美國，目前漢語在中小學課堂作爲外國語教學雖起步不久，但發展迅速。學生的來源及情況十分複雜。學生的年齡、年級、需要、語言文化背景、學習方式方法都不同；班級人數、授課時間、教學強度、教具和教材的裝備不一。教師的培訓不足。沒有一部教材是萬金油。要想教得好，就得找出好的教學辦法迎刃而上。很多老師早就開始根據學生情況，針對教學的需求，自己組織上課用的材料。這才是對路的教學：是"教學"而不是"教書"。這樣的教學不應是出於不得已，而應是必需。

This series is designed to facilitate true teaching. It aims at reflecting and encouraging a break from traditional practice by combining language materials, teaching references, and instructional design into a single series for easy, quick and solid practical use.

編這套書的目的就是要輔助這樣的教學。反映并鼓勵這種打破傳統的教學辦法，把教學的素材、教學參考資料和教案設計集中在一起。使教與學的索引，參考、運用簡便，省時，實際。

This series endeavors to face two essential questions for a teacher of K-12 world language：

What do I teach in a K-12 world language classroom?

How do I teach in a K-12 world language classroom?

這套書試圖面對中小學（幼兒園至 12 年級）漢語作爲外國語教學課堂教學的兩個根本問題：教什麼？怎麼教？

Let's consider these two questions in simple and realistic terms.

我們一起用簡單而現實的語言來探討這兩個問題。

"What"
"教什麼"

We expect young learners of Chinese to become world citizens and lifelong learners.

作爲教師，我們期望我們的學生能成爲世界公民和終身學者。

Language is a tool of communication, and thus, we teach learners a new communication tool. We teach interaction and good manners. We teach to develop high proficiency in Chinese.

語言是交際的工具。我們教我們的學生新的交際工具。教他們與人交流和交流的方式方法。教他們發展交際的技能。

Language is part of culture, and represents and reflects the world views and customs held by the people of a culture. Therefore, as language teachers, we teach learners a new perspective on life experience that is different in many ways from their own. We provoke curiosity and nurture respect and love through achieving understanding in another language.

語言是文化不可分割的部分。語言代表并反映不同文化中人們的世界觀和風俗習慣。在教語言的同時，我們介紹給我們的學生新的、與他們自己不同的對待人生的看法和角度。我們通過了解另一種語言引發好奇，培養尊重和愛。

Learning a foreign language is something with which most young learners have no experience. In addition to teaching a language, we teach learners how to learn something that is challenging and unfamiliar. We impart knowledge and skills so that at a young age, learners can discover a new world through studying a world language and discover their own strength in learning. We foster diligence and work ethic, and teach them develop knowledge and learning skills.

在課堂上學習外國語是學習一個對大多數幼小學生來説完全陌生的知識領域。我們教給他們怎麼學具有挑戰性的科目。我們傳授知識和方法。讓孩子們通過學習一種新的語言去學着探索新的世界，發現自己的能力和長處。我們培養勤奮和上進。我們教他們學會知識及學習方法并鍛煉學習能力。

"How"
"怎麼教"

A language teacher's job is to make the learning process easy, fun, and to make learning make sense to learners. We try to engage learners in this long-term, effective and fruitful endeavor.

教師的職責是將學習的過程和學習的内容化難爲易，做到寓教於樂，使

V

學習觸類旁通。通過這樣的教學理念與實踐讓學生致力於長期、有效的努力中。

Making learning easy, making it fun, and making it make sense are correlated. If something does not make sense, then it won't be fun, thus it won't be easy. If something is too hard, then it is not fun. If something is interesting, it must make sense one way or another and because it is fun it will be enjoyable and it won't feel too hard. If it feels easy the learner will be more inclined to continue.

化難爲易、寓教於樂、觸類旁通是相關的。不懂就沒意思，就不會容易；太難就不會有趣；有意思一定是理解了妙趣所在；而有趣使你更投入從而不感到太辛苦。感覺容易就不會因畏懼而退縮。

Make it Easy. Nothing is easy. Learning a language is not an easy endeavor. But this does not mean there is no way to make the learning process easier for learners. Making learning easy by no means implies a lowering of standards. It simply means finding sensible ways to set up learners for success instead of failure.

化難爲易。世上無易事。學習一門外國語絕非一件容易的事。但是這并不是説不能找出辦法簡化學習的過程。化難爲易也不是要降低標準。化難爲易是找出辦法幫助學生成功。

Make it Fun. Making it fun eases the anxiety, sustains interest, and lets learners enjoy the process. It promotes the active participation of learners.

寓教於樂是爲了消除緊張，保持學習興趣，讓學生在學習上感到滿足與愉快。鼓勵學生的積極參與。

Make it Make Sense. Making it understandable makes learning meaningful to learners. It requires the instructor to understand learners. What makes sense and what does not to these learners?

觸類旁通指的是學生的理解。一方面，學習的内容要在學生理解程度以内，并能加强學生對目的語言和文化的理解，達到舉一反三；另一方面，學生覺得學習的内容有意義，即與他們的生活有聯繫，學習的内容可以用來表達自己的思想感情。這需要教師了解學生。

Being able to speak in a foreign language is a rewarding experience, especially for a language like Chinese. Regardless of any scientific evidence, most of people have the notion that Chinese is a harder language to learn than most others. So, if a young learner speaks Chinese successfully, the sense of pride and achievement will be tremendous. This enthusiasm can translate into a passion and a motivation for more learning, even for other subject areas.

學會一門外國語是一個有回報的經歷，特別是學會説漢語。不管有否科學依據，多數人覺得漢語是種很難學的語言。要是一個小孩子會説漢語，就會感到自豪，會有很大的成就感。這樣的熱情鼓勵學習，不光是漢語還可以派生對其他學科的學習熱忱。

How does a teacher achieve the above objectives? The answer is: Know your students, know your subject, and know your methodologies.

教師怎麼才能做到"化難爲易、寓教於樂、觸類旁通"呢？答案是：懂得并了解你的學生，懂得并了解你要教什麼，懂得并了解你怎麼教。

This series will help you with the latter two areas.

這套書幫助你弄明白這後兩項。

Integration of "What" and "How"
"教什麼" 與 "怎麼教" 的結合

The "What" part of the book provides a series of building blocks. Each block is structured with a topic and connects functional language use with linguistic structures. Grammatical patterns are grouped according to functional use, and vocabulary is ordered by category and topic.

這套書的"什麼篇"介紹一系列的集裝板塊。每一個板塊都圍繞一個話題將語言材料與語言功用串聯在一起。也就是説，語言的語法結構是按語言的功用挑選組裝在一起的。詞彙是按話題和類別排列的。

The "How" part presents a progression and sequence of teaching and learning for Chinese in grades 6 ~ 12 classrooms. It demonstrates sampled thematic unit and lesson design variables and related instructional strategies, activities, and assessments to provide users with concrete "how" tips for good classroom practices and guides the user to connect "what" and "how." The unit design intends to be pragmatic, yet flexible and helpful to the users. At the same time, it respects the users' choice of methods and texts.

这套书的"怎麽篇"建议中小學、主要是 6 ~ 12 年級的漢語課堂教與學的進程和步驟。建議并示範以主題貫連的教學單元、教案設計，包括變量的設計；有關的教學指導建議、課堂活動和測試。并給使用者一些具體的課堂教學的小訣竅。引導使用者把"教什麽"和"怎麽教"——教學内容和教學方法聯繫起來。教學單元的設計力求具實用性、靈活性和支持性，同時尊重使用者對教材和教法的選擇。

The design comes from this analogy:

這套書的設計來自這樣一個比喻：

Building a house is a constructive process. When building a house, we must have basic building materials, such as bricks, a framework, a blueprint, etc. The process is initiated with a purpose, proceeds with a blueprint, and involves an architect and the work, skills, and creativity of builders.

蓋一座房子是一個建造過程。蓋房子要有基本的建造原料，如磚瓦泥沙等；要搭起架子來，還要有藍圖。這個全過程的展開首先需要一個明確目的，然後要圖紙設計，要有建築設計師和建築工人的參與，貢獻他們的智慧與勞動，他們的技術和創造精神。

In a language class, a teacher facilitates a creative, constructive process for learners engaging the target language. This resembles the process of building a house. The learners are builders. The teacher is an architect. The purpose of the tasks is to build learners' proficiency in the target language; the blueprints are unit designs and lesson plans — a carefully structured road map to success; the bricks are the vocabulary; the frameworks for connecting basic structures are sentence patterns.

在語言課堂上，老師協助學生參與學習目的語這樣一個創造性的、建設性的過程。就像蓋房子的過程一樣。學生是建築工人，老師是建築設計師；教學的目的是發展目的語的語言能力和水平；藍圖就是精心設計的教學大綱和教案，建築材料是詞彙及使用知識，框架是語法句型和運用。

However, the construction that takes place in a language classroom requires more when compared to constructing a building. 1) The classroom construction process is a hands-on experience using more experimentation. It is an interactive and on-going process with goals of long-term progress, requiring recycling and spiraling language materials. 2) The teacher is more than an architect. A teacher is a provider, a facilitator, a tutor, a motivator, and a mentor. A teacher must provide the learners with building materials, to help to develop the skills, and to give room and opportunity for the learners' creativity. More importantly, a teacher must demonstrate, model, and nurture love for learning and ways to achieve learning. 3) The learners are special builders. The learners are in different developmental stages in terms of physical, mental, and emotional maturity. They have specific characteristics and needs in terms of cognition, motivation, learning styles, and cultural and linguistic diversity. More importantly, the learners must feel ownership in this constructive process. They are decision-makers and critical thinkers in learning as well as active and creative users of the language. The new language should become a conduit for expressing their true feelings.

然而，課堂中的建設過程比蓋房更複雜。1) 這個過程不僅需要第一手參與的經歷，而且是一個不斷嘗試的過程；是一個有長遠目標的、互動的、進行的過程；需要不斷復習、重復，螺旋式上升性地運用語言材料。2) 老師不僅僅是一個建築工程師，還是一個供應師，不斷地提供建築的材料，幫助提高建築的技巧，并給予機會讓學生有創造發展的空間；同時老師還得展示、示範，培養學生對學習的熱愛和學習的技能。3) 學生是特別的建築工人。他們處於身、心、情感發育的不同成熟階段。他們在認知、學習動機、學習風格、語言文化背景方面的特點和需求不一。更重要的是，他們要在學習過程中有主人翁的態度和權益。他們是學習和語言運用的決策人、思考者。目的語將成爲他們表達真實情感的又一渠道。

This series is an endeavor to bring "What" and "How" together in an organic way by providing "what" as building materials with basic frameworks and demonstrating "how" as blueprints. It is written with a sincere hope to provide a service to K-12 Chinese language teachers and learners everywhere.

　　這套書以"什麽篇"提供建築材料和框架，"怎麽篇"做藍圖，兩部分所反映的教學理念和思路，探索的教學設計和框架，分享的教學經驗和技巧，力圖將"教什麽"和"怎麽教"有機地結合起來。這不是一套語法理論的書，也不是一套教學法研究的書。而是爲中小學漢語教學課堂提供的具體服務，是中小學漢語作爲外國語教與學的參考、輔助與必備。

Fu, Haiyan, Ed. D.

傅海燕

簡 介
Introduction

What do we teach in our grades 6 to 12 Chinese language classrooms? How do we teach effectively? These are two important questions. "What" and "how" are integrated in the sense that "what" supports and supplements "how", and "how" guides and implements "what". This series intends to look at these two questions from a practical perspective classroom teacher's point of view to share some wisdom and instructional tips. For the convenience of presentation, the series divides real 6-12 Chinese classroom practice into a "What" section and a "How" section. We begin with the section on "What" and followed with the section on "How".

在我們的 6～12 年級的漢語課堂上，我們到底教什麽、怎麽教才更有效果？這是兩個大而複雜的問題。在現實的課堂上，"教什麽" 和 "怎麽教" 是一個整體。"教什麽" 是 "怎麽教" 的框架和實體；"怎麽教" 引導并貫徹 "教什麽"。這套書試圖從一個實際的角度，一個課堂教師的視角來探討這兩個問題。爲了論述方便，將 6～12 年級漢語課堂教學的實際分成 "教什麽" 和 "怎麽教" 兩個部分。先討論 "教什麽" 再講 "怎麽教"。

The section "What: A Functional and Grammatical Walkthrough" provides a series of building blocks. Each block is structured with a topic to connect functional use with linguistic structures. Grammatical patterns are grouped according to functional use, and vocabulary is ordered by category and topic. The design and organization come from the following rationales:

- First, the ultimate purpose of language is communication, thus the starting point of language teaching and learning should be meaningful and functional.

- Second, grammatical patterns and vocabulary are fundamental to the construction of meaning. They are the organic part and substance of meaningful and functional communication.

- Thirdly, 6-12 graders are neither young children nor adults. They are adolescents. They are a special group of learners. Some of their learning characteristics are expressing individual identity and ideas, looking for patterns and thinking analytically and critically.

Effective classroom teaching and learning must reflect, incorporate and facilitate these needs and learning styles of young learners.

這套書的什麼篇：語用和語法走廊，介紹一系列的集裝板塊。每一個板塊都是圍繞一個話題將語言材料與語言功用串聯在一起。也就是説，語言的語法結構是按語言的功用挑選組裝在一起的。詞彙是按話題和分類出現的。這樣的設計與組織基於以下的理念：

首先，語言的使用目的是交流。語言教學的起點應是有意義和實用的。

其二，語法句型和詞彙是表達語意的基本材料，是實際交流的有機組成和實質。

第三，6～12年級的學生不是小孩子也非成人。他們是青少年。青少年是一組特殊的學習群體。表達自我與思想、搜尋概念模式、分析批判思考是他們學習的一些特點。

有效的課堂教學必須反映、包容、并支助學生的需求和學習風格。

The section aims at providing a service to 6-12 grades Chinese teachers (especially those new to the profession) with clear mapping, quick reference and supplementary materials for classroom teaching and learning.

這套書正是要爲課堂教師特別是剛入行的教師服務。爲課堂教與學提供清晰的路綫圖，一目了然地查閱資料和課堂用教材。

A teacher, no matter what methods and textbooks are used for classroom instruction, needs to take two important steps when designing a lesson plan. First, knowing what to teach: having a clear picture or framework of the content of teaching and learning and a general mapping of specifics and details of the content; Second, knowing how to teach: considering the needs and characteristics of the learners, then applying practical ideas and strategies for instruction and activities.

一個教師，不管在課堂教學時用哪種教學法、用什麼教科書，在設計教案時需要兩個重要的步驟：其一是知道教什麼。腦子里應該對教學内容有一個清楚的概念，對教學的種種細節有一個大致的規劃；其二是明白怎麼教。從學生的需求和特點出發想出課堂教學與活動的辦法，拿出招數來。

A learner, from time to time, needs more materials and references for intensive and extended learning.

學生呢，時不時地總是需要更多的材料和資料用來强化和擴展學習内容。

The purpose of this Section is to meet these challenges.

本書什麼篇的目的就是要面對這兩方面的挑戰。

Focusing on the first step "what," we provide quick, easy, and practical content to be applied in the 6-12 Chinese classrooms. The content of teaching and learning is organized by topic, theme-based grammatical patterns, and categories of vocabulary.

針對"教和學什麼"的問題，什麼篇爲6~12年級漢語課堂教學提供切實可行的教學内容。教學的内容是按題目編排的，按主題組織語法點、分類出詞彙。

The second step is "how." The sample unit designs map suggested teaching scope, sequence and content organization by themes. All unit designs and teaching tips are in Chapter Two.

"怎麼教和學"這部分内容均在怎麼篇裏。在這部分裏，介紹了十個主題教學單元及教學參考建議，教與學的範圍、步驟和內容都由主題連貫起來。

Intended Objectives　目標

1. To integrate content and context of language use;
2. To reveal vertical as well as horizontal connections between grammatical patterns and functions of language;
3. To make the content of teaching and learning more flexible and accessible for various and diverse classroom situations; and
4. To make reviewing, recycling and spiraling language materials for teaching and learning more convenient.

"什麼篇" 的設計構思的目的是：

1. 將語言使用的內涵和外延融會在一起；
2. 從而揭示語法與語用橫向與縱向的聯繫；
3. 使教學內容更具靈活性，便利多樣化的課堂教學；
4. 方便復習、重復和螺旋上升式地使用語言教學材料。

Format　編排

1. Topics are selected according to functional use of the language;
2. Teaching and learning foci and related cruxes are listed as a table of contents, and then demonstrated and explained in order under each topic;
3. Related grammatical patterns and vocabulary are listed under each topic; and
4. Cultural or other relevant notes, if any, are at the end of the topical section.

"什麼篇" 編排原則：

1. 題目按語用挑選；
2. 每個題目下的篇章的目錄列出本章節的教學重點及相關的教學難點，依次示範與講解；
3. 每一題目下列出相關的語法點及詞彙表；
4. 有關文化或其他注釋。

Application 使用

1. Teachers may use this Section to become familiar with the teaching and learning content in a context of young English speakers in 6-12 classrooms.

2. Teachers will find quick references and explanations about some of the difficulties experienced by young English speakers in 6-12 classrooms.

3. Teachers may incorporate the provided content materials to customize lesson plans or supplement other existing teaching and learning materials.

4. Teachers and learners may pinpoint the connection between grammatical patterns and functional language use.

5. Teachers may directly use or demonstrate the charts and vocabulary lists presented here.

6. Learners may expand their language use by using all the information provided.

7. Parents and administrators may get an overview of Chinese teaching and learning in 6-12 classrooms in order to provide supervision and feedback about the process.

"什麼篇"的適用對象:

1. 教師可以用本章全面熟悉 6~12 漢語課堂教學的内容;

2. 教師可以快速查閱 6~12 漢語課堂教學中出現的難點的注解;

3. 教師可以用本部分中提供的教學素材根據自己的需求編排教案或用來做補充教材;

4. 教師和學生都可以對語法點和語用的聯繫一目了然;

5. 教師可以直接使用或在課上展示本部分中的詞彙表;

6. 學生可以用本部書中的資料擴展語用範圍;

7. 家長和校方行政管理人員能對漢語教學的概況有一定的了解,從而對課堂的教與學有一定的監督指導。

語音——漢語拼音

Phonetics
—Hanyu *Pinyin*

現行使用的漢語語音拼寫系統有數個，拼音是其中之一。爲什麼我們教與學拼音呢？有幾個實用的原因。

There are several systems in use of Chinese pronunciation. *pinyin* is one of them. Why do we teach/learn *pinyin*? There are several practical reasons：

1）使用拼音的人口最多。

2）聯合國指定拼音爲拼寫中國城市和姓名的標準方式。

3）多數新出的字典和出版物用拼音作爲漢語語音的拼注方法。

4）拼音是一種計算機輸入方法。可以直接使用英文鍵盤。使用者不用重新背替代鍵碼。

這對母語爲英文的中文文字處理軟件使用者來説，是方便快捷的。

1）*pinyin* is used by most Chinese-speaking populations.

2）The United Nations has designated *pinyin* as the standard method for spelling Chinese names and cities.

3）Most newer dictionaries and publications use *pinyin* as phonetic spelling for Chinese characters.

4）*pinyin* as an input method for computerized word processing uses a standard English keyboard. It does not require the user to memorize a new keyboard arrangement.

Thus, it is convenient for English speakers to use.

校方、家長和學生可以根據學習的目的和需求作出教學上的選擇。如何有效地教語音請參照《怎麼篇：組織教學》中有關問答部分和列舉的教學活動。

School, parents and students should make the decision and choice based on the needs. As for how to teach writing characters effectively, please refer to its questions and answers and sample activities on teaching and learning phonetics in Section Two *Designing Teaching—How to Teach and Learn*.

本節簡單介紹中小學生學拼音應知道和注意的有關使用拼音的知識，重點是語音、聲調和拼讀。

This chapter introduces very basic practical knowledge about *pinyin* and its use in K-12 Chinese classroom instruction. It emphasizes pronunciation, tones, and phonetic spelling.

教 學 重 點　Content of Teaching and Learning

音節	Syllables
聲母及特點	Initials and Their Features
韵母及特點	Finals and Their Features
聲調	Tones
漢語語音表（見附錄）	Phonetic Chart（應加 bopomofo 符號）

教 學 難 點　Cruxes of Teaching and Learning

韵母的拼寫	Spelling of the Finals
聲母的讀法	Pronunciation of the Initials
拼讀	Pronunciation of Words
聲調標號	Tone Marks

教學重點

Content of Teaching and Learning

音節　Syllables

　　基礎的漢語詞語一般爲單音節詞，由一個聲母與一個韵母結合發聲。一共有差不多402個這樣的音節組合。

The basic Chinese word is monosyllable which consists of a consonant and a vowel. There are about 402 such units.

聲母及特點　Initials and Their Features

　　聲母也叫 Initials，因爲聲母發起一個音節。漢語的聲母不能單獨發音，必須與韵母拼讀才能發音。一共有21個聲母。

In the *pinyin* system, consonants are called "initials" because they usually begin with a syllable. Chinese initials cannot be pronounced without finals. There are 21 such initials.

韵母及特點　Finals and Their Features

　　韵母也叫 Finals，因爲音節以韵母結尾。一共有39個韵母。

In the *pinyin* system, finals end with syllables of sound. There are 39 such finals.

韵母的發音　Pronunciation of the Finals

　　讀韵母要注意如下方面：

1）英語的複合元音在發音時有從一個音向另一個音的過渡；漢語不同。

2）對學生來講幾個有問題的韵母：

　　"ian" 聽起來更像 "ien" 但拼做 "ian"。

"o" 只可跟 "b, p, m, f" 拼，獨自不能發聲。

"er" 只有三個聲調，沒有第一聲；第二聲如 "兒"；第三聲如 "耳"；第四聲與其他聲調略不同，如 "二"。

"e" 不是英文的 "ee"，而 "i" 雷同英文的 "ee"，不是英文的 "ai"。

跟 "zh, ch, sh, r, z, c, s" 相拼的 "-i" 不是同一個 "i"。

To pronounce Chinese finals correctly, pay attention to the followings:

1) When pronouncing compound vowels in English, there is a distinct, though smooth transition from one sound to the next. In Chinese, compound finals should be uttered as one sound. No transition should be detected.

2) Learner be aware: There are a few finals which are more problematic than others to English learners:

"ian" sounds more like "ien" but is spelled as "ian";

"o" only goes with "b, p, m and f." It cannot be pronounced without a consonant.

"er" has only 3 tones. The first tone is absent. The second tone is pronounced as in "兒", The third tone is as in "耳" and the fourth tone, is a little different, as in "二".

"e" is not an "ee" sound, while "i" is an "ee" sound, not an "ai" sound as in English. "-i" is not a real "i" and is not an "ee" sound either, it only goes with "zh, ch, sh, r, z, c, s".

韵母的拼寫　Spelling of the Finals

韵母按其發音特點可分成 4 組：

Vowels can be divided by articulation into four groups.

1) 第一組韵母是獨立的韵母。可自成音節，拼寫不變。有：

Group I: Independent vowels. When standing alone as a word, nothing changes. e. g.:

　　a, ai, ao, an, ang, e, ei, en, eng, er, o, ou, ong

2) 第二組韵母是以 i 開頭的韵母。有：

Group II: Any vowel started with an "i"

　　i, ia, iao, ian, iang, ie, in, ing, iu (iou), iong

3）第三組韵母是以 u 開頭的韵母。有：

Group III: Any vowel started with an "u"

　　u, ua, uai, uan, uang, ueng, ui (uei), un (uen), uo

4）第四組韵母是以 ü 開頭的韵母。有：

Group IV: Any vowel started with a "ü"

　　ü, üe, üan, ün

　　第二、三、四組的韵母在自成音節時，拼寫都有變化。請參看教學難點一"韵母的拼寫"。

　　All Groups II to VI vowels, as stand-alone syllables, need spelling changes. Please refer to Difficulty One "難點一 韵母的拼寫" below.

聲調　Tones

　　聲調是構成詞語意義不可缺少的一部分。

　　英語是一種有語調的語言：句尾的調高表示語氣，由此表明話語的情緒即意思。

　　漢語是一種有聲調的語言：聲調有區別語義的作用。漢語普通話有 4 個基本聲調和一個輕聲。

　　Tones are an important part of the meaning of words.

　　English is an intonation language. The pitch at the end of a sentence indicates mood. For example, pitch typically rises at the end of a question.

　　Chinese is a tone language. The tone of each sound differentiates meaning. In Common Speech（普通話 *Putonghua*）, there are four tones plus a neutral tone.

漢語語音表　Phonetic Chart（應加 bopomofo 符號）

　　（見附錄）

教與學提示　Tips for Teaching/Learning *Pinyin*

中小學生學習拼音應在有語義的上下文中進行。首先明確一些概念：
"音"和"詞"的區別："音"是發聲；"詞"是有語義的聲音。

Learn phonetics in meaningful contexts. First, some definitions: The difference between "sound" and "words": Sounds—noise and words—sounds with
meaning.

漢語的單音節詞/字有三個相輔相成的組成部分：形，聲，義。

三者缺一不可。對中小學生來説，學説話，哪怕是一個字一個字地、
一個詞一個詞地、一個句一個句地説，也比分開來學發音、聲調和拼讀更
有實際意義。在學説話的過程中學會正確地發音、正確的聲調、正確地使
用詞語、正確地拼讀和書寫。

In Chinese, a monosyllable word/character has three componants: Shape—
appearance; Pronunciation—sound, tone, symbol/spelling and Meaning (s).

They are inseparable. Therefore it will make more sense to K-12 learners
when teaching phonetics, we deal with these elements/aspects at once. Besides
learning all the sounds, spellings and phonetic rules, we learn how to say them
for meaningful purposes. That is to say, when learning words, we learn how to
pronounce them correctly and fluently and we learn how to spell and write them
correctly.

如何有效地教語音，請參照《怎麼篇：組織教學》中有關問答部分和
列舉的教學活動。

For teaching pronunciation effectively, please refer to Volume Two *How*: *Designing Teaching*. It also contains questions and answers and sample activities on
teaching and learning phonetics.

教學難點

Cruxes of Teaching and Learning

難點一 韵母的拼寫 Spelling of the Finals

韵母按其發音特點可分成4組。

There are four groups of vowels according to the articulation：

第一組韵母是獨立的韵母。可自成音節，拼寫不變。

Group I：Independent vowels. When standing alone as a word，nothing changes.

 a，ai，ao，an，ang，e，ei，en，eng，er，o，ou，ong

第二組韵母是以 i 開頭的韵母。

Group II：Any vowel starts with an "i".

 i，ia，iao，ian，iang，ie，in，ing，iu（iou），iong

這組韵母在自成音節時，拼寫有變化：

When standing alone as a word，two situations occur：

a. 當韵母有複合元音出現時，"i" 由 "y" 替代。

 "i" will be changed to "y" when the final consists of more than one vowel.

 羊　　　　yáng　　　sheep

b. 當韵母只有一個元音 "i" 時，前加 "y"。

 a "y" will be added at the front when the final has only one vowel.

 一　　　　yī　　　　　one

第三組韵母是以 u 開頭的韵母。

Group III：Any vowel starts with an "u".

 u，ua，uai，uan，uang，ueng，ui，un，uo

這組韵母在自成音節時，拼寫有變化：

When standing alone as a word, two situations occur:

a. 當韵母有複合元音出現時，"u"由"w"替代。

"u" will be changed to "w" when the final consists of more than one vowel.

完　　　wán　　　finish

b. 當韵母只有一個元音"u"時，前加"w"。

a "w" will be added at the front when the final has only one vowel.

五　　　wǔ　　　five

第四組韵母是以 ü 開頭的韵母。

Group IV: Any vowel starts with a "ü".

　　ü, üe, üan, ün

這組韵母在自成音節時，拼寫有變化。在韵母前加"y"。

When standing alone as a word, spelling changes and a "y" will be added at the front.

語　　　yǔ　　　language

其他應注意　Spelling Exceptions

第一組，没問題。Group I: Trouble free.

第二組，"iou"與聲母拼時，寫成"iu"：

Group II: "iou" when spelled with a consonant, appears as "iu" as in:

六　　　liù　　　six

在自成音節時，拼寫成"you"：

When standing alone as a word, it becomes "you," as in:

有　　　yǒu　　　have

第三組，"uei"和"uen"

"uei"與聲母拼時，寫成"ui"：

"uei" when spelled with a consonant, appears as "ui" as in:

會　　　huì　　　know how

在自成音節時，拼寫成 "wei"：

When standing alone as a word, it becomes "wei" as in：

爲　　wèi　　　be

"uen" 與聲母拼時，寫成 "un"：

"uen," when spelled with a consonant, appears as "un" as in：

混　　hùn　　　mix

在自成音節時，拼寫成 "wen"：

When standing alone as a word, it becomes "wen" as in：

問　　wèn　　　ask

第四組的韵母只可以跟 5 個聲母拼："j, q, x, n, l"。

Group IV: This group goes with only five initials："j, q, x, n and l".

跟 "j, q, x" 拼時，去掉韵母上面的兩個小點。

When spelled with "j", "q" and "x", they drop the two dots on top of the vowel, as in：

句　jù　sentence　　群　qún　group　　學　xué　learning

跟 "n, l" 拼時，保持兩個小點 ü：

When spelled with "n" and "l", they keep the two dots on top of the vowel, as in：

女　nǚ　woman　　　绿　lǜ　green

難點二　聲母的讀法 Pronunciation of Initials

漢語的聲母本身不發音，只有在跟韵母結合時才發音。由於拼音用英文的字母做書寫符號，請注意發音上的不同。幼小的學生如果同時學習英文的拼讀，更要在教學中強調區分。

Initials in Chinese cannot be pronounced without the help of vowels. The *pinyin* system utilizes Western alphabets for spelling. The learner should be aware of the differences in pronunciation. For K-3 students, if learning *pinyin* at the same time with English spelling, differentiation is needed.

難點三 拼讀 Pronunciation of Words

在語流中，拼讀時有變聲變調的情況。

Some words, when in combination with others, change tone.

變調 Changing of the Tones

1) 兩個三聲相遇，第一個三聲變成二聲。

When a third tone meets with another third tone the first third tone changes into a second tone.

$$\check{}\ +\ \check{}\ =\ \acute{}\ +\ \check{}$$
$$你\ 好\ =\ 你\ 好$$

2) "不 not, no" 是第四聲。當 "不" 後面跟了四聲詞時變成二聲。

When "不 not, no" of being fourth tone is followed by another fourth tone "不" changes into a second tone.

$$\grave{}\ \grave{}\ =\ \acute{}\ \grave{}$$
$$不\ 對\ =\ 不\ 對$$

3) "一" 是一聲。但若 "一" 後跟了一聲或三聲詞時變成四聲。

When "一 one" of first tone is followed by another first tone or third tone "一" changes into a fourth tone.

$$\bar{}\ \bar{}\ =\ \grave{}\ \bar{}\qquad\bar{}\ \check{}\ =\ \grave{}\ \check{}$$
$$一\ 些\ =\ 一\ 些\qquad一\ 點\ =\ 一\ 點$$

"一" 後跟了四聲詞時變二聲。

When "yi" of first tone is followed by another fourth tone "yi" changes into a second tone.

$$\bar{}\ \grave{}\ =\ \acute{}\ \grave{}$$
$$一\ 件\ =\ 一\ 件$$

難點四　聲調標號 Tone Marks

在哪兒標聲調號？ Where do we put the tone marks?

在元音 “ɑ e o i/u” 上。先後的優先順序也是如此。

Tone marks are put on vowels. But if the vowel contains more than one of the above letters, in general, the priority order goes like this：

　　ɑ e o i/u.

In other words, in a situation like：

　　“ɑi”, the tone mark should be on the “ɑ”;

　　“ei” , on the “e”;

　　“ou”, on the “o”;

　　“iu”, on the “u”;

　　“ui”, on the “i”.

B

漢字　Characters

漢字是漢語的文字表達符號。學習漢字包括認讀和書寫。記憶和書寫漢字是英語爲母語背景的學生學習上的一個難點。

本節針對幼兒園至十二年級學生學習上的難點，簡單介紹學習漢字所應具有的知識。其中包括：漢字的使用，漢字的形成與漢字的書寫和漢字文字處理軟件的使用。如何有效地教漢字，請參照《怎麼篇：組織教學》中有關問答部分和列舉的教學活動。

Chinese characters are the basic symbols of the Chinese written system. Learning Chinese characters includes the recognition and production of texts using characters. Memorizing and writing characters present challenges to English-speaking learners.

This chapter introduces the basic knowledge of learning characters keeping the needs of K-12 learners in mind. The basic knowledge includes the use of Chinese characters, the composition and writing of Chinese character, and the use of Chinese word processors. As for how to teach writing characters effectively, please refer to the question and answer and sample activities on teaching and learning characters in chapters in Volume Two *How: Designing Teaching.*

教 學 重 點　Content of Teaching and Learning

漢字的使用	The Use of Chinese Characters
漢字的書寫形成	Chinese Characters and Composition
書寫漢字	Writing Characters
用計算機寫漢字	Computerized Writing

教 學 難 點　Cruxes of Teaching and Learning

記憶漢字	Memorizing Chinese Characters

教學重點

Content of Teaching and Learning

漢字的使用　The Use of Chinese Characters

漢字有兩個書寫版本：繁體和簡體。有的地區、有的人用繁體字；有的地區、有的人用簡體字。古代的文獻用繁體字，現代很多地區和大多數人在日常生活中用簡體字。K-12 的學生應知道、接受和尊重這一語言文字使用的歷史與現狀。校方、家長和學生可以根據學習的目的和需求作出教學上的選擇。

現在的計算機技術可以使兩種字體在轉換時易如反掌。同時爲不同需要的學生提供兩個版本也不是一個大的技術問題。

There are often two systems of Chinese characters: traditional and simplified. Some Chinese-speaking regions and people use traditional characters and others use the simplified versions. Ancient historical documents and texts were written in traditional characters. In modern times, many regions and the majority of Chinese users employ the simplified version of characters. K-12 learners should be aware of this and accept and respect the history and reality of this aspect of Chinese. As for which version to study, school, parents and students should make the decision based on the needs of the students.

Computer technology, namely the word processor, has simplified use of both versions along with the easy conversion of texts from one system to the other. Making texts available in both or either version according to student requests should not be a big technical problem.

漢字的書寫形成　Chinese Characters and Composition

一般對中小學生簡單介紹三個類型的漢字。（參考摘録書目：胡雙實《漢字史話》中華書局 1980）

We usually introduce three kinds of characters to K-12 learners. （Reference：Hu，Shuangbao《漢字史話》中華書局 1980）

象形字　Pictographs

象形字來源於古代人對自然事物、事件及景物形象的圖畫描繪。這樣的字一般爲獨體字。這樣的字雖不多，但是形象能引起學生的興趣，吸引學生的注意力。

Pictographs originated from ancient drawings of nature，objects，and events. Most pictographs have only single element. Although they are not in great numbers，introducing this kind of characters can stimulate student's interest and attention to learning.

會意字　Ideographs

會意字是象形字的引申，常由兩個象形字組合而成，把兩個或更多的形象放在一起力圖表達一個新的或抽象的意思。可以在學習象形字的基礎上學習。

Ideographs are mostly the combination of two pictographs. Two or more images together express a new or abstract meaning. We should use pictographs as the basis for introducing ideographs.

形聲字　Pictophonetics

我們今天用的多數的漢字是形聲字。形聲字也是合體字。一般由兩部分組成：一部分表意思，一部分表讀音。由於長時間的進化演變，表義的部分可能已失去原來的意思，表音的部分并不規律。切忌"望文生義"造成理解錯誤，或"望字生音"念錯字。

The great majority of the characters we use today fall into this category. A pictophonetic character has two parts：A picto part indicates meaning and a phonetic part indicates sound. Due to centuries of evolution，changes in meaning and pronunciation occurred. Many characters have lost their original meanings and，usually，the sound indicators of characters are not regular or accurate. Be aware of this in actual use.

書寫漢字　Writing Characters

書寫漢字主要是談手寫與用計算機寫。如何有效地教漢字，請參照《怎麼篇：組織教學》中有關問答部分和列舉的教學活動。

Writing characters refers to producing characters by hand and creating texts with a computer. As for how to teach writing characters effectively, please refer to the question and answer and sample activities on teaching and learning characters chapters in Volume Two *How*: *Designing Teaching*.

手寫漢字　Writing by Hand

手寫漢字可以用至少三個方法來提高書寫記憶的能力。一個是利用對偏旁部首的記憶和提示，一個是理順筆畫熟練筆順，還有一個是通過書法藝術。

There are at least three methods to help with memorizing characters. First, relies on radicals for hints; the second is to practise through correct stroke orders, and the third is to use calligraphy.

偏旁部首　Radicals

（參考摘録書目：胡雙寶《漢字史話》中華書局 1980）

偏旁部首被稱爲義符，其本身曾有一定的意義。每個偏旁部首都能有數個至多個組合。偏旁部首不僅可以用來查新字。從記憶的角度講，重復出現的符號容易記得牢。新出現的字中如有已知會寫的部件容易記住。另外，偏旁部首自有定義對一些新字的字義有提示作用。按偏旁部首或已知的獨體字來學寫新字容易幫助記憶。

Radicals are pictographs used in character dictionary indices. (Reference: Hu, Shuangbao《漢字史話》中華書局 1980) From the view point of memory, symbols that appear repeatedly have a better chance to be remembered. If a new character has a familiar radical, it will be easier to learn. Also, radicals were originally pictographs. They have their own orginal meanings. They often provide hints to the meanings or nature of the characters they are used in.

筆畫筆順　Stroke Orders

老一輩的人學漢字都十分強調正確的筆畫和筆順。理順筆畫熟練筆順，熟能生巧，順理成章，不失爲幫助記憶的好辦法之一。幫助學生養成書寫的好習慣。但不可認定這是唯一的辦法，過分偏頗而顧此失彼，使幼小學生失去寫字的興趣。多鼓勵少批評。

Older generations of Chinese learners learned writing characters with prescribed stroke orders. Practising the right way of writing helps the students to make progress and achieve fluency. Younger learners should be encouraged to foster good writing habits. However, no one way is the only way. Gaining encouragement and learning through successful experience is the key. It is important to constantly give young students positive reinforcement rather than a negative one.

書法藝術　Art of Calligraphy

書法是一門藝術。練習書法不僅是學習文化的一部分，也可以幫助中小學生加強對漢字的記憶理解。同時對書法藝術的學習與欣賞還能幫助學生增加對漢字書寫的熱情，激發其更大的學習動力。

Calligraphy is an art form. Practising Chinese calligraphy is not only an integral part of learning the Chinese culture, but will also be helpful in remembering and understanding characters. Learning and appreciating Chinese calligraphy will inspire and motivate young students to write and practise characters.

用計算機寫漢字　Computerized Writing

用計算機寫漢字的好處

用計算機寫漢字是件好事情。首先，文章可以隨意編排。重整段落，修改内容，轉換字體都不在話下。可用的字體數不勝數。還有，用文字處理軟件可以念文章，翻譯文章，并能幫助和極大地支持初學者閱讀和編寫中文文章。

The Benifits：

Using a word processor to create Chinese texts is a great thing. First, texts can be easily manipulated and the transfer of passages or the revision of texts is no longer a major issue. Conversion back and forth between traditional and simplified versions requires only a few mouse clicks and choices of fonts are numerous. Second, with a word processor, a beginning learner can access and create texts in Chinese with tremendous assistance and support. For example, written texts can be read by the computers for listening or be translated from one language to another.

用計算機寫漢字的三個可能的麻煩

A. "ü" 在哪兒？

這是一個技術問題。用拼音輸入時的方便在於可以直接使用英文鍵盤。但是英文鍵盤没有 "ü"。不同的中文文字處理軟件有不同的解決辦法：例如，微軟用 "V" 鍵，其他的一些用 "uu" 替代。

B. 爲什麽寫的漢字常不對？

這個問題大得多。語言轉換漢字不能達到絕對的準確。漢語的每個語音都會有很多相應的漢字。計算機文字處理的能力不盡人意。打字時得不斷選字、改字，以保證準確性。這又費精力又費時間。對初學者來説很具挑戰性，得特別留心。尤其是在 AP 中文測試這樣的應試當中，速度和準確性缺一不可。

C. 對手寫漢字有什麽影響呢？

用計算機寫漢字方便，若更多的時間和精力放在這，漸漸地對手寫漢字會有副作用。人們不用動腦記憶也不用動手書寫了。更別提練書法了。

有利有弊。揚長避短才難能可貴。

The Drawbacks:

There are three important issues related to using a Chinese word processor.

A. Where is "ü"?

This is a little technical problem. The *pinyin* input method seems to be a preferable one due to the fact that it utilises an English keyboard. An English keyboard can satisfy all of the letters except "ü." Different word processors find different solutions. For example:

Key designates " ~ " for this feature; Microsoft word employs "v," others may use "uu."

B. How does one get the characters right?

This is a bigger problem. Typing characters on a computer by phonetic spelling is still not as convenient as one would like it to be: Each sound/ spelling is associated with multiple characters. With almost no exception, word processors require inputer to identify and choose the correct characters. This operation can be time-consuming and tedious. The learner must be aware and be careful when creating texts so as to choose the correct character matching the given *pinyin*. Also, for testing situations like the online AP Chinese test, practicing typing with speed and accuracy is a must.

C. What happens to writing by hand?

This is a by-product. Some concerns have already been raised that as more time and effort are put into using word processors to create text in Chinese, writing by hand as a skill and a means of memorization of characters has been negatively affected. Not to mention the negative impact on calligraphy as an art.

There are obvious advantages and disadvantages in Chinese computing. Taking advantages of the positives and trying to avoid the negatives are rare and commendable.

教學難點
Cruxes of Teaching and Learning

記憶漢字 Memorizing Chinese Characters

記憶漢字可能是多數學生的難點。雖然記住和正確書寫漢字不容易，但是學習的趣處正在於其挑戰性。千萬不能把學認學寫漢字變成一件頭疼的事，總是有挫敗感。還是要通過成功的經驗鼓勵學生的學習興趣，幫助學生找到有效的方法和知識記住更多的漢字。

如何有效地教與學漢字，請參照《怎麼篇：組織教學》中有關問答部分和列舉的教學活動。

Memorizing characters is a difficult job for most learners. Challenging as it is, learners should be encouraged to find practical ways to expand their knowledge and memory of more characters. Doesn't the fun part of learning come from its challenge? The key is to inspire learning through successful learning experiences not through failure.

As for how to teach writing characters effectively, please refer to the question and answer and sample activities on teaching and learning characters in chapters in Volume Two *How*: *Designing Teaching*.

1

數字與生活　Numbers in Life

　　數字是日常生活中經常用到的。不管多大的孩子學習漢語，從一開始就可以學習數字。爲什麼要學數字呢？涉及數字的話題有很多。

　　最簡單的有：數數兒，數東西/人，做算術；稍複雜一點的有：談年齡、號碼，如：電話號碼、門牌號碼、公共汽車號，等等；再難一點的還有：錢、日曆；更難的還有：大數目、數學計算，等等。

　　請參考以下的內容，按教與學的需求，選擇使用。

"Numbers" is a topic used daily. Beginning students of Chinese, regardless of age, may learn numbers from the very beginning. Why do we learn numbers? Many basic topics in life require numbers.

The simplest situations are: counting, numbering objects/people, doing basic arithmetic. More complicated topics include: talking about age, or numbers such as telephone number, street number, bus number, and so on. More sophisticated topics are: money, calendar. Larger numbers and mathematical calculations are even more difficult.

Select from the content listed below according to teaching and learning needs. Customize them as needed.

教學重點　Content of Teaching and Learning

數字/數目	Number, Amount, Quantity, Digit
數學用語	Mathematical Terms
名量詞	Measure Words for Noun (Nominal Measure Word)
錢	Cash, Money
年齡	Age
電話號碼	Telephone Number
日曆	Calendar

教學難點　Cruxes of Teaching and Learning

年齡	Age
"一" vs. "幺"	
"二" vs. "兩"	

換算	Conversion of Big Numbers from English to Chinese
對數字的聽力理解	Listening Comprehension of Numbers
名量詞	Measure Word for Noun（Nominal Measure Word）
"多" 的使用	Use of "多"

詞　彙　表　Glossary

數目表	Number
數學用語表	Mathematical Terms
常用量詞表	List of Commonly Used Measure Words

教學重點

Content of Teaching and Learning

數字/數目 Numeral, Number, Amount, Quantity, Digit

基本數字 Basic 10 Numbers

yī	èr	sān	sì	wǔ	liù	qī	bā	jiǔ	shí
一	二	三	四	五	六	七	八	九	十

大數目 Large Numbers

shí	èrshí	sānshí	sìshí	wǔshí	liùshí	qīshí	bāshí	jiǔshí
十	二十	三十	四十	五十	六十	七十	八十	九十

yìbǎi ......
一百

yìqiān ......
一千

Basic Units：

qiān	bǎi	shí	gè
千	百	十	個
1,	0	0	0

中文數目每4位數爲一新單元。英文用的阿拉伯數字是3位進制。常用數字單位：

For Chinese numbers, every four digits consist of a unit. While in English it is three. The commonly used units are as follows：

zhào	yì	wàn	gè
兆	億	萬	個
千百十兆	千百十億	千百十萬	千百十個

換算的關鍵 Critical Units for Conversion

10,000	ten thousand	一萬
100,000	a hundred thousand	十萬

1，000，000	a million	一百萬
100，000，000	a hundred million	一億
1，000，000，000	a billion	十億

e. g. :

2，031	二千〇三十一
12，345	一萬　二千三百四十五
356，005	三十五萬　六千〇五
4，507，889	四百五十萬　七千八百八十九
80，008，000	八千萬　八千
900，675，000	九億　〇六十七萬　五千
1，300，000，000	十三億

Jiānádà de rénkǒu yuē wéi (approximately)： liǎngqiān qībǎi wàn
加拿大　的　人口　約　爲　　　　　　　　兩千　　七百　萬

Měiguó de rénkǒu yuē wéi　　　　　　　　sān yì
美國　　的　人口　約　爲：　　　　　　　三　億

Zhōngguó de rénkǒu yuē wéi　　　　　　　shísān yì
中國　　　的　人口　約　爲：　　　　　　十三　億

數學用語　Mathematical Terms

整數　zhěngshù　{math} integer, whole number, round number

　正數　　zhèngshù　{math} positive number

　負數　　fùshù　　{math} negative number

　零　　　líng　　　zero

小數　xiǎoshù　　{math} decimal

　　　　　　　　　yì diǎn qī wǔ
1. 75　　　　　　　一　點　七　五

　　　　　　　　　líng diǎn èr wǔ
0. 25　　　　　　　〇　點　二　五

分數	fēnshù	{math} fraction	
		èr fēn zhī yī	
1/2		二 分 之 一	
		sān fēn zhī èr	
2/3		三 分 之 二	
		sì fēn zhī sān	
3/4		四 分 之 三	
		shíliù fēn zhī yī	
1/16		十 六 分 之 一	
		bǎifēnzhī wǔshí	
50%		百分之 五十	
		bǎifēnzhī qīshíwǔ	
75%		百分之 七十五	

算術	suànshù	arithmetic	
加	jiā	" + "	add
		yī jiā yī děngyú èr	
1 + 1 = 2		一加 一 等於 二	
減	jiǎn	" – "	subtract
		sì jiǎnqù èr děngyú èr	
4 – 2 = 2		四 減去 二 等於 二	
乘	chéng	" × "	multiply
		èr chéngyǐ èr děngyú sì	
2 × 2 = 4		二 乘以 二 等於 四	
除	chú	" ÷ "	divide
		liù chúyǐ sān děngyú èr	
6 ÷ 3 = 2		六 除以 三 等於 二	
等於	děngyú	" = "	be equivalent to
以	yǐ	by	
進位	jìnwèi	{math} carry	

數學	shùwué	mathematics (as a subject)	
代數	dàishù	algebra	
幾何	jǐhé	geometry	

三角	sānjiǎo	trigonometry
函數	hánshù	{math} function
統計	tǒngjì	statistics

名量詞 Measure Words for Noun (Nominal Measure Word)

漢語的名詞和數詞之間必須用量詞。

When describing an amount/quantity of objects, a measure word is needed to connect the number with the noun.

量詞的使用 Rules of Using Measure Words

1）數詞加量詞修飾名詞

When a number is used to quantify a noun, a measure word is needed：

+ Measure Word + Noun

liǎng	ge		rén	
兩	個		人	two persons

2）"這""那""哪"加量詞修飾名詞

When "this/these", "that /those" or "which" is used to designate a noun, a measure word is needed：

"這/那/哪" + Measure Word + Noun

nà		ge	rén	
那		個	人	that person

錢 Cash, Money

中國錢

人民幣　rénmínbì　RMB (unit of currency in the PRC)

		Written	Colloquial
yuan unit		元 yuán	塊 kuài
Ten cent unit (one – tenth of a yuan)		角 jiǎo	毛 máo

Cent unit（one – tenth of a jiao）　　　　　　分 fēn

"二" is a problematic number in terms of money：

èr（liǎng）yuán èr jiǎo	liǎng kuài èr（máo）
二（兩）　元　二　角	兩　塊　二（毛）
èrshí yuán èr jiǎo èr fēn	èrshí kuài èr máo èr（fēn）
二十　元　二角　二分	二十　塊　二　毛　二（分）
èrbǎi èrshí èr yuán èr jiǎo	èrbǎi èrshí èr kuài èr
二百　二十　二　元　二　角	二百　二十二　塊　二

美國錢　American Money

美金　　mĕijīn／美元 mĕiyuán　　　US dollar, American dollar

Dollar unit　　　美元 mĕiyuán

Cent unit　　　美分 mĕifēn

其他　Other

歐元　　ōuyuán　　Euro

換算　huànsuàn　Convert；Conversion（from one system of calculation to another）

Yì mĕiyuán dĕngyú bā yuán rénmínbì
一　美元　等於　八　元　人民幣。
One U. S. dollar equals eight RMB Yuan.

錢的使用　Other Expressions Related to Use of Money

價錢	jiàqián	Price	零錢	língqián	Small change
花錢	huā qián	Spend money	用錢	yòng qián	Spend money
付錢	fù qián	Pay	找錢	zhǎo qián	Give change
一共	yígòng	Altogether, Total			
多少錢	duōshao qián	How much			

一共多少錢？　How much is it in total？

錢的所有　How Much Money Do You Have?

"塊"　kuài　is a measure word for Chinese currency.

"錢"　qián　is the noun.

Wǒ yǒu liǎng kuài qián
我　有　兩　塊　錢 。I have two dollars.

問句　Questions & Answers

1) 數目小於十，用"幾"　If the number is less than 10, use "幾".

Nǐ yǒu jǐ kuài qián
你　有　幾　塊　錢？
How much money do you have?

Wǒ yǒu liǎng kuài qián
我　有　兩　塊　錢 。
I have two dollars.

2) 數目大於十，用"多少"

If the number is more than 10, use "多少".

Nǐmen yǒu duōshao qián
你們　有　多少　錢？
How much money do you have?

Wǒmen yǒu èrshí kuài qián
我們　有　二十　塊　錢 。
We have twenty dollars.

年齡　Age（of a person, animal, plant）

1) 談年齡，用"歲"。

When talking about one's age, use "歲 suì years of age".

2) 問年齡，用"多大?"

To ask about one's age, use "多大?". （"大" and "小" are used to describe people's age, not size.）

Jīnnián nǐ duō dà
今年　你多　大？How old are you this year?

Wǒ (shì) shísì suì
我　（是）十四 歲。I am 14.

電話號碼　Telephone Number

（See chapter 2：Self Introduction for more details）

電話號碼用個位數字。

To say a telephone number, use single digit.

Wǒ de diànhuà shì（qī qī sān）èr sān líng wǔ liù qī bā
我　的　電話　是（七七三）二 三 〇 五六七八。

日曆　Calendar

（See chapter 6：Time for more details）

中文日期的排列順序總是從大到小。

When discussing calendar units, longer（time）concepts go before smaller

ones.

年　　　nián　　　year
月　　　yuè　　　month
日　　　rì　　　　day

èr líng líng liù nián bā yuè sānshí rì
二 〇 〇 六 年 八 月 三 十 日

教學難點

Cruxes of Teaching and Learning

難點一　年齡 Age

對不同年齡的人問年齡要用不同的說法以示敬重。

For different age group, a different question may be more appropriate：

For little children：

你幾歲（suì）？

For young people or people of your own age group：

你多大？

For senior citizens：

Nín duō dà suìshu　／Nín duō dà niánjì
您　多　大　歲數？／您　多　大　年紀？

難點二　"一" vs. "幺"

數數兒的時候，排順序的時候，用"一"：

"一" is used for counting：

一二三……（numeral）

第一，第二，第三……（ordinal number）

連續讀單個數字的組合時，用"幺"或"一"。

"幺" can be used for reading digital numbers in sequence.

e. g.：telephone number or room number.

Room "105" can be read as

"一○五" 或 "幺○五".

Telephone：（312）1456781：

"三一二一四五六七八一"，或者"三幺二幺四五六七八幺"

難點三　"二" vs. "兩"

數數兒的時候，排順序的時候，用"二"。

"二" is used for counting.

一二三……（numeral）

第一，第二，第三……（ordinal number）

"兩"作爲起始數用在量詞前。

"兩"，as an initial number for 2，has to be used if a measure word follows it （but only as a whole number, not a fraction）.

	2 people	兩個人
	2 o'clock	兩點（鐘）
	2 dollars	兩塊錢
but：	2.20 dollars	兩塊二
	2.02 dollars	兩塊〇二
	2:22pm	下午兩點二十二（分）

難點四　換算 Conversion of Big Numbers from English to Chinese

英文數目的進制分隔是每 3 個數字出現一個新的單位：

English numbers（Arabic numbers）have 3 digits per unit：

1，000，000，000.

（billions，millions，thousands，000）

中文是四個。換算時有 5 點要注意：

Chinese numbers have 4 digits per unit. Five points need to be emphasized：

1）Unit：Every four digits begin a new unit.

2）When to read unit word：

Do not say the unit word until all digits in the unit are mentioned.

1/23，45/6，789 一億二千三百四十五萬六千七百八十九

3）When to read "0"：

When "0" is at the beginning of the unit.

1/0001/0001 　　　　　　　　　一億〇一萬〇一

When "0" is in the middle of the unit.

1/0101/1011 　　　　　　一億〇一千〇一萬一千〇一十一

Not when it is at the very end of the number.

1/00，00/0，000 　　　　　　　一億

1/11, 00/1, 110	一億一千萬（○）一千一百一十
10/10, 00/1, 100	十億一千萬（○）一千一百

4）"10" in sequence can be read "一十"：

　　111：一百一十一

5）The most important/difficult conversions are：（Remember！）

10, 000	10 thousand	一萬
100, 000	100 thousand	十萬
1, 000, 000	a million	一百萬
10, 000, 000	10 million	一千萬
100, 000, 000	100 million	一億
1, 000, 000, 000	a billion	十億

難點五　對數字的聽力理解 Listening Comprehension of Numbers

數字的聽力理解比較難，需要多練習。

It is always hard to listen to and comprehend numbers. It will require constant practice.

難點六　名量詞 Measure Words for Noun（Nominal Measwre Word）

名量詞的使用　Rules of Using Measure Words for Noun

1）數字加名詞時，必須使用量詞：

When a number is used to quantify a noun, a measure word is needed：

＋ Measure Word ＋ Noun

liǎng	ge	rén	
兩	個	人	two persons

2）"這/那/哪"指示名詞時，應使用量詞：

When "this/these"，"that /those" or "which" is used to designate a noun, a measure word is needed：

"這/那/哪" ＋ Measure Word ＋ Noun

nà   ge   rén
那   個   人   that person

3）"幾" 詢問小於 10 的量，放在量詞前：

For numbers between 1 and 10, Chinese uses "幾" before a measure
word for questions：

jǐ ge   jǐ suì
幾 個   For amount   幾 歲   For age

jǐ yuán   jǐ diǎn
幾 元   For money   幾 點   For time

jǐ jīn
幾 斤   For weight

4）"多少" 詢問大於 10 的量，放在量詞前：

For numbers bigger than 10, Chinese uses "多少" before a measure
word for question：

duōshao gè   duōshao suì
多少   個   For amount   多少   歲   For age

duōshao yuán   duōshao jīn
多少   元   For money   多少   斤   For weight

名量詞的其他用法 Other Functions of Measure Words for Noun

1）量詞重疊表示 "每"，無例外：

Measure words can also be duplicated meaning "every one"：

gègè：Tāmen gègè dōu hěn bàng
個個：他們   個個   都   很   棒 。

Everyone of them is wonderful.

2）數詞與量詞重疊做狀語表示順序：

Numerals and measure words can be duplicated, showing the order of
actions：

yí ge yí ge de：yí ge yí ge de chī
一 個 一 個 地：一 個 一 個 地 吃

Eat one by one.

yì bǐ yì bǐ de：qǐng yì bǐ yì bǐ de xiě
一 筆 一 筆 地：請   一 筆 一 筆 地 寫

Please write it stroke by stroke.

難點七 "多"的使用 Use of "多"

1) "多"和"少"作爲形容詞在描述時，不可脫離副詞單用。

"多" and "少" are adjectives that cannot be used by themselves when describing something. They require adverbs in company to form descriptions.

wrong	correct
我有多朋友。	我有很多朋友。

2) "多"作爲副詞，與一個形容詞結合表示疑問。

"多" as an adverb together with an adjective can forma question：

Duō cháng   Duō cū
多　　長 ？ For length 　多　粗？ For thickness

Duō kuān   Duō jiǔ
多　寬 ？ For width 　多　久？ For time

Duō gāo   Duō yuǎn
多　　高 ？ For height 　多　　遠 ？ For distance

Duō dà
多　大？　 For age，area，capacity and volume

3) "多"作爲副詞，與一個形容詞結合表示感歎。

The same structure as above can also be used to show exclamations：

Duō gāo a
多　高 啊！ How high（tall）！

Duō dà a
多　大 啊！ How big！

Duō yuǎn a
多　　遠 啊！ How far away！

詞彙表

常用量詞表 List of Commonly Used Measure Words

(Some measure words in Chinese can find their equivalents in English while a lot others do not.)

把 bǎ   For things with a handle or for things that can be grasped (like a chair)

一把

椅子	yǐzi	chair
刀子	dāozi	pocket knife
雨傘	yǔsǎn	umbrella

杯 bēi   Glass, cup of liquid

一杯

水	shuǐ	water
酒	jiǔ	alcoholic beverage, wine
果汁	guǒzhī	fruit juice, syrup

本 běn   Copy of books

一本

書	shū	book
字典	zìdiǎn	Chinese character dictionary
詞典	cídiǎn	dictionary
雜誌	zázhì	(news, etc.) magazine
課本	kèběn	textbook
畫報	huàbào	pictorial

場 chǎng   For recreation or sporting events, performances and speeches

一場

球賽	qiúsài	ball game
電影	diànyǐng	movie, motion picture
話劇	huàjù	modern drama
音樂會	yīnyuèhuì	concert, musical recital
演說	yǎnshuō	speech
辯論	biànlùn	debate, argue

頂 dǐng   Top (of the head, a thing)

一頂

帽子	màozi	cap, hat

段 duàn   Section, part, period of time

一段

路	lù	road, path
樹枝	shùzhī	branch, twig
文章	wénzhāng	article, essay
音樂	yīnyuè	music
時間	shíjiān	time
故事	gùshi	story, plot (like of a novel)

副 fù   For a set of things

一副

眼鏡	yǎnjìng	eyeglasses
鞋帶	xiédài	shoelace
耳環	ěrhuán	earring

個 gè   General classifier

一個

人	rén	person

學校	xuéxiào	school
東西	dōngxi	thing, object
故事	gùshi	story, plot (like of a novel)

件 jiàn　For an item of clothing, luggage, or an incident
一件

東西	dōngxi	thing, object
事	shì	affair, matter, thing, incident, event
行李	xíngli	baggage, luggage
衣服	yīfu	clothes, clothing
家具	jiājù	furniture

節 jié　Length or sections
一節

課	kè	lesson, class
車厢	chēxiāng	compartment (of a train)
繩子	shéngzi	rope, string, cord
音樂	yīnyuè	music

句 jù　For sentences or lines of verse
一句

話	huà	sentence (spoken or written)
詩	shī	poetry, poem, verse

棵 kē　For plants
一棵

花	huā	flower
草	cǎo	grass
樹	shù	tree
莊稼	zhuāngjia	crop (mostly grain or cereal crop)

顆 kē　For small and round things (like bean, pearl)

一顆

豆子	dòuzi	beans, peas, legumes
珍珠	zhēnzhū	pearl
心	xīn	heart

塊 kuài For lump or chunk of things, things in shape of a flat sheet or the colloquial term for money

一塊

蛋糕	dàngāo	cake
巧克力	qiǎokèlì	chocolate
糖	táng	candy, sweets
地	dì	land, floor
錢	qián	cash, money

輛 liàng For vehicles

一輛

汽車	qìchē	motor vehicle, automobile, car
坦克	tǎnkè	tank (the military vehicle)
摩托車	mótuōchē	motorbike, motorcycle
自行車	zìxíngchē	bicycle
卡車	kǎchē	truck

門 mén For academic subjects

一門

課	kè	lesson, class
科學	kēxué	science
學問	xuéwèn	knowledge, scholarship
技術	jìshù	skill, technique, technology

篇 piān For articles, journals or pages

一篇

文章	wénzhāng	article, essay
講義	jiǎngyì	lecture notes
日記	rìjì	diary, journal

瓶 píng   Bottle, vase, jar

一瓶

水	shuǐ	water
牛奶	niúnǎi	milk (from a cow)
酒	jiǔ	alcoholic beverage

首 shǒu   For songs, poems

一首

詩	shī	poetry, poem, verse
歌	gē	song

雙 shuāng   Set of two

一雙

鞋	xié	shoes
筷子	kuàizi	chopsticks

艘 sōu   For ships or large vessels

一艘

船	chuán	boat, ship, vessel
快艇	kuàitǐng	speedboat, motor launch

所 suǒ   For schools, hospitals and houses

一所

學校	xuéxiào	school
醫院	yīyuàn	hospital
房子	fángzi	house, building

條 tiáo   For long and usually soft objects, some animals or items of news

一條

褲子	kùzi	pants, trousers
裙子	qúnzi	skirt
圍巾	wéijīn	scarf, muffler
領帶	lǐngdài	necktie
河	hé	river
魚	yú	fish
狗	gǒu	dog
新聞	xīnwén	news
消息	xiāoxi	news, tidings

聽 tīng　Tin, can (from the English "tin")

一聽

可口可樂	Kěkǒukělè	Coca-cola
雪碧	Xuěbì	Sprit
七喜	Qīxǐ	Seven Up
啤酒	píjiǔ	beer

位 wèi　Formal classifier for people

一位

老師	lǎoshī	teacher
先生	xiānsheng	Mister, sir
小姐	xiǎojie	young (unmarried) lady

張 zhāng　For flat things like a sheet of paper, a table, etc.

一張

紙	zhǐ	paper
報紙	bàozhǐ	newspaper
票	piào	ticket
地圖	dìtú	map

畫	huà	painting, drawing
照片	zhàopiàn	photograph
桌子	zhuōzi	table, desk
床	chuáng	bed, couch, bench

支 zhī   For long, narrow and stiff object

一支

筆	bǐ	pen
香煙	xiāngyān	cigarette
槍	qiāng	gun, rifle

枝 zhī   Branch

一枝

花	huā	flower
玫瑰	méigui	rose

隻 zhī   For one of a pair of things, especially body parts, or small animals

一隻

眼睛	yǎnjing	eye
腳	jiǎo	foot
手	shǒu	hand
耳朵	ěrduo	ear
鞋	xié	shoe
襪子	wàzi	sock
貓	māo	cat
老鼠	lǎoshu	rat, mouse
鳥	niǎo	bird
雞	jī	chicken
手套	shǒutào	glove, mitten

座 zuò   For large and fixed structures (like mountains, bridges)

一座

山	shān	mountain
橋	qiáo	bridge
大樓	dàlóu	multi-storied building

Note

有些名詞可用數個不同的量詞。

Some nouns can be quantified by several different measure words.

a dog：

yì zhī gǒu　yì tiáo gǒu
一　隻　狗　一　條　狗

a boat/ship：

yì zhī chuán　yì tiáo chuán　yì sōu chuán
一　隻　船　一　條　船　一　艘　船

(*Measure Word List – Compiled by Yu Hongwei*)

2

自我介紹　Self Introduction

　　自我介紹是人際交流的第一步。這一話題涉及的內容可有：問候、介紹姓名、年齡、家庭住址和電話等。

　　在每一個小話題裏我們都將提示相關的句式的結構和用法以及難點。請根據需求加減使用。

　　Self introduction is the initial step of an interpersonal communication. This topic covers greetings, an introduction to names, age, home addresses, telephone numbers, etc.

　　In each sub-topic, we provide related grammatical structures and explain functional usages as well as grammatical difficulties . Please make your selections for teaching and learning as needed.

教學重點 Content of Teaching and Learning

問好	Greetings
介紹姓名	Introducing Names
介紹年齡	Introducing Age
介紹電話號碼	Introducing Telephone Numbers
介紹家庭住址	Introducing Home Addresses
稱謂	Titles

教學難點 Cruxes of Teaching and Learning

形容詞謂語句	Adjective as Predicate
"不"的變調	Tone Sandhi for "不"
漢語的 "Yes/No"	Yes and No in Chinese
"姓"與"名"的位置	Positions of "姓" and "名"
"姓"與"叫"的使用	Practical Uses of "姓" and "叫"
"姓" and "名" vs. "是"	
請教尊姓大名	Formal and Informal Ways of Inquiring Names

文化聯繫 Cultural Relations

其他問候方式	Other ways of Greeting
請教尊姓大名	Respectful Ways of Asking about Names
姓名的排行	Order of Naming the Children
男孩名和女孩名	Meanings of Chinese Names: Boys Vs. Girls
介紹年齡	Introducing Age
稱謂	Titles

詞彙表 Glossary

常用（人與物）代詞表	List of Commonly Used Pronouns for People/ Animals and Objects

教學重點

Content of Teaching and Learning

問好　Greetings

In Chinese，we use the following patterns to say "Hi!"：

句型　Sentence Patterns

Subject	+	Adjective	

A： Nǐ　　　hǎo
　　你　　　好!　　　　Hi!

B： Nǐ　　　hǎo
　　你　　　好!　　　　Hi!

提問與回答　Questions and Answers

Subject	+	(Adverb)	+	Adjective

A： Nǐ　　　　　　　　hǎo　　ma
　　你　　　　　　　　好　　　嗎?

How are you doing?

B： Wǒ　　　hěn　　　hǎo
　　我　　　很　　　好。

I am very well.

A： Nǐ　　　　　　　　máng bu máng
　　你　　　　　　　　忙　　不　　忙?

Are you busy?

B： Wǒ　　　bú tài　　máng
　　我　　　不 太　　忙。

Not really.

否定形式　Negative："不"

A： Nǐ　　　　　　　　máng ma
　　你　　　　　　　　忙　　嗎?

Are you busy?

B：　Wǒ　　　　　bù　　　　　máng
　　　我　　　　　不　　　　　忙。

I am not busy.

Note

1）漢語的形容詞可以直接做謂語描述情形，不用動詞的幫助。

In Chinese, adjectives can be directly used without the help of verbs to describe a situation.

2）否定形式"不"直接放在形容詞前。

The negator "不" goes right in front of the adjective.

3）有兩種"肯定/否定"的問句。(請參閱 Chapter：Questions.)

There are two major ways to ask a "yes/no" question. (For more detail, see Chapter 14：Questions.)

a. Add a "嗎" at the end of the sentence.

Nǐ hǎo ma
你　好　嗎？

b. Use positive/negative form of an adjective.

Nǐ máng bu máng
你　忙　不　忙？

文化聯繫　Cultural Relations

日常生活中還有以下問候方式：

In daily life you may ask about a person's action as a form of greeting：

　　in the morning：

Zǎo
早　! Good morning! (meaning：You got up early)

　　during the day：

Chīle ma
吃了　嗎？Have you eaten?

Qù nǎr
去　哪兒? Where are you going?

Mángzhe na
忙着　　　哪！／？ You are busy！／Are you busy?

You're working hard！／Are you working hard?

You don't really expect a serious answer.

介紹姓名　Introducing Names

In Chinese：

介紹姓　　　Introducing one's last name：

Wǒ xìng Wáng
我　姓　王　。My Last name is Wang.

介紹名　　　Introducing one's first name/full name：

Wǒ jiào Xiǎomíng
我　叫　小明　。（Introducing first name）

Wǒ jiào Wáng Xiǎomíng
我　叫　王　小明　。（Introducing full name）

也可以說　　　Also you may say：

Wǒ de míngzi jiào Wáng Xiǎomíng
我　的　名字　叫　王　小明　。

（Introducing full name）

問姓名　Inquiring Names

英文的 "What is your name?" 既問姓又問名。中文要用兩個不同的
問題。

In English，we use "What is your name?" to ask for one's first or full name.
In Chinese，we must use different verbs to ask for one's first or full name.

（last name）

Nǐ xìng shénme
你　姓　什麼 ?

（first name/full name）

Nǐ jiào shénme
你　叫　什麼 ?

Nǐ jiào shénme míngzi
你 叫　什麼　名字？

Nǐ de míngzi jiào shénme
你 的　名字 叫　什麼？

若問中文或英文名字：

To ask about one's name specifically in Chinese or in English：

Nǐ de Zhōngwén míngzi jiào shénme
你 的　中文　　名字 叫　什麼？
What is your Chinese name?

Nǐ de Yīngwén míngzi jiào shénme
你 的　英文　名字 叫　什麼？
What is you English name?

文化聯繫　Cultural Relations

請教尊姓大名　Respecful Ways of Asking about Name

可以介紹另外兩種更禮貌的或在正式場合請教姓名的方式。

We may also ask adult names with respect or at a formal occasion by using：

Qǐng wèn　nín jiào shénme
請　　問，您 叫　什麼？May I ask, what your name is?

Nín guì xìng
您 貴 姓？　　　　　　May I have your honorable last name?

姓名的排行/男孩名和女孩名

Order of Naming the Children/Meanings of Chinese Names：Boys vs. Girls

這兩個題目都可以作爲文化學習來討論。

在此扼要説明的是，中文的名字一般由兩個或三個字組成：姓（也有少數雙姓的），雙字（或單字）的名。不少家庭的名字有傳統的排行。形式不同。家裏同一代人的名字常用一種形式。

傳統上，名字多選用褒義的詞語。一些有陽剛氣的字詞被選來做男孩名，而女孩名多爲表美好的字與詞。現代的名字則五花八門，不一定強調男女之分。

Both topics can be used for cultural discussions.

Generally speaking, Chinese names used to have two or three characters. However, there are exceptions. Chinese families would have part of their first names chosen by their ancestors to distinguish different generations. So siblings of the same generation in the extended family were easily identified.

Traditionally, words with positive meanings are chosen for names. Some words are specifically chosen for boy names, and some are favored for girls. However, modern names can be gender mutual.

介紹年齡　Introducing Age

介紹年齡用"歲"。

To introduce age, we use a number plus "歲." No verb is needed.

Wǒ (shì) shíwǔ suì
我 （是）十五 歲。I am 15.

Tā jīn nián jiǔ suì
他 今 年 九 歲。　He is nine this year.

根據長幼用不同方法問年齡。

To ask about one's age is more complicated. It depends on the age of the person.

1）10 歲以下的：

For people younger than 10 years of age：

Nǐ (jīn nián) jǐ suì
你（今 年）幾 歲？

2）10 歲以上的：

For people who are older than 10：

Nǐ (jīn nián) duō dà
你（今 年）多 大？

3）長者/長輩：

For people who are adults (to show respect)：

Nín duō dà suìshu　　Nǐ duō dà niánjì
您　多　大　歲數？／你　多　大　年紀？

文化聯繫　Cultural Relations

介紹年齡是漢語裏一個經常的話題。這與西方文化習慣不同。

In Chinese, age is an often used ice-breaker in conversation. Students should be aware of the cultural differences between the East and the West.

介紹電話號碼　Introducing Telephone Numbers

電話號碼要讀單個數碼。Telephone numbers are read digit by digit.

(312) 7738209：（三幺二）七七三八二○九

(For the use of "一" and "幺", see the details in Chapterl: Numbers in Life.)

問電話號碼　Inquiring a Telephone Number

問電話號碼的標準形式是：Use either of the following standard formats：

Qǐng wèn　nín de diànhuà (hàomǎ) shì shénme
請　　問，您　的　電話　（號碼）　是　什麼？ or
Nǐ de diànhuà shì duōshao (hào)
你　的　電話　是　多少　（號）？
What is your telephone number?

實際上：　For practical use, we simply say：

(Qǐng) gěi wǒ nǐ de diànhuà (hàomǎ)
（請）　給我你的　電話　（號碼）。
Qǐng bǎ diànhuà (hàomǎ) gěi wǒ
請　把　電話　（號碼）　給我。
(Please) give me your telephone number.

介紹家庭住址　Introducing Home Addresses

有三個句子可用來介紹你的家庭住址：

In Chinese, there are three structures that may be used to introduce your home addresses: (They have the same meaning.)

Wǒ jiā zài Zhījiāgē
我　家　在　芝加哥。

Wǒ zài Zhījiāgē zhù
我　在　芝加哥　住。　　} I live/My family lives in Chicago.

Wǒ zhù zài Zhījiāgē
我　住　在　芝加哥。

介紹具體的地址　Introducing a street address

1）英文先說門牌號碼，後說街名。

In English, we say the street number first, then the street name.

e. g. : 1050 S. Clark Street

2）漢語先說街名，後說門牌號碼。（由大至小）

In Chinese, all addresses go from larger concepts to smaller ones.

　　　　　　nán jiē　　hào
e. g. : Clark　南　街 1050　號

問家庭住址　Inquiring Locations/Home Addresses

In Chinese, there are, again, three structures that may be used to inquire your home addresses: (They have the same meaning.)

Nǐ jiā zhù nǎr　　Nǐ jiā zài nǎr
你　家　住　哪兒？/你　家　在　哪兒？

Nǐ zài nǎr zhù
你　在　哪兒　住？　　} Where do you /does your family live?

Nǐ jiā zhù zài shénme dìfang
你　家　住　在　什麼　地方？

完整回答　Complete Answer

Wǒ (jiā) zhù zài Zhījiāgē　　nán jiē　　hào
我　（家）住　在　芝加哥 Clark　南　街 1050　號。

稱謂　Titles

1）英文，頭銜在姓前。

In English, the title goes before the family name: Mr. Smith

中文，姓在頭銜前。

In Chinese, the title goes after the family name: 王先生

2）英文的稱謂/頭銜簡單。

In English, title use is not complex.

For male: Mr.

For female: Mrs. /Miss. /Ms.

中文的稱謂複雜。

In Chinese, titles reflect political conditions and social status.

For male: 先生

For female: 太太（夫人）/小姐/女士

文化聯繫　Cultural Relations

A. 不同的地方/區域流行不同的稱法。例如天津人習慣稱熟人"張哥""李姐"等；臺灣人習慣用"先生""太太"。

There are many Chinese-speaking regions in the world. A title can be regionally specific. For example, people from Tianjin like to address one another by using family terms, such as "張哥—brother" and "李姐—sister"; people from Taiwan have the habit to use "先生—Mr., 太太—Mrs."

B. 中國大陸的婦女婚後多不改姓夫姓。不能輕易認爲一個王女士就是王太太。用"女士"安全些。

Women from mainland China mostly do not change their maiden names after marriage. Therefore it is incorrect to assume that a Ms. Wang is a "王太太". In formal situations, it is advisable (safer) to speak to a woman as "女士", rather than other titles.

C. 通常"先生"也指丈夫，"太太"指某人之妻。例如："我先生""我太太"，"你先生""你太太"。

People often use "先生" to refer to one's husband and "太太" to one's wife, e. g. "我先生—my husband", "我太太—my wife"; "你先生—your husband", "你太太—your wife".

D. 不少人喜歡被人冠以學術頭銜和職位頭銜。例如“王大夫”“李處長”等。

People formally prefer academic/job titles to other titles, for example, “王大夫 Dr. Wang”, “李處長 Director Li.”

E. 長期以來，“同志”是在中國大陸一個普遍又普通的稱謂。現在“同志”一般在工作單位或年紀大的人中間使用。

For a long time “同志” had been a term to address everyone in PRC. But now “同志” is used in the work units or among aged people.

F. 熟人之間或非正式場合，中國人喜歡用如下的稱謂：

Among acquaintances or in informal situations, Chinese people sometimes use the following prefixes：

For young people：“小 xiǎo little” + last name, e. g. “小王，小李……”
   – A term of endearment used in front of people's names
For older people：“老 lǎo old” + last name, e. g. “老王，老李……”
   – A prefix to names to indicate affection, respect or familiarity
For tall and big people：“大 dà big” + last name, e. g. “大王，大李……”
   – A prefix to names to indicate endearment

G. 用家庭親屬的稱謂稱呼他人或陌生人也是一種常用的禮貌方式。

As a common practice, it is courteous to address strangers on street according to age by using terms for family members or relatives, e. g.

For a man about your father's age：“叔叔” – Uncle
For a woman about your mother's age：“阿姨” – Aunt
For a man of your grandfather's age：“老大爺，老爺爺” – Grandpa
For a woman of your grandmother's age：“老大媽，老奶奶” – Grandma
For people more or less of your own age：
   “大哥，大姐，小弟弟，小妹妹” – Brother/Sister
For little children：“小朋友”, etc. – Little friends

教學難點
Cruxes of Teaching and Learning

難點一　形容詞謂語句 Adjective as Predicate

英文形容和描述時要用動詞 "to be"。漢語直接用形容詞。

In Chinese, we use adjectives directly to describe (without use of a verb).

Subject ＋ Adjective
你　　　　好。
他　不　　好。

When translating from English to Chinese, the learner must avoid using "是".

難點二　"不" 的變調 Tone Sandhi for "不"

常用詞有常有的麻煩。"不" 後跟四聲的單音節詞時，變二聲。

When "不 bù not; no" is followed by a 4th tone, it changes to 2nd tone.

難點三　漢語的 "Yes" ／ "No" Yes and No in Chinese

英文的肯定是 Yes，否定是 No。

In English, "Yes" means yes, and "No" means no!

中文沒有一對一的表達方式。接受就肯定，否則否定。

In Chinese, there are no exact, equivalent expressions. To agree or to accept uses the positive form of an expression; otherwise uses the negative form.

　　A：你去不去？（Are you going?）

　　B：去，你呢？（Yes. And you?）

　　A：不去。（No.）

或用 "對/好" 表示贊同。Or use "對/好" to agree.

英文的 Yes 是表示説話人自己的肯定意見。No 是表示説話人自己的否定意見。不是同意不同意別人的意見。

Also, once again, generally, in English, "yes" means yes and "no" means no as far as actions are concerned, e. g. :

	A：Are you going?	B：Yes, I am going.
	A：Aren't you going?	B：Yes, I am going.
or：	A：Are you going?	B：No, I am not going.
	A：Aren't you going?	B：No, I am not going.

漢語的點頭肯定是同意或接受別人的意見；搖頭否定是不同意或不接受別人的意見。

While, in Chinese, depending on the question, we can answer positively to agree with or accept the other speaker's words by nodding our heads, or not by shaking our heads, e. g. :

　　　　A：你去嗎？(Speaker uses the positive：Are you going?)

　　　　B：去，我去。(Agree：Yes, I am.)

or：　B：不，我不去。(Disagree：No, I am not.)

　　　　A：你不去嗎？(Speaker uses the negative：Aren't you going?)

　　　　B：不，我去。(Disagree：No, I am.)

or：　B：對，我不去。(Agree：Yes, I am not)

難點四　姓與名的位置 Positions of "姓" and "名"

在口語中，英文先表名後表姓。

In English：Surname/family name is usually stated after the given name.

　　　　e. g. ：John Smith

　　　　John（given name）　　Smith（family name）

中文總是先表姓後表名。

In Chinese：Surname/last name is always stated first.

e. g. ：Yao，Ming 姚明

Yao（family name）   Ming（given name）

難點五　“姓”與“叫”的使用 Practical Uses of “姓”and “叫”

“姓” 只介紹姓。

“叫” 介紹名或全名。

“姓” introduces family name only.

“叫” introduces either a given name or full name.

難點六　“姓” and “名” vs. “是”

英文介紹姓名時説：“My name is Jane Smith.”

In English，we say “My name is Jane Smith.”

中文用“姓”介紹姓，“叫”介紹名。説：我姓王，我叫王小明。當然也可以説：“我是王小明。”用來認證自己是那個人。有細微的差別。

In Chinese：“姓” and “叫” are verbs which introduce names. We say：我姓王，我叫王小明。

However，one can says “我是王小明。” to identify oneself. Please pay attention to the subtleness of usages.

難點七　請教尊姓大名
Formal and Informal Ways of Inquiring Names

1）正式場合，用“您”表示禮貌與尊重。

Formal way of inquiry：Use “您” to show respect.

您姓什麼？

2）非正式場合，用“你”。

Informal way of inquiry：Use “你”.

　　　　　你姓什麼？

3）鄭重請教尊姓大名時，問：

Very formal way to inquire one's last name (in this case, first name is a-
voided)：

Qǐng wèn, nín guì xìng
請　　問，您貴　姓？

詞彙表

常用（人與物）代詞表
List of Commonly Used Pronouns for People/Animal and Objects

人稱代詞　Personal Pronoun

我	wǒ	I
你	nǐ	you
他	tā	he
她	tā	she
我們	wǒmen	we
你們	nǐmen	you
他們	tāmen	they (including both genders)
她們	tāmen	they (feminine)

非人稱代詞　Other Pronoun

它	tā	it (third person singular, neutral)

指示代詞　Demonstrative Pronoun

這	zhè/ "zhèi"	this
那	nà/nèi	that

每   měi   each, every

疑問代詞   Interrogative Pronoun

（See Chapter 14：Questions）

> **Note**
>
> 漢語的名詞没有數的概念。"們 men"是一個後綴，只用來表人稱代詞的複數。很少的名詞在極少的情況下可以用"們"表複數，如：人們/人們 rénmen。這與英文不同。
>
> Chinese, in general, has no plural forms for nouns. "們 men" is a suffix added to the above personal pronouns to indicate plurality. It is occasionally added to nouns indicating people, e. g.：人們/人們 rénmen people. It does not apply to other nouns/situations.

3

家人　**Family Members**

　　這一節的話題是談家庭、家人和親屬關係。除了詞彙以外，重點是動詞 "有" 及量詞的使用。家庭關係和稱謂是文化的傳統、觀念和習俗的一部分。在語言的使用上有很多反映。并且也可以引出不少對文化的討論。請酌情參考使用有關部分。

This chapter is about family, family members and relatives. Besides vocabulary, the major grammatical points are "to have" as predicate and the use of measure words. Family relations and titles are part of the cultural tradition, cultural values and practices in Chinese-speaking regions. Language usage significantly reflects culture in this regard. This topic can provoke many discussions about culture. Select the relevant content for teaching and learning.

教 學 重 點　Content of Teaching and Learning

家人	Family Members
有/沒有	Have /Not to Have
量詞	Measure Words
問答	Questions and Answers

教 學 難 點　Cruxes of Teaching and Learning

兄弟姐妹排行	Order of Your Siblings
非嫡系兄弟姐妹	Half/Step Siblings
親戚	Relatives
不/沒有	Negatives
名量詞	Measure Words for Noun (Nominal Measure Words)

文 化 聯 繫　Cultural Relations

中國家庭	Chinese Family

詞 彙 表 Glossary

家人與關係	Family Members and Relationships
親戚	Relatives

教學重點

Content of Teaching and Learning

家人　jiārén　Family Members

家庭成員　Family Members

Immediate Family：

爸爸	bàba	papa，daddy
媽媽	māma	mother，mom
哥哥	gēge	elder brother
弟弟	dìdi	younger brother
姐姐	jiějie	elder sister
妹妹	mèimei	younger sister

Grandparents：

Paternal：

爺爺	yéye	grandfather
	formal：	祖父 zǔfù
奶奶	nǎinai	grandmother
	formal：	祖母 zǔmǔ

Maternal：

姥爺	lǎoye	grandfather
	formal：	外公 wàigōng／外祖父 wàizǔfù
姥姥	lǎolao	grandmother
	formal：	外婆 wàipó／外祖母 wàizǔmǔ

家庭關係　Family Relationships

父母	fùmǔ	father and mother，parents

Biological Parents：

生父	shēngfù	birth father
生母	shēngmǔ	birth mother

Step Parents：

繼父	jìfù	stepfather
繼母	jìmǔ	stepmother
孩子	háizi	child, children
男孩子	nán háizi	boy
女孩子	nǚ háizi	girl
兒子	érzi	son
女兒	nǚ'ér	daughter
獨生子	dúshēngzǐ	only son
獨生女	dúshēngnǚ	only daughter

Siblings：

兄弟姐妹	xiōngdì jiěmèi	siblings
雙胞胎	shuāngbāotāi	twins

Spouse：

丈夫	zhàngfu	husband (legal)
妻子	qīzi	wife (legal)
先生	xiānsheng	husband (Mr.)
太太	tàitai	(夫人 fūrén wife) (Mrs.)

親戚　qīnqi　Relatives

Paternal

伯父	bófù	uncle (father's elder brother)
伯母	bómǔ	aunt (wife of father's elder brother)
叔叔	shūshu	uncle (father's younger brother)
嬸	shěn	aunt (wife of father's younger brother)
姑姑	gūgu	aunt (father's sister)
姑父	gūfù	uncle (husband of father's sister)

Maternal：

舅舅	jiùjiu	uncle (mother's elder or younger brother)
舅媽	jiùmā	aunt (wife of mother's brother)
姨	yí	mother's sister; wife's sister
姨父	yífù	uncle (husband of mother's sister)

表親　biǎoqīn　Cousin；Relationship between Cousins

(First cousins：Call them brothers and sisters according to age.)

paternal　堂　táng　　(with the same family name)

堂哥	堂姐
堂弟	堂妹

maternal　表　biǎo　　(with different family name)

表哥	表姐
表弟	表妹

(Second cousins：Call your parents' cousins uncles and aunts.)

堂叔	表舅
堂姑	表姨

其他親屬關係　qítā qīnshǔ guānxi

Other Relationships among Relatives (by blood or marriage)

孫子	sūnzi	grandson
孫女	sūnnü	granddaughter
外孫	wàisūn	grandson (daughter's son)
外孫女	wàisūnnü	granddaughter (daughter's daughter)
侄子	zhízi	nephew (brother's son)
侄女	zhínü	niece (brother's daughter)
外甥	wàisheng	nephew (sister's son)
外甥女	wàishengnǚ	niece (sister's daughter)

公公	gōnggong	father-in-law (husband's father)
婆婆	pópo	mother-in-law (husband's mother)
岳父	yuèfù	father-in-law (wife's father)
岳母	yuèmǔ	mother-in-law (wife's mother)
女婿	nǚxu	son-in-law
兒媳	érxí	daughter-in-law

有/没有　yǒu/méiyǒu　Have/Not to Have

功用 Function：表所有　To specify prossession

句型 Sentence Patterns：

Subject	+	Verb	+	(# ge)	+	object.

Wǒ　　　　yǒu　　　　　　　　　dìdi
我　　　　有　　　　　　　　　弟弟。

Wǒ　　　méiyǒu　　　　　　　mèimei
我　　　没有　　　　　　　　妹妹 。

否定形式　Negative Form：　　（没有 méiyǒu not have）

Never say "不有".

量詞　Measure Words

量詞連接數詞與名詞。

When numbering objects, a measure word is needed to connect the number with the noun.

Wǒ　　yǒu　　liǎng ge　　dìdi
我　　有　　兩　個　　弟弟。

問答　Questions & Answers

If a number is less than 10, use "幾 jǐ how many".

Nǐ bàba māma yǒu jǐ ge háizi

你 爸爸 媽媽 有 幾個 孩子？

Tāmen yǒu liǎng ge érzi hé yí ge nǚ'ér

他們 有 兩 個兒子和一個女兒。

If a number is greater than 10, use "多少 duōshao how many".

Nǐmen bān yǒu duōshao xuésheng

你們 班 有 多少 學生 ？

Wǒmen bān yǒu shí'èr ge xuésheng

我們 班 有 十二 個 學生 。

教學難點

Cruxes of Teaching and Learning

難點一　兄弟姐妹排行 Order of Your Siblings

中英對比 Compare English and Chinese：

1）中文的 "brother" 分哥哥和弟弟；"sister" 分姐姐和妹妹。

In English, we refer all our male siblings as "brothers" and all our female siblings as "sister".

In Chinese, we call older male siblings as "哥哥" and younger ones "弟弟", older female siblings as "姐姐", and younger female siblings as "妹妹".

2）中文可按年齡的大小分。

In Chinese, we also number our siblings or relatives in order by age："大哥""二哥""三哥""四哥"，"大表姐""二表姐""三表姐" "四表姐" 等。

難點二　非嫡系兄弟姐妹 Half/Step Siblings

按中國的文化，在一個家庭裏，不管有無血緣關係，按年齡大小互稱兄弟姐妹。

In English, we refer to half/step siblings directly as "step brothers/sisters" or "half brothers/sisters."

In Chinese, we normally don't differentiate half/step siblings from other siblings.

If needed, half sibings may be called:

tóng fù yì mǔ tóng mǔ yì fù de xiōngdì jiěmèi
同　父異母／同　　母異父的　兄弟　姐妹

難點三　親戚 Relatives

中文沒有"second cousin"這個概念。父母的"cousin"是你的堂（叔/姑/舅/姨）或表（叔/姑/舅/姨）。

In English, parents' cousins are second cousins.

In Chinese, we refer to our parents' cousins as our parental/maternal uncles and aunts.

paternal	maternal
堂（叔/姑/舅/姨）	表（叔/姑/舅/姨）

文化聯繫　Cultural Relations

出於禮貌，非親屬之間也可以用親屬稱謂互相稱呼。

To be polite, usually, we refer to other people in terms of relatives, e. g.

　　For older adults："爺爺，奶奶"；

　　For adults closer in age to parents："叔叔，阿姨"；

　　For people of our own age："哥哥，姐姐", etc.

難點四　不/沒有 Negatives

1）"有"的否定是"沒有"。

The negative form for "有" is "没有".

Never say "不有". This cannot be overly emphasized.

"不" 和 "没" 的不同

Both "不" and "没" are negatives. However, they have different emphases:

a. "不" 否定日常重復的行爲動作。

"不" denies the occurrence of a habitual/repeated action.

> 我每天都不吃早飯。

I don't eat breakfast. (everyday/without exception)

b. "不" 否定意願。

"不" also denies the willingness of an action.

> 昨天他怎麼説都不來（不肯/不願意）。

He would not come (no matter what, he was unwilling.)

c. "没" 否定一件特定事件/行爲的發生。

"没" simply denies the completion of a specific action.

> 我每天都吃早飯，可是今天没吃。

I eat breakfast daily but did not this morning (missed one meal.)

難點五　名量詞 Measure Words for Noun (Nominal Measure Words)

請參閱數字節中的量詞注釋和量詞表。

This is an important grammatical point. Please see the List of Commonly Used Measure Words for beginning learners Chapter 1: Numbers in Life.

文化聯繫

中國家庭　　Chinese Family

這裏有很多話題可談。中國傳統的居住習慣如有"四代同堂"等。傳統的中國人家庭觀念包括"尊老愛幼""孝敬父母"等，以及現代中國的"獨生子女"一代。

There are many cultural traditions, values, and practices under this topic to learn about. We may begin with phrases like"四代同堂","尊老愛幼","孝敬父母", and"獨生子女".

4

國家/人/語言

Country/
People/Language

　　談論國家、人和語言不僅是自我介紹的一部分，也是學習地理、文化、社會風情等有關的內容。可考慮酌情編入不同的教學單元。

　　本節教學重點之一是詞彙。故詞彙放在首要位置。漢語的國名、國人和語言的聯繫明確，容易學習記憶。美國作為一個多元民族、多元文化的國家，學生的家庭背景情況不一，在提供詞彙時，不要保守，讓學生各得其所。

　　其他句型和語法點是這個話題的必需，請參考使用。新老師務請審閱教學難點以防患於未然。

Speaking about countries, people, and languages is part of self introduction. It is also an opportunity to study geography, culture, and other customs. Combine it with any topic according to the class instructional needs.

This chapter takes advantage of clear and easy connections between vocabularies of country, people and language. It emphasizes learning vocabulary. It puts vocabulary in the forefront. The USA is a country of immigrants with multi-cultural and multi-lingual backgrounds. Provide the necessary vocabulary to all students for convenient use.

The sentences patterns and instructional difficulties are musts for this topic. Make sure to be thoroughly familiar with them for proper classroom instruction and explanation.

教 學 重 點　Content of Teaching and Learning

談國籍與語言	Speaking about Citizenship and Language
談地點	Speaking about Locations
簡單問句	Simple Questions
複雜問句	Complex Questions

教 學 難 點　Cruxes of Teaching and Learning

"Chinese"	Function of "哪"
"是" vs. "在"	"也" vs. "和"
"Latin" vs. "Spanish"	"And" vs. "和"

"在" vs. "在住 " vs. "住在"   "也 " vs. "還"

"說" vs. "告訴"   "都不" vs. "不都"

"Where are you from?"   "都" vs. "All"

文化聯繫 Cultural Relations

我們都是美國人   We are all Americans

漢語/中文/華文   Chinese Language

詞彙表 Glossary

國家/人   Country/People

語言   Language

有關地理詞   Related Geographical Terms

教學重點

Content of Teaching and Learning

談國籍與語言　Speaking about Citizenship and Language

功用 Function：Identifying People and Language

句型 Sentence Patterns：

是　shì　to be

Tā shì Zhōngguórén
他 是　中國人　　。
He is a Chinese.

Wǒ shì Měiguórén
我 是　美國人 。
I am an American.

Wǒmen shì Zhōngguórén yě shì Měiguórén
我 們 是　中國人　，也 是　美國人　。
We are Chinese and American.

說　shuō　to speak

Zhōngguórén shuō Zhōngwén
中國人　　說　中文　　。
Chinese people speak Chinese.

Měiguórén shuō Yīngyǔ
美國人　　說　英語 。
American people speak English.

其他句型：副詞和連詞

也 yě also, too；還　hái still, yet, also, as well；
都 dōu all；和 hé and, with

Wǒmen shuō Hànyǔ yě shuō Yīngyǔ
我們　說　漢語，也 說　英語 。
We speak Chinese and English, too.

Tāmen yě shuō Yīngyǔ bù dōu shuō Hànyǔ
他們　也 說　英語，不 都　說　漢語 。

They also speak English but not all of them speak Chinese.

Tā shuō Yīngyǔ yě shuō Fǎyǔ hái huì shuō yìdiǎnr Hànyǔ
他 説 英語 ，也 説 法語，還 會 説 一點兒 漢語 。
He speaks English, French, also a little Chinese.

Wǒ de péngyou shì Mòxīgērén hé Měiguórén
我 的 朋友 是 墨西哥人 和 美國人 。
My freinds are Mexican and American.

Tā shuō Xībānyáyǔ hé Fǎyǔ
他 説 西班牙語 和 法語。
He speaks Spanish and French.

談地點   Speaking about Locations

功用 Function：Identifying Locations

句型 Sentence Patterns：

是 shì to be

Wǒ shì Zhōngguórén
我 是 中國人。
I am a Chinese.

Tā shì Fǎguórén
他 是 法國人 。
He is a French.

在 zài to be at

Zhōngguó zài Yàzhōu
中國 在 亞洲。
China is located in Asia.

Fǎguó zài Ōuzhōu
法國 在 歐洲 。
France is located in Europe.

簡單問句   Simple Questions

Nǐ shì nǎ（guó）rén
你 是 哪（國）人？   Where are you from?

Wǒ shì Zhōngguórén
我 是　中國人　。　　　　　　　I am a Chinese.

Zhōngguó zài nǎr
中國　　在 哪兒?　　　　　　　Where is China?

Zhōngguó zài Yàzhōu
中國　　在　亞洲　　　　　　　China is located in Asia.

Nǐ shuō shénme yǔ
你 說　什麼 語?　　　　　　　What language do you speak?

Wǒ shuō Hànyǔ
我　說　漢語　。　　　　　　　I speak Chinese.

Tā ne
他 呢?　　　　　　　　　　　What about him?

Tā shuō Yīngyǔ yě shuō Xībānyáyǔ
他 說　英語 ,也 說　西班牙語 。　He speaks English and Spanish.

複雜問句　Complex Questions

wèn dá　fùzá jù　zhíjiē yǐnyǔ yǔ jiànjiē yǐnyǔ
問　答 :(複雜 句: 直接 引語 與 間接 引語)

　　Direct quote:

　　　　Wǒ wèn tā　(Nǐ) shì nǎ (li) rén
　　　　我　問 他 "(你) 是 哪 (裏) 人 ?"
　　　　Tā shuō　　Wǒ shì Měiguórén
　　　　他 說 : "我 是　美國人　。"

　　I asked him, "Where are you from?" He said, "I am an American."

　　Indirect quote:

　　　　Wǒ wèn tā Nǐ shì nǎ (guó) rén
　　　　我　問 他 :你 是 哪 (國) 人 ?
　　　　Tā shuō tā shì Měiguórén
　　　　他　說 他 是　美國人　。

　　I asked him where he is from. He said he is an American.

　　Direct quote:

　　　　Wǒ wèn tā　nǐ shì nǎr rén
　　　　我　問 他 : "你 是 哪兒 人 ?"

Tā gàosu wǒ　　Wǒ shì Měiguórén
他　告訴　我："我　是　美國人　。"

I asked him,"where are you from?"He told me,"I am an American."

Indirect quote：

Wǒ wèn tā　(nǐ)　shì nǎ　(guó) rén
我　問　他:(你)　是　哪　(國)　人？

Tā gàosu wǒ tā shì Měiguórén
他　告訴　我　他　是　美國人　。

I asked him where he is from. He told me that he is an American.

Look at the following examples to summarize your own rules：

亞洲：

越南	Yuènán	Vietnam	
	越南人		越南語
泰國	Tàiguó	Thailand	
	泰國人		泰國語
韓國	Hánguó	(South) Korea	
	韓國人		韓國語

歐洲：

波蘭	Bōlán	Poland	
	波蘭人		波蘭語
意大利	Yìdàlì	Italy	
	意大利人		意大利語

教學難點

Cruxes of Teaching and Learning

難點一　"Chinese"

怎麼翻譯"Chinese"這個詞？這個詞的英文意思一個是名詞，指中國人和中國語言；一個是形容詞，指跟中國有關的或從中國來的。這是初學者、特別是中小學生容易搞亂的。

In English, the word "Chinese" can be used two ways：

1）As a noun to refer to a person of Chinese origin or the Chinese language.

2）As an adjective to modify a noun：a Chinese movie or a Chinese restaurant.

Learners sometimes say,"漢語飯館" instead of "中國飯館"。

The correct usages need to be emphasized.

難點二　"是" vs. "在"

初學者，特別是中小學生常把"是"和"在"放在一個句子裡。區別的辦法是：

"是"——to be 是用來定義、鑒別身份的。

"在"——to be at 是用來明確地點與時間的。

Learners, often, use "是" and "在" in the same sentence, which is wrong in Chinese.

"是" is "to be". The function of this word is to identify what is what and who is whom.

"在" is "to be at". (If translate "在" as "to be at" it helps English speakers.) The function of this word is to identify the location.

Even though English the following sentences are more or less the same in meaning, they do not have the same structure：

"I am a student at Chicago High School."

"I attend school at Chicago High (I go to Chicago High)."

"是" and "在" have different grammatical functions. See below：

Subject + Location + Verb + Object

Wǒ　　　　　　　　shì Zhījiāgē Zhōngxué de xuésheng
我　　　　　　　　是 芝加哥　中學　的　學生　。
I am a Chicago High School student.

Wǒ zài Zhījiāgē Zhōngxué shàngxué
我　在 芝加哥　中學　上學　　　。
I attend school at Chicago High School.

難點三　"Latin" vs. "Spanish"

Be prepared to address the following:

Very rarely, some children are confused about "Latin", "Latinos", "Spanish".

A simple answer:

The language most Latinos speak is called Spanish.

Latin is a classical written language.

難點四　"在" vs. "在住" vs. "住在"

I live/My family lives in Chicago.

Wǒ jiā zài Zhījiāgē
我 家 在 芝加哥。("在"as a verb)

Wǒ jiā zài Zhījiāgē zhù
我 家 在 芝加哥 住。("在"as a proposition)

Wǒ jiā zhù zài Zhījiāgē
我 家 住 在 芝加哥。("在"as resultative complement)

難點五　"說" vs. "告訴"

"說" is "to speak/say". It takes a direct or indirect quote. For example:

Tā shuō　Wǒ shì xuésheng
他 說:"我 是 學生 。"(A)

Tā shuō tā shì xuésheng
他 說 他 是 學生 。(B)

"告訴" is "to tell". It takes direct and indirect object and quote. For example:

Tā gàosu wǒ　Wǒ shì xuésheng
他 告訴 我:"我 是 學生 。"(C)

Tā gàosu wǒ tā shì xuésheng
他 告訴 我 他是 學生 。(D)

In (A) and (C) the quotes (with quotation marks " ...") are direct quotes.

In (B) and (D) the quotes (without quotation marks) are indirect quotes.

In (C) and (D), "我" is the indirect object, the quotes (direct and indirect) are the direct objects.

難點六 "Where are you from?"

"Where are you from?" 這句話很難翻譯成中文。特別是在美國這樣一個多民族的移民國家裏，情況太複雜了，一言難問清。我們建議説：

This question is hard to translate into Chinese, if you ask this in the US, a country of immigrants. In order not to alienate anyone, the possible solutions we suggest are：

Nǐ jiā zǔ shàng shì nǎr rén
你（家/祖 上 ancestors, forefathers）是 哪兒 人？

Nǐ jiā zǔ shàng shì nǎ guó rén
你（家/祖 上 ）是 哪 國 人？

下面的兩句有政治敏感的嫌疑，不太合適。

It could be politically sensitive and inappropriate to say：

Nǐ (jiā) shì cóng nǎr lái de
你（家）是 從 哪兒來 的？

Nǐ shì nǎ guó rén
你是 哪 國 人？

難點七 Function of "哪"

哪兒 nǎ (r) where

Zài nǎr
在 哪兒？

Qù nǎr
去 哪兒?
Cóng nǎr dào nǎr qù
從 哪兒 到 哪兒 去?

哪 nǎ/něi which, what

    Nǐ zài nǎ ge xuéxiào shàngxué
    你 在 哪個 學校   上學 ?
     Nǐ zài shénme xuéxiào shàngxué
    (你 在 什麼   學校   上學 ?)
    Nǐ shì nǎ ge dìfang de rén
    你 是 哪個 地方 的 人?
     Nǐ shì shénme dìfang de rén
    (你 是 什麼   地方 的 人?)

難點八　"也" vs. "和"

"也"和"和"也是學生常用錯的。

Often, learners think "也" and "和" are both like the English "and/also". The differences must be emphasized, and can be simply emphasized like this:

"也" connects two verbal phrases:

    Wǒ shuō Yīngyǔ yě shuō Hànyǔ
    我 説 英語,也 説 漢語。
    Tā yǒu gēge yě yǒu dìdi
    他 有 哥哥,也 有 弟弟。

"和" connects two noun phrases:

    Wǒ shuō Yīngyǔ hé Hànyǔ
    我 説 英語 和 漢語。
    Tā yǒu gēge hé dìdi
    他 有 哥哥 和 弟弟。

難點九　"And" vs. "和"

英語的"And"可以連接句子，"和"不能。請比較。

Often, learners assume "And" and "和" have the same grammatical functions in both English and Chinese. However, they do not. "And" can connect words, phrases, clauses, and sentences. "和" can connect words or phrases, but cannot connect clauses/sentences.

(words) He and I

　　　　tā hé wǒ
　　　　他 和 我

(phrases) Watch movie and play on the computer

　　　　kàn diànyǐng hé wán diànnǎo
　　　　看　電影　和 玩　電腦

(clauses) I watched a movie at home and also watched one at school.

　　　　Wǒ zài jiā kànle yí gè diànyǐng zài xuéxiào kànle yí ge
　　　　我　在家 看了 一個　電影 ，在　學校　看了 一 個
　　　　diànyǐng　　　hé
　　　　電影　　。(No"和")

(sentences) I have two brothers. And he has no brother.

　　　　Wǒ yǒu liǎng ge gēge Tā méiyǒu gēge　　hé
　　　　我 有　兩 個 哥哥。他 沒有　哥哥。(No"和")

Note

It can never be over-emphasized that "和" cannot connect sentences.

難點十　"也" vs. "還"

"也" and "還" both can be translated into "also" and "too".

"也" and "還" both are used to connect verbal phrases.

However, what "也" connects usually has equal weight, while "還" also means "still", it has a notation of "in addition to".

Wǒmen shuō Yīngyǔ yě shuō Hànyǔ
我們   説 英語 ,也 説   漢語 。
Tā shuō Yīngyǔ Hànyǔ hái shuō yìdiǎn Fǎyǔ
他 説   英語 、漢語 、還 説   一點 法語。

難點十一   "都不" vs. "不都"

The first word controls the following one：

"都不" means "all not"；"不都" means "not all"

他們都不是中國人。

They are all not Chinese/ None of them is Chinese.

他們不都是中國人。

They are not all Chinese/Not all of them are Chinese.

難點十二   "都" vs. "All"

"都" 在漢語裡是一個副詞，只能放在動詞的前面。"All" 是無所不在的。

"都" in Chinese is an adverb. It can only be put before a verb to modify the verb. "都" can never be put before a noun or at the beginning of a sentence while the English "all" can.

都   dōu   all（"All" at the beginning of a sentence）

我們都是學生。（"都" before the verb）All of us are students.

所有 suǒyǒu   all（"All" before a noun）

我們認識所有的人。

（You cannot say "都人" because "人" is not a verb.）

Unless, you say：這兒的人我們都認識。We know all the people.

Other words meaning "All"：

全 quán   1）complete, total, whole, entire, all

2）completely，totally，entirely

全家	quán jiā	entire family
全國	quán guó	whole country，entire nation，nationwide
全年	quán nián	annual，yearly
全天	quán tiān	entire day

我們全都是中學生。　　We are all high school students.

他們全都沒有中文書。　None of them has a Chinese book.

整　zhěng　whole，complete，entire

整天	zhěng tiān	all day，whole day，all day long
整年	zhěng nián	all year，whole year，all year long
整個國家	zhěnggè guójiā	whole nation

文化聯繫

Cultural Relations

我們都是美國人　We are all Americans

In Chinese，there are two ways to specify the ethnicity/origin of a U. S. citizen.
For Chinese Americans：

1）華裔（Huá yì）美國人

華裔，refers to the Chinese origin or Chinese descent of citizens of countries other than China. "華" refers to China/Chinese. "裔" means origin/descent，especially the citizens of countries other than the countries of origin.

2）美籍華人（Měi jí Huárén）American Citizen of Chinese descent. "籍" means "citizenship/registry". As such，there can be other Americans：

　　　　　　　　　Rì yì Měiguórén　Měi jí Rìběnrén
Japanese-American：　日裔　美國人　/美　籍　日本人

	Fǎ yì Měiguórén　Měi jí Fǎguórén
French-American：	法　裔　美國人　/　美　籍　法國人

	Fēi yì Měiguórén　Měi jí Fēizhōurén
African-American：	非　裔　美國人　/　美　籍　非洲人

	Lādīng yì Měiguórén　Měi jí Lādīngrén
Latin-American：	拉　丁　裔　美國人　/　美　籍　拉丁人

漢語/中文/華文　Chinese Language

我們學的是"漢語/中文/華文"，也叫"普通話"或"國語"。中國有很多種方言，例如：廣東人說廣東話。

The Chinese we are learning is "普通話 pǔtōnghuà", common spoken language, standard spoken Chinese, modern standard Chinese (based on the Beijing dialect, also known as Mandarin or Guoyu).

Many Chinese and Chinese Americans speak different dialects. For example：

Guǎngdōngrén shuō Guǎngdōnghuà
廣東人　　　　說　　　廣東話　　。

or：

Shànghǎirén shuō Shànghǎihuà
上海人　　　說　　　上海話　　。

Tiānjīnrén shuō Tiānjīnhuà
天津人　　　說　　　天津話　。

詞彙表

Glossary

國家/人　guójiā/rén　Country/People

國家 (Nation, Country)：　　人 (People)：

China	中國	Zhōngguó	中國人	Zhōngguórén
The United States of America	美國	Měiguó	美國人	Měiguórén
The United Kingdom	英國	Yīngguó	英國人	Yīngguórén

France	法國	Fǎguó	法國人	Fǎguórén
Germany	德國	Déguó	德國人	Déguórén
Japan	日本	Rìběn	日本人	Rìběnrén
Mexico	墨西哥	Mòxīgē	墨西哥人	Móxīgērén
Puerto Rico	波多黎各	Bōduōlígè	波多黎各人	Bōduōlígèrén
Poland	波蘭	Bōlán	波蘭人	Bōlánrén
Canada	加拿大	Jiānádà	加拿大人	Jiānádàrén
Russia	俄羅斯	Éluósī	俄羅斯人	Éluósīrén
The Philippines	菲律賓	Fēilǜbīn	菲律賓人	Fēilǜbīnrén
(South) Korea	韓國	Hánguó	韓國人	Hánguórén
(North) Korea	朝鮮	Cháoxiǎn	朝鮮人	Cháoxiǎnrén
Thailand	泰國	Tàiguó	泰國人	Tàiguórén
India	印度	Yìndù	印度人	Yìndùrén
Pakistan	巴基斯坦	Bājīsītǎn	巴基斯坦人	Bājīsītǎnrén

語言　yǔyán　Language

	yǔ 語 Spoken Language		wén 文 Written Language	
Chinese	漢語	Hànyǔ	中文	Zhōngwén
English	英語	Yīngyǔ	英文	Yīngwén
French	法語	Fǎyǔ	法文	Fǎwén
German	德語	Déyǔ	德文	Déwén
Japanese	日語	Rìyǔ	日文	Rìwén
Spanish	西班牙語	Xībānyáyǔ	西班牙文	Xībānyáwén
Latin	拉丁語	Lādīngyǔ	拉丁文	Lādīngwén

有關地理詞　Related Geographical Terms

地球	dìqiú	earth, globe
大洲	dàzhōu	continent
亞洲	Yàzhōu	Asia

非洲	Fēizhōu	Africa
歐洲	Ōuzhōu	Europe
美洲	Měizhōu	America

	北美州	Běiměizhōu	North America
	中美洲	Zhōngměizhōu	Central America
	南美洲	Nánměizhōu	South America
	拉丁美洲	Lādīngměizhōu	Latin America

大洋洲	Dàyángzhōu	Oceania
南極洲	Nānjízhōu	Antarctic
北極	běijí	North Pole, Arctic Pole

大洋　dàyáng　Ocean

太平洋	Tàipíngyáng	Pacific Ocean
大西洋	Dàxīyáng	Atlantic Ocean
印度洋	Yìndùyáng	Indian Ocean
北冰洋	Běibīngyáng	Arctic Ocean

中國　Zhōngguó　China

首都	shǒudū	Capital, capital city
省	shěng	Province
城市	chéngshì	Big city
農村	nóngcūn	Village, countryside

北京	Běijīng	Beijing (capital, PRC)
上海	Shànghǎi	Shanghai (municipality, PRC)
天津	Tiānjīn	Tianjin (municipalcity, PRC)
重慶	chóngqìng	Chongqing (municipal city, PRC)

香港	Xiānggǎng	Hong Kong (SAR)
澳門	Àomén	Macao, Aomen (SAR)
廣東	Guǎngdōng	Guangdong (Province)

| 臺灣 | Táiwān | Taiwan（Province） |
| 臺北 | Táiběi | Taipei（Provincial capital，Taiwan） |

大河	dàhé	Great river	
	黄河	Huáng Hé	Huang he River，Yellow River
	長江	Cháng Jiāng	Changjiang，Yangtse River
名山	míngshān	Famous mountains	
	泰山	Tài Shān	Mount Tai（in Shandong Province）
	華山	Huà Shān	Mount Hua（in Shaanxi Province）
	阿裡山	Ālǐ Shān	Mount Ali（in Taiwan Province）
古迹	gǔjì	Historic sites	
	長城	Chángchéng	Great Wall of China
	故宫	Gùgōng	Imperial Palace

5

Work and
Occupation

工作與職業

　　工作與職業的話題牽扯兩方面的詞彙：工作／職業和工作地點。本節着重討論學習這兩方面的詢問、表述和連貫表達。

　　這個話題也與文化社會的因素有很多聯繫。漢語的學習可與學生的家庭背景與社區文化相結合擴展討論學習。

　　Work and occupation is a topic involving two kinds of vocabularies: work/ occupation and the workplace. This chapter stresses the facilitation of inquiry, the statement of each aspect and the combination of the two.

　　This topic also has connections with cultural and social vocabularies. Language learning creates an opportunity for further discussion about students' families and community backgrounds.

教 學 重 點　Content of Teaching and Learning

工作與職業	Work and Occupation
詢問／表述職業	Asking and Speaking about Occupation
工作地點	Workplace
詢問／表述工作地點	Asking and Speaking about Workplace

教 學 難 點　Cruxes of Teaching and Learning

"做" vs. "是"	
地點在句中的位置	Position of Location Word in a Sentence

文 化 聯 繫　Cultural Relations

工作與職業	Work and Occupation

詞 彙 表　Glossary

職業	Occupations
工作地點	Workplace
跟學習相關的詞彙	Words Related to Study

工作與職業　Work and Occupation

職業　Occupations

老師	lǎoshī	Teacher
律師	lǜshī	Lawyer, attorney
工程師	gōngchéngshī	Engineer
醫生	yīshēng（大夫 dàifu）	Doctor, physician
護士	hùshi	Nurse（in a hospital）
經理	jīnglǐ	Manage, director
職員	zhíyuán	Employee, office worker, staff member
商人	shāngrén	Merchant, businessman, trader
演員	yǎnyuán	Performer, actor, actress
藝術家	yìshùjiā	Artist
警察	jǐngchá	Police officer
消防隊員	xiāofáng duìyuán	Fireman, fire fighter
售貨員	shòuhuòyuán	Shop assistant, salesperson
秘書	mìshū	Secretary
保安員	bǎo'ānyuán	Security guard
工人	gōngrén	Worker
學生	xuésheng	Student, pupil

大學生	dàxuéshēng	University student, college student
中學生	zhōngxuéshēng	Middle-school student
小學生	xiǎoxuéshēng	Elementary school student

詢問／表述職業　Asking and Speaking about Occupation

句型　Sentence Patterns：

工作	gōngzuò	work, occupation, job
做	zuò	act as, work, do
	Zuò shénme gōngzuò	
	做　什麼　工作？	
是	shì	am, is, are …
	Shì lǎoshī	
	是　老師。	

工作地點　Workplace

公司	gōngsī	Company, corporation, firm
醫院	yīyuàn	Hospital
商店	shāngdiàn	Shop, store
書店	shūdiàn	Bookstore
飯館	fànguǎn	Restaurant
餐館	cānguǎn	Restaurant
飯店	fàndiàn	Hotel, restaurant
咖啡館	kāfēiguǎn	Coffee shop
酒吧	jiǔbā	Bar (especially Western-style), pub
圖書館	túshūguǎn	Library
警察局	jǐngchájú	Police station
派出所	pàichūsuǒ	Police substation
銀行	yínháng	Bank
幼兒園	yòu'éryuán	Kindergarten, nursery school
劇院	jùyuàn	Theater, theater club
政府機構	zhèngfǔ jīgòu	Government institution

學校	xuéxiào	School
大學	dàxué	University, college
中學	zhōngxué	Middle school, high school
小學	xiǎoxué	Elementary school, primary school

詢問╱表述工作地點　Asking and Speaking about Workplace

句型　Sentence Patterns：

地方　dìfang　place, location

Zài shénme dìfang gōngzuò
（在　什麼　地方　工作　?）
Zài nǎr gōngzuò
在　哪兒　工作　?
Zài gōngsī gōngzuò
在　公司　工作　。

文化聯繫

Cultural Relations

　　這個話題可與現實生活緊密聯繫，也可作文化對比。但公立學校學生的家庭背景各不相同，這個話題會有敏感區。一方面鼓勵學生與生活實際聯繫，另一方面不應讓學生感到不舒服。

　　Applying this topic is a good opportunity to make real-life connections and cultural comparisons. However, be aware, in K-12 schools, especially public schools, students come from all social-economical backgrounds. This topic, potentially, may be sensitive to some students. The teacher needs to encourage the use of language in real-life situations, while avoiding situations that may cause discomfort.

教學難點

Cruxes of Teaching and Learning

難點一　"做" vs. "是"

Asking about a person's profession uses the verb "做", but the answer uses the verb "是".

句型　Sentence Patterns

Subject	+	Place	+	Verb	+	Object.

Nǐ bàba　　　　　　　　　　zuò　shénme gōngzuò
你 爸爸　　　　　　　　　　做　什麼　工作 ？

Wǒ bàba　　　　　　　　　　shì　lǎoshī
我 爸爸　　　　　　　　　　是　老師。

Nǐ bàba　zài nǎr　　gōngzuò
你 爸爸　在 哪兒　　工作 ？

Tā　　zài zhōngxué　gōngzuò
他　　在 中學　　　工作 。

難點二　地點在句中的位置
Position of Location Word in a Sentence

Location word is always placed before the action verb. A name of a place can be used as the location of an action or as a modifier of a noun. (Learners often confuse the two in use.)

句型　Sentence Patterns：

| Subject | + | Place | + | Verb | + | Object. |

Tā　　　　　　　　shì　　Zhījiāgē Dàxué de xuésheng
A. 他　　　　　　　是　　芝加哥 大學 的 學生 。

He is a student in the University of Chicago.

（A：U of C defines the student as part of the identification.）

Tā zài Zhījiāgē Dàxué shàng xué
B. 他 在 芝加哥 大學 上 學 。

He studies at the University of Chicago.

（B：U of C is the location where action happens.）

Combination：

| Subject | + | Adverb | + | Verb | + | Object |

Nǐ　　　　　　　　　　zuò　　shénme
你　　　　　　　　　　做　　什麼 ？
Wǒ　　　　　　　　　　shì　　dàxuéshēng
我　　　　　　　　　　是　　大學生 。

Nǐ　　　zài nǎr　　shàng xué
你　　　在 哪兒　　上 學 ？
Wǒ　　　zài Díbǎo Dàxué shàng xué
我　　　在 迪堡 大學 上 學 。
Wǒ　　　　　　　　shì　　Díbǎo Dàxué de xuésheng
我　　　　　　　　是　　迪堡 大學 的 學生 。

Nǐ bàba　　　　　　zuò　　shénme
你 爸爸　　　　　　做　　什麼 ？
Wǒ bàba　　　　　shì　　jīnglǐ
我 爸爸　　　　　是　　經理 。

Tā　　　zài nǎr　　gōngzuò
他　　　在 哪兒　　工作 ？
Tā zài　　shāngdiàn　　gōngzuò
他 在　　商店　　　工作 。
Tā　　　　　　　　shì　　shāngdiàn de jīnglǐ
他　　　　　　　　是　　商店 的 經理 。

Tā	bú	shì	fànguǎn de jīnglǐ
他	不	是	飯館 的 經理。

Tā māma		zuò	shénme
他 媽媽		做	什麼 ？

Tā		shì	dàifu
她		是	大夫。

Tā	zài nǎr	gōngzuò
她	在 哪兒	工作 ？

Tā	zài dàxué yīyuàn	gōngzuò
她	在 大學 醫院	工作 。

Tā		shì	nàge yīyuàn de dàifu
她		是	那個 醫院 的 大夫。

詞彙表

跟學習相關的詞彙　Words Related to Study

學		Learn, study

	學習	xuéxí	Study, learn
	上學	shàng xué	Go to school, attend school

學校	xuéxiào	School

	大學	dàxué	University, college
	中學	zhōngxué	Middle school, high school
	小學	xiǎoxué	Elementary school, primary school

學生	xuésheng	Student, pupil

	大學生	dàxuéshēng	University student; college student
	中學生	zhōngxuéshēng	Middle-school student
	小學生	xiǎoxuéshēng	(Elementary) school child; pupil

Dàxuéshēng shàng dàxué
大學生　　　上　大學。

Dàxuéshēng zài dàxué xuéxí
大學生　　在 大學 學習。

Zhōngxuéshēng shàng zhōngxué
中學　　生　上　中學　。

Zhōngxuéshēng zài zhōngxué xuéxí
中學生　　　　在　中學　學習。

Xiǎoxuéshēng shàng xiǎoxué
小學生　　　　上　　小學　。

Xiǎoxuéshēng zài xiǎoxué xuéxí
小學生　　　在　小學　學習。

Wǒmen zhù zài Zhījiāgē　Wǒmen dōu shì xuésheng　zài Zhījiāgē
我們　　住 在 芝加哥。我們　都　是　　學生　，在　芝加哥

shàng xué
上　　學。

Wǒ gēge shì dàxuéshēng
我　哥哥 是　大學生　。

Wǒ gēge xuéxí Hànyǔ
我　哥哥 學習　漢語。

Wǒ gēge zài Díbǎo Dàxué xuéxí Hànyǔ
我　哥哥 在 迪堡　大學　學習　漢語。

Wǒ gēge de Hànyǔ lǎoshī shì Wáng lǎoshī
我　哥哥 的 漢語　老師 是　王　老師。

Nǐmen shì zhōngxuéshēng
你們　是　　中學生

Nǐmen yě xuéxí Hànyǔ
你們　也 學習 漢語。

Nǐmen zài Lādīng Zhōngxué xuéxí Hànyǔ
你們　在 拉丁　中學　學習 漢語。

Nǐmen de Hànyǔ lǎoshī bú shì Wáng lǎoshī
你們　的 漢語 老師 不 是　王　老師。

Tāmen shì xiǎoxuéshēng
他們　是　小學生　。

Tāmen yě dōu xuéxí Hànyǔ
他們　也　都　學習　漢語。

Tāmen zài Bài'ěr Xiǎoxué xuéxí Hànyǔ
他們　在　拜爾　小學　學習　漢語。

Tāmen de Hànyǔ lǎoshī yě bú shì Wáng lǎoshī
他們　的漢語　老師也不是　王　老師。

Zhè shì wǒmen de Hànyǔ lǎoshī Tā xìng Wáng
這是　我們　的　漢語　老師，他姓　王。

Wáng lǎoshī bú shì Měiguórén Tā shì Zhōngguórén yě shì
王　老師不是　美國人。他是　中國人，也是

Jiānádàrén
加拿大人。

Tā shuō Yīngyǔ Fǎyǔ hé Hànyǔ
他　説　英語、法語和　漢語。

Tā fùmǔ de jiā zài Běijīng Tā zhù zài Zhījiāgē
他父母的　家在　北京。他住在　芝加哥。

6

時間　Time

　　時間是非常重要的概念。在日常生活中我們談論時間，談論行爲發生的時間，特別是漢語的動詞本身沒有時態，時間詞因此更爲關鍵。

　　本節按時間詞的語用功能將時間詞分爲兩類：時間點與時間段。并介紹簡單常用時間詞、其他時間詞的組成、時間詞在句中的位置、與時間有關的問句形式。

　　時間的表達與兩個成分休戚相關。第一，時間的表達不僅與行爲動作有緊密聯繫，而且有時是通過行爲動作表達的。其二，很多時間詞是通過數字表達的。學了數字再學時間，兩者可以在教學上相輔相成。

　　Time is an important concept. In our daily life, we talk about time itself as well as its relationship to actions and events. Chinese verbs have no tenses, and thus do not reflect time themselves. Time expressions, therefore, become more critical in language use.

　　This chapter divides time expressions into two categories according to pragmatic functions: moment in time and periods of time. It also introduces simple daily time expressions, compositions of other time expressions, position of time expressions in sentences, and question forms relating to time.

　　Time expressions relate to two other language elements: verbs and numbers. Firstly, time indicates the moment and duration of actions, while actions can be used to indicate time. Secondly, many time expressions have a numeric component. This points to the natural connections and possible sequence of instruction.

教 學 重 點　Content of Teaching and Learning

時間點	Point in time—Moment
日曆	Calendar
一天	A Day
鐘點	O'clock
過去/現在/未來	Past/Present/Future
動詞組指示時間	Actions Indicating Time
時間段	Period of time—Duration
度量	Measurements

對比	Compare
句型與提問	Sentence Patterns and Questions
時間點句型	Point in Time
時間段句型	Time Duration

教 學 難 點　Cruxes of Teaching and Learning

時間點在句中的位置	Position of Time Phrase in the Sentence
行為指示時間	Actions Indicate Time
時間點做名詞定語	Point in Time as Attributive
"Year" vs. "年"	
上? 下?	Last and Next
時間點與時間段	Point in Time vs. Period of Time

教學重點

Content of Teaching and Learning

時間點　Point in Time —Moment

使用規則　Rules：

1）時間的表達總是從大概念到小概念。

　　Time expressions always proceed from the larger concept to the smaller one.

2）時間點在動詞前。

　　Time expressions（moment of time）are always put before verbs.

日曆　rìlì　calendar

年　　　nián　　　　　　year

　　　yī jiǔ jiǔ jiǔ nián
　　　一 九 九 九　年

　　　èr líng líng líng nián　èr líng líng líng nián
　　　二 零 零 零 年 （二 ○ ○ ○ 年 ）

In English, we say,"the year nineteen ninety-nine or the year two thousand" or "ninety-nine" refering to the year.

In Chinese, we read each digit and always use the word "年 nián" at the end：

　　　一九九九年　yī jiǔ jiǔ jiǔ nián　or　九九年　jiǔ jiǔ nián

月　　　yuè　　　　　　month

In English, each month has a name.

In Chinese, the months are numbered in sequence starting from January.

yīyuè	èryuè	sānyuè	sìyuè	wǔyuè	liùyuè
一月，	二月，	三月，	四月，	五月，	六月，
January	February	March	April	May	June

qīyuè	bāyuè	jiǔyuè	shíyuè	shíyīyuè	shí'èryuè
七月，	八月，	九月，	十月，	十一月，	十二月

July   August   September   October   November   December

日   rì   Day of the month（formal）

èr yuè yī rì

二 月 一 日

號   hào   Day of the month（informal）

shí'èr yuè èrshíyī hào

十二 月 二十一 號

星期   xīngqī   week

禮拜 lǐbài   Week（colloquial expression）

周   zhōu   Week（written expression）

星期一	禮拜一	周一
星期二	禮拜二	周二
星期三	禮拜三	周三
星期四	禮拜四	周四
星期五	禮拜五	周五
星期六	禮拜六	周六
星期日（星期天）	禮拜日（禮拜天）	
周末	zhōumò	Weekend
周日	zhōurì	Weekday

一天   yì tiān   A day

早上	zǎoshang	Early morning
上午	shàngwǔ	Morning
中午	zhōngwǔ	Noon, midday
下午	xiàwǔ	Afternoon
晚上	wǎnshang	Evening, night
半夜	bànyè	Midnight

前半夜	qiánbànyè	The first half of the night
後半夜	hòubànyè	After midnight

鐘點　zhōngdiǎn　O'clock

點鐘　diǎnzhōng　Hour, o'clock（Also See 1：Numbers in Life Chapter）

yì diǎn　　　　liǎng diǎn
一　點　　　　　兩　點

For two o'clock, always say "兩點." Never say "二點".

半　　　bàn　　　　Half, semi-（點鐘）
（According to the rule #1, "half" is smaller than "a whole hour" therefore：）

liǎng diǎn bàn
2：30　兩　點　半

刻　　　kè　　　　Quarter of an hour

liǎng diǎn yí kè　　　　liǎng diǎn sān kè
2：15　兩　點　一　刻　　2：45　兩　點　三　刻

分　　　fēn　　　　Minute（of time）

liǎng diǎn wǔ fēn　　　　liǎng diǎn shí fēn
2：05　兩　點　五　分　　2：10　兩　點　十　分

However, in expressions more than 10 minutes, "fen" can be omitted：

liǎng diǎn shíwǔ(fēn)
2：15　兩　點　十五（分）

差　　　chà　　　　Lack, be short of
Whatever is lacking, comes before mentioning of the whole clock.

chà wǔ fēn sān diǎn　　　　chà yí kè sān diǎn
2：55　差　五　分　三　點　　2：45　差　一　刻　三　點

According to the patterns above, there are at least three ways to say 2：45

liǎng diǎn sìshíwǔ（fēn）
2：45　兩　點　四十五（分）

liǎng diǎn sān kè

兩　　點　三　刻

chà yí kè sān diǎn

差　一　刻　三　點

Think：What are the other possible ways to say it? Can other times be told in similar ways?

Variations of telling the time：

	liǎng diǎn wǔ fēn	liǎng diǎn líng wǔ(fēn)
2：05	兩　點　五　分	兩　　點　○　五（分）
	liǎng diǎn shíwǔ (fēn)	liǎng diǎn yí kè
2：15	兩　點　十五　（分）	兩　　點　一　刻
	liǎng diǎn sānshí (fēn)	liǎng diǎn bàn
2：30	兩　點　三十　（分）	兩　點　半
	liǎng diǎn sìshíwǔ (fēn)	
2：45	兩　點　四十五　（分）	
	chà yí kè sān diǎn	chà shíwǔ fēn sān diǎn
	差　一　刻　三　點	差　十五　分　三　點
	liǎng diǎn wǔshíwǔ (fēn)	chà wǔ fēn sān diǎn
2：55	兩　點　五十五　（分）	差　五　分　三　點

其他時間詞　Other Related Expressions

世紀	shìjì	century：
	19 世紀	21 世紀
	19 Century	21 Century
年代	niándài	decade（e. g. the 1980s）
	60 年代	80 年代
	the 60s	the 80s
每	měi	each，every
	每年	每天
	every year	every day
清晨	qīngchén	early morning
半夜	bànyè	midnight，in the middle of the night
秒	miǎo	second
有時候	yǒu shíhou	sometimes，at times，occasionally

過去/現在/未來　Past/ Present/ Future

Past	Present	Future
qiánnián　qùnián 前年　　去年 year before last　last year	jīnnián 今年 this year	míngnián　hòunián 明年　　　後年 next year　year after next
qiántiān　zuótiān 前天　　昨天 day before yesterday　yesterday	jīntiān 今天 today	míngtiān　hòutiān 明天　　後天 tomorrow　day after tomorrow
shàng ge yuè 上　個　月 last month	zhège yuè 這個　月 this month	xià ge yuè 下　個　月 next month
shàng ge xīngqī 上　個　星期 last week	zhège xīngqī 這個　星期 this week	xià ge xīngqī 下　個　星期 next week

其他　Other Expressions

過去	guòqù	in the past
從前	cóngqián	in the past
現在	xiànzài	now，at the present time
目前	mùqián	at present
將來	jiānglái	(in the) future
未來	wèilái	coming (of time)，future

míngnián wǔ yuè　　　　　　　qùnián bā yuè
明年　　五　月　Next May　去年　八　月　Last August

jīntiān zǎoshang　　　　　　　zuótiān zhōngwǔ
今天　　早上　This morning　昨天　　中午　Yesterday noon

qī yuè sān hào shàngwǔ
七　月　三　號　上午　The morning of July 3

xīngqīliù wǎnshang
星期六　　晚上　Saturday night

shàng xīngqīsì zǎoshang jiǔ diǎn yí kè
上　　星期四　早上　九　點　一　刻

Last Thursday at 9：15 am（in the morning）

xià xīngqītiān xiàwǔ sān diǎn bàn

下　星期天　下午　三　點　半

3：30 pm（in the afternoon）next Sunday

動詞組指示時間　Actions Indicating Time

用動作行爲指示時間有三個詞組。請注意中英文的不同。

There are three patterns help to form time expressions with actions：

（Pay attention to the structural differences in English and Chinese.）

1）During an action（while ... , When ...）action 的時候 shíhou

<table>
<tr><td></td><td>shàng kè de shíhou</td></tr>
<tr><td>during class：</td><td>上　課的　時候</td></tr>
<tr><td></td><td>kàn diànyǐng de shíhou</td></tr>
<tr><td>while watching a movie：</td><td>看　電影　的　時候</td></tr>
</table>

> T（V ＋的時候）＋ Main Action in Sentence.

吃飯的時候，我看書。

While eating, I read books. ／ I read books while eating.

2）Before an action　action 以前　yǐqián

<table>
<tr><td></td><td>shàng kè yǐqián</td></tr>
<tr><td>before class：</td><td>上　課 以前</td></tr>
<tr><td></td><td>kàn diànyǐng yǐqián</td></tr>
<tr><td>before watching a movie：</td><td>看　電影　以前</td></tr>
</table>

> T（V ＋以前）＋ Main Action in Sentence.

吃飯以前，我學習漢語。

Before eating, I study Chinese. ／ I study Chinese before eating.

3）After an action　action 以後　yǐhòu

<table>
<tr><td></td><td>shàng kè yǐhòu</td></tr>
<tr><td>after class</td><td>上　課 以後</td></tr>
<tr><td></td><td>kàn diànyǐng yǐhòu</td></tr>
<tr><td>after watching a movie：</td><td>看　電影　以後</td></tr>
</table>

> T（V ＋以後）＋ Main Action in Sentence.

吃飯以後，我看電視。

After eating, I watch TV. ∕ I watch TV after eating.

時間段　Period of Time—Duration

度量　Measurements

> \# (whole number) + measure word + more (or less) than the whole measurement

1) "年", "天", "分", "刻", "秒" are used as measurements:

　　一年　　　　一年半/一年多

　　兩天　　　　兩天半/兩天多

　　五分鐘　　　五分多鐘

　　一刻鐘　　　一刻多鐘

　　三秒鐘　　　三秒半

2) "個" is used to measure other specified lengths of time:

The time periods to be measured are: "世紀", "月", "星期", "早上", "小時/鐘頭", 等.

兩個月

半個月

　　　　　　一個多月

　　　　　　一個半月

一個星期　　一個多星期

一個早上

兩個小時/兩個鐘頭

半個小時/半個鐘頭

　　　　　　兩個半小時 (鐘頭)

　　　　　　兩個多小時 (鐘頭)

3) "從……到" pattern is used to specify a starting point to an ending point

of a duration.

從一月到六月　From January to June

從八點到九點　From eight o'clock to nine o'clock

對比　Compare

時間點　Point in Time	時間段　Period of Time
2000 年	一年 　　　　半年 　　　　一年多 　　　　一年半
二月	兩個月 　　　　半個月 　　　　一個多月 　　　　一個半月
星期一	一個星期 　　　　一個多星期
今天 明天 昨天	一天 　　　　半天 　　　　一天多
早上，晚上， 上午，中午，下午，	一個早上
兩點 兩點半	兩個小時，兩個鐘頭 　　　　半個鐘頭 　　　　兩個半小時 　　　　兩個多小時
兩點一刻 兩點十五分	一刻鐘 十五分鐘 一秒鐘 一會兒 半天

| 一月 | 從一月到六月 |
| 八點 | 從八點到九點 |

句型與提問　Sentence Patterns and Questions

時間點句型　Sentence Patterns：Point in Time

Remember：From large to small

èr líng líng liù nián sānyuè èrshíèr rì xīngqīsān shàngwǔ shíyī
二 ○ ○ 六 年　三月　二十二日　星期三　　上午　十一
diǎn èrshíwǔ fēn
點　二十五　分

Remember：The point in time comes before the action：

| Subject　Time | + | Verb + Object |

Wǒmen měitiān zǎoshang qī diǎn wǔshíwǔ fēn shàng dì yī jié kè
我 們　每天　早上　七 點　五十五　分　上　第一 節 課。
We everyday morning at 7：55 have the first period of class.

or

| Time | + | Subject + Verb + Object |

Měitiān zǎoshang qī diǎn wǔshíwǔ fēn wǒmen shàng dì yī jié kè
每天　早上　七 點　五十五　分 我們　上　第 一 節 課。
Every morning at 7：55, we have the first period of class.

問題　Questions：

General time：什麼時候？

Specific time：幾點？

Year, date：哪年？幾月幾日（號）？

Point in time phrases are always before the verbs.

| Subject | + | Time | + | Verb | + | Object |

Nǐ shénme shíhou shàng kè
你 什麼　時候　上　課？
When do you have class?

Nǐ jǐ diǎn xià kè
你 幾 點 下 課?
At what time do you end class?

時間段句型　Sentence Patterns：Time Duration

Subject + Verb + Object + Verb + Duration

habitual：
Tā (cháng) kàn shū kàn liǎng ge zhōngtóu
他 (常) 看 書 看 兩 個 鐘頭 。
He (often) reads (books) for two hours.

done：
Tā kàn shū kànle liǎng ge zhōngtóu
他 看 書 看了 兩 個 鐘頭 。
He read (books) for two hours.

doing：
Tā kàn shū kànle liǎng ge zhōngtóu le
他 看 書 看了 兩 個 鐘頭 了。
He has been reading (books) for two hours.

Plan：
Tā kàn shū yào kànliǎng ge zhōngtóu
他 看 書 要看 兩 個 鐘頭 。
He is going to read (books) for two hours.

問題　Questions

Duō cháng shíjiān　　Duō jiǔ
多 長 時間? ／多 久?
For how long?

Nǐ měi tiān kàn shū (yào) kàn duō cháng shíjiān (habitual)
你 每 天 看 書 (要) 看 多 長 時間 ?
How long do you read everyday?

Nǐ jīntiān kàn shū yào kàn duō cháng shíjiān
你 今天 看 書 要 看 多 長 時間 ?(plan)
How long are you going to read today?

Nǐ kàn shū kànle duō cháng shíjiān
你 看 書 看了 多 長 時間 ?(done)
How long did you read?

Nǐ kàn shū kànle duō cháng shíjiān le
你 看 書 看了 多 長 時間 了?(up to now)
How long have you been reading?

Nǐ chángcháng kàn shū kàn duō jiǔ
你 常常 看 書 看 多 久?(habitual)
How long do you usually read?

Nǐ jīntiān kàn shū yào kàn duō jiǔ

你 今天 看 書 要 看 多 久?（plan）

How long are you going to read today?

Nǐ kàn shū kànle duō jiǔ

你 看 書 看了 多 久?（done）

How long did you read?

Nǐ kàn shū kànle duō jiǔ le

你 看 書 看了 多 久 了?（up to now）

How long have you been reading?

教學難點

Cruxes of Teaching and Learning

難點一　時間點在句中的位置

Position of Time Phrase in the Sentence

在句首：before or after the subject（but always before the verb）

　　我每天八點上課。

　　每天八點我都上課。

難點二　行爲指示時間 Actions Indicating Time

讓學生困惑的地方有兩個：時間詞本身、時間詞在句中的位置。

This is most confusing to English speakers for two resaons: the time phrase itself, the time phrase in a sentence.

1）時間詞本身 The time phrase itself:（See Chapter 18: Noun Phrases.）

　　In English, "during, before, after" are adverbs which go before verbs.

　　In Chinese, "時候, 以前, 以後" are nouns which go after verbs.

　　　　During an action（While ... , When ... ）　　action 的時候（shíhou）

　　　　　　During class:　　　　　　　　　　　　上課的時候

　　　　　　While watching a movie:　　　　　　看電影的時候

Before an action   action 以前 （yǐqián）

     Before class：   上課以前

     Before watching a movie：   看電影以前

After an action   action 以後 （yǐhòu）

     After class   上課以後

     After watching a movie：   看電影以後

2）時間詞在句中的位置 The time phrase in the sentence：

英文的時間狀語可以在動詞前或後。

In English, the time phrase may go either before or after the main action：

     Before (I attended) class I read.

     I read before (I attended) class.

中文的時間狀語只可以在動詞前。

In Chinese, the time phrase must go before the main action.

     上課以前我看書。

Tip：Two "Reversals" of words order may be needed.

One Reversal：

     When translating "Before class I read.", reverse the phrase itself：

         Before class：上課以前

Two Reversals：

     When translating " I read before class".

     Firstly reverse the time and action：

         before class, then read

     Secondly, reverse the word order within the time phrase itself as above.

     上課以前我看書。

難點三　時間點做名詞定語 Point of Time as Attributive

The point in time can be used to define a noun such as "7 o'clock movie", e. g. ：

     我想看七點的電影。

他要坐八點的火車。

難點四　"Year" vs. "年"

There are two differences in English and Chinese in reading a year：

1） Numbers vs. digits

　　In English, a year is usually read every two digits：

　　　　the year 1991 is read：Nineteen Ninety-One

　　or as a whole number in case of the years of 2000：

　　　　the year 2006 is read：Two Thousand and Six

　　In Chinese, a year is read by each individual digit：

　　　　the year 1991 is read：yi, jiu, jiu, yi 一九九一年

　　　　Note："九十一年" means ninety-one years.

2） "年" must be used

　　In English, when reading a year, the word "year" is not needed.

　　In Chinese, when reading a year, the word "年" must be used.

　　　　一九九一年 or simply 九一年

難點五　上？ 下？ Last and Next

這恐怕是時間詞裡最難的。

This is most complicated in conversion from English to Chinese.

常犯的錯誤 Most frequent mistakes are：

1） Using "This and That"

　　"這個""那個" when referring to "今年，今天".

　　This year：　　　　今年

　　Today：　　　　　今天

2） Overly generalized use of "last"：

　　Last year：　　　　去年

　　Yesterday：　　　　昨天

3) Reversed use of "上" and "下":

Somehow it is hard for some English speakers to think

Last　　　　上　　　　(past)

Next　　　　下　　　　(future)

4) "Last September" is in which year?

In English, "last September" is the September that has most recently passed. It could be last year's or this year's.

In Chinese, months are put in the context of a year:

　　　今年九月 the September of this year,

　　　去年九月 the September of last year.

The same principle applies to "next".

　　　明年九月 the September of next year

Seasons are just like months. They should be put in the context of a year.

難點六　時間點與時間段 Point of Time vs. Period of Time

在句中的位置 Positions in a Sentence:

時間點在動詞前

Point in Time (Moment of Time) is before the action.

時間段在動詞後

Period of Time (Time Duration) is used after the action.

時間詞的構成　Formation of time expressions (See Time Lists and the Comparison List)

時間點不用量詞

Point in Time (Time Moment) uses no measure word.

時間段用量詞

Period of Time (Time Duration) uses a measure word (though some measure words are time expressions themselves).

7

**Actions
& Events**

行爲與事件

　　叙述行爲與事件需要動詞。本節把動詞另列一節是爲了提供教與學擴展的需要，同時方便與其他話題組合。

　　本節出現的動詞一是最常用的；二是按功用分類的；三是以詞組形式排列的。其他的教學重點與難點分析都與動詞的使用有關。

　　Describing and recounting actions and events require verbs. The subject of action verbs and verb phrases is provided as a whole section for convenience of expanded teaching and learning. So they may be combined with other topics.

　　The verbs in this chapter are commonly used. They are categorized by function, and they appear in phrases. Also listed are grammatical points and explanations that relate to the use of verbs.

教 學 重 點　Content of Teaching and Learning

常用動詞與動詞詞組　　　　　Commonly Used Verbs and Verbal Phrases

教 學 難 點　Cruxes of Teaching and Learning

動詞的分類　　　　　　　　　Category of Verbs

漢語形容詞的動詞性　　　　　Adjectives as Verbs

動詞作時間詞　　　　　　　　Actions Indicating Time

狀語與動作的關係（對比英語）

　　　　　　　　　　　　　　Relationship between Adverbial and Action
　　　　　　　　　　　　　　(Comparing with English)

英語中的"看"　　　　　　　"看" in English

漢語中的"To know"　　　　　"to know" in Chinese

漢語中的"To visit"　　　　　"to visit" in Chinese

補 充 語 法 點　Supplementary Notes

雙賓語　　　　　　　　　　　Double Object

文 化 聯 繫　Cultural Relations

借："A borrower or a lender be?"

教學重點

Content of Teaching and Learning

常用動詞與動詞詞組　Commonly Used Verbs and Verbal Phrases

Coming and Going：

Verb		Verbal Phrase	
上	shàng	go up, get on	
	上學	shàng xué	go to school, attend school
	上課	shàng kè	go to class, attend class
	上班	shàng bān	go to work, go on duty
	上廁所	shàng cèsuǒ	go to the toilet, use the toilet
	上車	shàng chē	get into or board a vehicle
	上街	shàng jiē	go out into the streets (shopping)
	上網	shàng wǎng	{IT} get on line, get on the Internet
下	xià	go down, get off	
	下課	xià kè	get out of class
	下班	xià bān	come off duty, go off work
	下棋	xià qí	play chess (or similar board games)
	下車	xià chē	alight (from a vehicle), de-board
放	fàng	release, set free, let go, put down	
	放學	fàng xué	dismiss students from school
	放假	fàng jià	have (or grant) vacation or holiday
	放屁	fàng pì	fart; {abusive} talk nonsense
來	lái	come	
	來上學	lái shàngxué	come to school
去	qù	go, go away, leave, depart	
	去上學	qù shàngxué	go to school

回	huí	return, go back
回家	huí jiā	return home
回國	huí guó	return to one's native country
回學校	huí xuéxiào	go back to school
走	zǒu	walk, travel on foot
走路	zǒu lù	walk, travel on foot
坐	zuò	sit; seat, place; travel by, go by (car, airplane, etc.)
坐車	zuò chē	go by train (bus or car)

Daily Life

起	qǐ	rise, stand up
起床	qǐ chuáng	get out of bed (in the morning)
睡	shuì	sleep, go to sleep
睡覺	shuì jiào	sleep, go to sleep
吃	chī	eat
吃飯	chī fàn	eat a meal
吃早飯	chī zǎofàn	have breakfast
吃中飯（午飯）	chī zhōngfàn (wǔfàn)	have lunch
吃晚飯	chī wǎnfàn	have supper (dinner)
吃中國菜	chī Zhōngguócài	eat Chinese food
吃墨西哥菜	chī Mòxīgēcài	eat Mexican food
吃水果	chī shuǐguǒ	eat fruit (s)
喝	hē	drink
喝水	hē shuǐ	drink water or tea
喝茶	hē chá	have tea, drink tea
喝可口可樂	hē Kěkǒukělè	drink Coca-cola
喝咖啡	hē kāfēi	drink coffee
喝牛奶	hē niúnǎi	drink (cow's) milk
喝酒	hē jiǔ	drink alcoholic beverages

喝啤酒	hē píjiǔ	drink beer
喝橘子水（汁）	hē júzishuǐ(zhī)	drink orange juice
喝果汁	hē guǒzhī	drink fruit juice（syrup）
看 kàn		look，see，read，watch，visit，call on（friends，etc.）
看書	kàn shū	read a book
看電視	kàn diànshì	watch television/TV
看電影	kàn diànyǐng	watch a movie/motion picture
看球賽	kàn qiúsài	watch a ball game
看朋友	kàn péngyou	visit friend
看病	kàn bìng	see a doctor
聽 tīng		hear，listen
聽音樂	tīng yīnyuè	listen to music
聽歌	tīng gē	listen to songs
說 shuō		say，speak
說漢語	shuō Hànyǔ	speak Chinese（spoken language）
說話	shuō huà	speak，talk，chat
打 dǎ		strike，hit，beat，play
打電話	dǎ diànhuà	make a phone call
打球	dǎ qiú	play a ball game
打乒乓球	dǎ pīngpāngqiú	play ping-pong
打橄欖球	dǎ gǎnlǎnqiú	play rugby/American football
打棒球	dǎ bàngqiú	play baseball
打籃球	dǎ lánqiú	play basketball
打排球	dǎ páiqiú	play volleyball
打網球	dǎ wǎngqiú	play tennis
打羽毛球	dǎ yǔmáoqiú	play badminton
打高爾夫球	dǎ gāo'ěrfūqiú	play golf
打保齡球	dǎbǎolíngqiú	play Bowling
玩 wán		play，have fun，relax

	玩電腦	wán diànnǎo	play on the computer
	玩電動	wán diàndòng	play computer games
	玩球	wán qiú	play a ball
用	yòng	use	
	用計算機	yòng jìsuànjī	use a computer
	用筆	yòng bǐ	use a pen (writing tools)
	用漢語	yòng Hànyǔ	use Chinese
騎	qí	ride	
	騎馬	qí mǎ	ride a horse
	騎車	qí chē	ride a bicycle
	騎自行車	qí zìxíngchē	ride a bicycle
	騎摩托車	qí mótuōchē	ride a motorcycle
開	kāi	open up, turn on (a light), operate (a machine)	
	開門	kāi mén	open a door, open for business
	開燈	kāi dēng	turn on a light
	開車	kāi chē	start/drive a vehicle(car,train,etc.)
	開會	kāi huì	hold a meeting, attend a meeting
滑	huá	slip, slide	
	滑冰	huá bīng	skateing, ice-skating
	滑旱冰	huá hànbīng	roller-skate
	滑雪	huá xuě	ski
	滑板	huá bǎn	skateboard
游	yóu	swim, float	
	游泳	yóu yǒng	swim
	游水	yóu shuǐ	swim
唱	chàng	sing	
	唱歌	chàng gē	sing, sing a song
跳	tiào	jump, leap	
	跳舞	tiào wǔ	dance

跳高	tiào gāo	high jump
跳遠	tiào yuǎn	broad jump, long jump
跳水	tiào shuǐ	dive（into water）
跑 pǎo		run
跑步	pǎo bù	run, jogging
寫 xiě		write, compose, portray, depict, draw, paint
寫字	xiě zì	write, practise calligraphy
寫信	xiě xìn	write a letter
寫文章	xiě wénzhāng	write an article
作(做) zuò		do, make, be, serve as
做飯	zuò fàn	cook, prepare a meal（especially rice）
做作業	zuò zuòyè	do one's（school）assignment
做功課	zuò gōngkè	do schoolwork/homework
買 mǎi		buy, purchase
買東西	mǎi dōngxi	buy things
賣 mài		sell
賣東西	mài dōngxi	sell things
逛 guàng		take a stroll, stroll roam
逛商店	guàng shāngdiàn	go window-shopping

Two-word Verbs

學習 xuéxí		study, learn
學習英語		study Englsih
學習漢語		learn Chinese
練習 liànxí		practise, drill; exercise
練習口語		practice oral speeches
復習 fùxí		review（lessons, etc.）
復習語法		review grammar

預習	yùxí	prepare/preview a lesson (of a student)
	預習生詞	preview new words
準備	zhǔnbèi	prepare, get ready
	準備上課	prepare to go to class
打算	dǎsuan	plan, intend; plan, intention
計劃	jìhuà	plan, program; plan
休息	xiūxi	rest, take a break, relax
	休息休息	need a good rest
鍛煉	duànliàn	work out; exercise
	鍛煉身體	do exercise
參加	cānjiā	join, participate in, take part in
	參加課外活動	participate in extracurricular activities
參觀	cānguān	visit (e. g. as an observer, tourist, etc.)
訪問	fǎngwèn	visit, call on
游覽	yóulǎn	sight-see, tour
知道	zhīdao	know, understand, realize
認識	rènshi	know, understand, recognize
理解	lǐjiě	comprehend, understand
了解	liǎojiě	understand, comprehend, discover, find out about
同情	tóngqíng	sympathize with, have sympathy for

教學難點

Cruxes of Teaching and Learning

難點一　動詞的分類 Category of Verbs

Verb "是 shì to be"

"是" in Chinese has a more limited function than "to be" in English.

1）It is used to identify what is what and who is whom. Negative form is "不是".

> 她是學生，她不是老師。
>
> She is a student. She is not a teacher.
>
> 這是書，不是本子。
>
> This is a book not a notebook.
>
> 這本書是我的，不是你的。
>
> This book is mine, not yours.

2）It is used to identify time, location, and manner of a specific action.

> 他真的來了嗎？是什麼時候來的？是怎麼來的？
>
> Has he really come? When did he come? How did he get here?

Important Note：Unlike in English, it cannot be used to describe a person/situation.

Verb "有 yǒu to Have"

"有" basically has three functions in Chinese. Negative form is "没有".

1）Possession：

> 我有一個弟弟，没有妹妹。
>
> I have a little brother, I don't have a little sister.

2）"There is/are ..."

> 書架上只有幾本書，没有報紙。
>
> There are only a few books on the bookshelf, there are no newspapers.

3）Comparison/estimation：

> 他只有五英尺一英寸，還没有我高。
>
> He is only 5′1″, not as tall as I am.

行爲動詞　Action Verbs

1）英文的很多動詞在中文是動詞性詞組，用的時候得注意。

Many action verbs in English are verbal phrases in Chinese.

> Sleep – 睡覺 shuìjiào　　"睡" is a verb；"覺" is a noun

You can say：睡個好覺 have a good sleep

When you ask about（evaluate）the action，you ask，"睡得好不好？"

2）有些動詞不是動詞性詞組，是雙音節動詞。

There are also two-word verbs.

Study － 學習 xuéxí "學" is a verb；"習" is also a verb.

情態動詞/助動詞

Model Verbs/Auxiliary Verbs（See Model Verbs List）

Model verbs/auxiliary verbs emphasize mood/desire/capability/obligation/possibility of an action.

See Chapter 8 for more details.

難點二 漢語形容詞的動詞性 Adjectives as Verbs

漢語的形容詞可以直接做謂語，直接形容對象和情況，不需要動詞。

In Chinese，adjectives are used to describe people and situations directly as predicate.

我很好。I am fine.

直接用形容詞還有比較的意思。

However，when an adjective is used by itself，it has the implication of comparing.

我好。（我比他好。）

難點三 動詞做時間詞 Actions Indicating Time

行爲動詞還可以指定時間。

Action verbs（verbal phrases）are used to indicate time.

Usually with the help of "... 的時候"，"... 以前"，"... 以後" to form time expressions.

（For more detailed explanation, see Chapter 6：Time.）

難點四　狀語與動作的關係（對比英語）Relationship between Adverbial and Action（Comparing with English）

表時間、地點和行爲方式的狀語在英文句中的位置靈活，可在動詞前或後。

Adverbial phrases include phrases that indicate time, location, and manner of an action.

In English, adverbial phrases are placed flexibly within a sentence. They may go before or after the verbs.

（Time）	I come to school everyday at 7：30 am.
	Everyday at 7：30 am., I come to school.
（Place）	I come to school from my house.
	From my house, I come to school.
（Manner）	I come to school by bus with my friends.
	With my friends, I come to school by bus.

表時間、地點和行爲方式的狀語在中文句中的位置固定，只可在動詞前。

In Chinese, all adverbial phrases indicating time, location, and the conditions of an action must come before the verb in a sentence.

（Time）	我每天早上七點半去上學。
（Place）	我從我家來學校上學。
（Manner）	我跟我的朋友坐公共汽車來上學。

難點五　英語中的"看""看" in Enghish

沒有一對一的翻譯。

Remember：there is no exact one to one equavalent of words in any two languages. Some words in a language refer to one thing in another language or one word may have many meanings in another language.

中文的"看"譯成英文有不少定義。

The verb "看" refers to many functions of the eyes in English：

read/watch/see/observe/look/visit/view, even viewpoint, etc.

看書	kàn shū	read a book
看電影	kàn diànyǐng	watch/see a movie
看那兒	kàn nàr	look at that/there
看朋友	kàn péngyou	visit/go see friends
你怎麼看?	What do you think about it? /How do you see it? /	
	What is your opinion?	

"看", when pronounced "kān", means to "look after, take care of, keep under surveillance, keep an eye on, detain, etc."

難點六　漢語中的 "to know" "To know" in Chinese

英文的"to know"譯成中文含義也很多。

Another commonly used word in English that has many different functions in Chinese is "to know". When learners try to translate from English to Chinese, confusions may rise.

1) When "to know" is related to "to know/ to understand ", there are a few expressions to show nuances in functional use：

知道	zhīdao	emphasizes knowing information, knowledge
認識	rènshi	emphasizes knowing through recognition
會	huì	emphasizes knowing how, being able to do somthing through a learned skill

2) When "to know" is related to comprehension and understanding, there are several expressions to show nuances in functional use：

懂得	dǒngde	emphasizes comprehension of meaning, method, etc.
明白	míngbai	emphasizes comprehending with clarity and sensibility

理解	lǐjiě	emphasizes comprehending with rational think-ing and depth
了解	liǎojiě	emphasizes comprehension of detailed informa-tion
同情	tóngqíng	emphasizes comprehension with compassion/sympathy

難點七　漢語中的 "to visit"　"To visit" in Chinese

"to visit" 也是一個麻煩。There are many kinds of visiting in Chinese：

訪問	fǎngwèn	(formal) visit, call on
參觀	cānguān	visit (e. g. as an observer, tourist, etc.)
游覽	yóulǎn	sight-see, tour
旅游	lǚyóu	travel, be a tourist
看	kàn	(informal) visit, call on (friends, etc.)
去玩	qù wán	go to play, visit a place to have fun/to relax

補充語法點

Supplementary Notes

雙賓語　Double Object

A few verbs take two objects：Direct object and indirect object.

有的動詞後跟兩個賓語：直接賓語和間接賓語。

請你給我一本書。Please give me a book.

In this sentence，"我" is an indirect object of the action. and "一本書" is the direct object of the action.

Rarely, this will cause confusions. However, in the situations of using the Chinese verb "借", we need caution.

在一般情況下，直接賓語和間接賓語的使用不是一個問題。但用

"借"時，要注意。

借："A borrower or a lender be?"

借　　jiè　　　borrow, lend

As you can see, "借" is both to borrow and to lend. Thus theoretically, the sentence below can be confusing.

"借"既可借出也可借進。不明確，語義容易混淆。

Tā jièle wǒ liǎng kuài qián
他 借了 我 兩 塊 錢。

It could mean：

他借給了我兩塊錢。He lent me two dollars.

他跟我借了兩塊錢。or 他借了我的兩塊錢。

He borrowed two dollars from me (of mine).

By the way, the opposite word is "還 huán return, repay".

文化聯繫　Cultural Relations (for your learning pleasure)

A famous quote from Shakespeare's "Hamlet"：

"Never a lender nor a borrower be."

不要借給別人錢，也不要借別人的錢。

8

Hobby/
Preference/
Obligation

愛好/選擇/責任

　　談愛好也要談選擇和責任。這些表達可能和願望的話題都離不開使用能願動詞/助動詞。

　　本節爲方便話題的展開介紹常用的能願動詞及例句。希望詞彙表方便教與學的選擇，并通過例句給出一些能願動詞使用的情景。

　　教學的難點着重強調英語學生可能遇到的困難。

Talking about hobbies also relates to choices, possibilities, responsibilities and obligations. In all these topics, modal verbs (auxiliary verbs) are indispensable.

This chapter provides a modal verbs list and usage examples. The list aims to make expanded teaching and learning convenient, and the sample sentences provide examples with situational usages.

The explanation stresses the cruxes that English speaking students might encounter.

教 學 重 點　Content of Teaching and Learning

　　能願動詞/助動詞表　　　　　List of Modal Verbs (Auxiliary Verbs)
　　能願動詞的使用:例句與比較　Use of Modal Verbs：Example & Comparison

教 學 難 點　Cruxes of Teaching and Learning

　　"想" vs. "要"

　　"想" and "要" vs. "喜歡"

　　"想" vs. "Want"

　　"Ask" in Chinese

　　"Can" in Chinese

　　"會" vs. "能" vs. "可以"

　　"不用" vs. "甭" & "不要" vs. "別"

　　Negative for "得" and "不得不"

教學重點

Content of Teaching and Learning

能願動詞/助動詞表　List of Modal Verbs（Auxiliary Verbs）

想　　　xiǎng　　Intend, want to, would like to
　　　　　　　　（as verb：think, long for, recall with fondness, miss）

要　　　yào　　　Want; will
　　　　　　　　（as verb：demand; as adjective：important）

別　　　bié　　　Don't
　　　　　　　　（as verb：depart, leave, separate）
　　　　　　　　（other usages：other, another, different）

不用　　búyòng　　Need not, no use to; dispense with

會　　　huì　　　Know how, be able to
　　　　　　　　（for prediction：be likely to）

能　　　néng　　Capable of; be possible

可以　　kěyǐ　　Be permitted to; may, can
　　　　　　　　（as adjective：not bad, pretty good）

應該　　yīnggāi　Should, ought to, must

必須　　bìxū　　Be obliged to, have to

得　　　děi　　　Must, have to

不得不　bùdébù　Cannot but, cannot help but be obliged to, have no alternative

（一定）要　（yídìng）yào　Must, (surely) have to

能願動詞的使用：例句與比較

Use of Modal Verbs：Examples & Comparison

想 xiǎng want

positive：
Wǒ xiǎng gēn péngyou qù kàn diànyǐng
我 想 跟 朋友 去 看 電影 。
I want to go to see a movie with my friends.

negative：
Wǒ bù xiǎng jīntiān wǎnshang qù kàn diànyǐng
我 不 想 今天 晚上 去 看 電影 。
I don't want to go to see a movie tonight.

question：
Nǐ xiǎng bu xiǎng zài jiā kàn diànshì
你 想 不 想 在 家 看 電視 ？
Do you want to watch TV at home?

要 yào want

positive：
Wǒ yào gēn tāmen yìqǐ qù Zhōngguó
我 要 跟 他們 一起 去 中國 。
I want to go with them to China.

negative：
Wǒ bù xiǎng gēn tāmen qù Zhōngguó
我 不 想 跟 他們 去 中國 。
I don't want to go with them to China.

question：
Nǐ xiǎng bu xiǎng gēn tāmen qù Zhōngguó
你 想 不 想 跟 他們 去 中國 ？
Do you want to go with them to China?

會 huì know how (of a learned skill)

Wǒ huì shuō Yīngyǔ yě huì shuō Déyǔ kěshì wǒ shuō de bú tài hǎo
我 會 説 英語,也 會 説 德語,可是 我 説 得 不太 好。
I know how to speak English and I also know how to speak German but I don't speak well.

Zhège háizi tài xiǎo hái bú huì zǒu lù kěshì tā huì jiào bàba
這個 孩子 太 小 , 還 不 會 走 路,可是 他 會 叫 "爸爸、
māma
媽媽 "。
This child is too young, and has not yet learned to walk, but he knows how to say "daddy and mommy".

能　néng　able to, capable of（from a subjective view point）

Wǒmen huì shuō yìdiǎn Hànyǔ yě néng xiě hěn duō Hànzì kěshì bù
我們　會　説　一點　漢語，也　能　寫　很　多　漢字，可是　不
néng kàn Zhōngwén bào
能　看　中文　報。
We know how to speak a little Chinese and we also are capable of writing many characters, but we are not proficient enough to read Chinese newspapers.

Jīntiān wǎnshang tā bù néng kàn diànshì yīnwèi tā yǒu hěn duō
今天　晚上　他 不　能　看　電視，因爲 他 有　很　多
gōngkè yào zuò
功課　要　做。
He is not able to watch TV tonight because he has too much homework.

Nàge dìfang tài yuǎn méiyǒu chē bù néng qù
那個　地方　太　遠，没有　車　不　能　去。
That place is too far away and you won't be able to go there without a car.

可以　kěyǐ　may, to be permitted, to be allowed（from an objective view
　　　　point）

Shàng kè de shíhou bù kěyǐ wán diànnǎo
上　課 的 時候 不 可以 玩　電腦　。
Playing computer is not allowed during class.

Chī zhōngfàn de shíhou kěyǐ qù túshūguǎn kàn shū
吃　中飯　的 時候 可以 去　圖書館　看　書。
It is allowed to go to read in the library during lunch.

Yàoshi nǐ yǒu qián jiù kěyǐ mǎi méiyǒu qián jiù bù néng mǎi
要是　你 有　錢　就 可以 買，没有　錢　就 不　能　買。
If you have money, you can buy it; without money, you can't.

應該　yīnggāi　should, ought to, must（suggest/ the right thing to do）

Wǒ（yīng）gāi zǒu le
我 （應）該 走了。
I must（should）go now.

Nǐ bù（yīng）gāi lái
你 不（應）該 來。
You should not have come.

必須　bìxū　be obliged to, have to（obligated, be required/demanded to）

Xuésheng bìxū měitiān xuéxí
學生　　必須　每天　學習。
A student must study everyday.

Míngtiān nǐ bìxū lái
明天　　你 必須 來。
You must come tomorrow.

得　děi　must, have to（no choice）

Wǒ jīntiān bù néng dǎ qiú wǒ děi zuò gōngkè
我　今天 不　能　打　球，我　得　做　功課　。
I cannot play ball today, I have to do homework.

Yào xiǎng dǎ de hǎo měitiān dōu děi liànxí
要　　想 打 得　好，每天　都　得　練習。
If you want to play well, you have to practice everyday.

不得不　bùdébù　cannot help but be obliged to, unwilling but have no alter-

n'ative

Wǒ bù xiǎng qù kěshì bùdébù qù
我 不　想　去，可是 不得不 去。
I don't want to go but have no choice.

（一定）要　yídìng yào　must, surely have to（give order/demand）

Nǐmen yídìng yào zǎo diǎnr lái
你們　一定 要 早 點兒 來。
Make sure you come early.

教學難點

Cruxes of Teaching and Learning

難點一　"想" vs. "要"

"想"和"要"都可以譯成"want"／"intend to do"，但是確切的意思和在句中的用法都不同。請比較。

"想" and "要", as modal verbs, both mean "want／intend to do". However, the differences are：

1）In meaning：要 is more determined than 想.

2）In structure：

要, meaning want, can be followed by either an object or a verbal phrase.

As a verb　我要這個。(a direct object)

As a modal verb　我要跟他們一起去中國。(a verbal phrase)

想 can only be followed by a verbal phrase.

As a modal verb　我想跟朋友去看電影。(a verbal phrase)

When "想" is followed directly by an object, it means "miss".

As a verb 我想我媽媽。　(an object) I miss my mom.

3）Negative：The negative form of 要 VP is 不想 VP.

As a verb　我不要那個。(a direct object)

As a modal verb　我不想跟他們去中國。(a verbal phrase)

難點二　"想" and "要" vs. "喜歡"

"想"、"要"容易和"喜歡"混淆。學生要説"想""要"却用"喜歡"。這跟英文的"would like"有"want"／"intend to do"的意思有關。

Learners often confuse "想" and "要" with "喜歡". Often when a learner means to say "想" or "要", he/she uses "喜歡." "想" and "要", as model verbs, mean "intend, want", but in English they may also be translated as "would like". "喜歡" may also refers to preferences but it is "like", meaning "to be fond of", which is different from "would like".

Compare：

Would you like (to have) some tea?

Nǐ xiǎng (yào) hē diǎnr chá ma

你　想　（要）喝 點兒 茶　嗎？

Do you like tea?

Nǐ xǐhuan hē chá ma
你 喜歡 喝茶 嗎？

難點三 "想" vs. "Want"

中文的"想"有數個用法

"想" has more usages：

（As a modal verb） intend, want to, would like to

Wǒ xiǎng qù Zhōngguó
我 想 去 中國 。
I want to go to China.

（As a verb） think

Wǒ xiǎng méiyǒu wèntí
我 想 沒有 問題。
I don't think there is any probelm.

（As a verb） long for, recall with fondness, miss

Wǒ xiǎng Běijīng wǒ xiǎng wǒ māma
我 想 北京，我 想 我 媽媽。
I miss Beijing, I miss my mom.

"想"後跟兼語句

In English, we may "want" someone to do something directly.

But in Chinese, you have to have another verb after "想" to convey the same meaning：

I want you to come with us.

Wǒ xiǎng qǐng nǐ gēn wǒmen yìqǐ qù
我 想 請 你 跟 我們 一起 去。

My mom does not want me to go.

Wǒ mā bù（xiǎng）ràng wǒ qù
我 媽 不（想） 讓 我 去。

Wanting someone to do something in Chinese implies "letting/allowing/making" someone do it.

For that effect，"請/讓/叫" are needed after "想"。（See the Chapter 22：Giving Instructions.）

難點四 "Ask" in Chinese

英文的 "Ask" 可以提問也可以請求別人做事。漢語不同，"問" 只能提問，請別人做事要用兼語句。請看對比。

In English, you may use the word "Ask" for two things：

Ask a question：

    May I ask you a question?

    Can I ask you what that is?

Ask someone to do something：

    Could I ask you to do this for me?

    He asked me to give him this book.

In Chinese, the above two functions of "ask" must be conveyed differently：

Ask a question (direct/indirect question)：use "問 wèn ask, inquire"

    Tā wèn wǒ yí ge xiǎo wèntí

    他 問 我 一 個 小 問題。

    He asked me a little question.

    Tā wèn wǒ   Nǐ jiào shénme míngzi

    他 問 我："你 叫 什麼 名字？"

    He asked me, "What is your name?"

To ask someone to do something, use one of the following three expressions：

請 qǐng ask/request/invite (somebody to do something politely)

    Jīntiān tā qǐng wǒ chī wǎnfàn

    今天 他 請 我 吃 晚飯 。

    Today, he invites me to dinner.

讓 ràng let/allow/have/make (somebody do something)

    Lǎoshī ràng wǒmen yí gè zì xiě wǔ biàn

    老師 讓 我們 一個字寫五 遍 。

    Our teacher asked us to write each character five times.

叫 jiào call on/order/make (somebody do something)

    Wǒ māma jiào nǐ zài wǒ jiā chī wǎnfàn

    我 媽媽 叫 你 在 我 家 吃 晚飯 。

    My mom asked you to have dinner at our house.

難點五　　"Can" in Chinese

英文的"Can"是一個常用詞，也是一個麻煩。因爲漢語没有確切的對應。請對比。

A. "Can" is a simple word in English, but in Chinese, there are subtle nuances. The differences in meaning are emphasized below:

English	Chinese
can: know how (a learned skill)	會
can: capacity, capable of, proficient	能
can: capacity, allowed to conditionally	可以

還有，"Can"可以直接評估行爲能否與狀況。在漢語不行，會不會與做得好與否是兩個概念，得用兩個不同的句子表達。

B. "Can" may be used to evaluate an action:

I can swim very well.

But in Chinese, the meaning of the above sentence has to be conveyed in two:

我會游泳。　　　　　（know how）

我（游泳）游得很好。　（how well）

（See Complement of Degree in Chapter 9.）

Never say:

我會游泳游得好。　　（×）

難點六　　"會" vs. "能" vs. "可以"

注意"會""能""可以"的差別。

"會"，"能" and "可以" may overlap in meaning. But to use them appropriately, we must recognize that they emphasize different aspects of one's ability.

會　　know how (a learned skill)

能　　capacity, capable of, proficient (subjective)

可以　capacity, allowed to conditionally (objective)

難點七　"不用" vs. "甭" & "不要" vs. "別"

"不用"：speak faster and faster, and you get "甭".

"不要"：speak faster and faster, and you get "別".

難點八　Negative for "得" and "不得不"

"得"和"不得不"的否定都是"不用"。請比較。

The negative of "得" and "不得不" is "不用".

(positive)　　Wǒ jīntiān děi zuò hǎo duō gōngkè
　　　　　　　我　今天　得　做　好　多　功課　。
　　　　　　　I have to do a lot of homework today.

(negative)　　Wǒ jīntiān bú yòng zuò gōngkè
　　　　　　　我　今天　不　用　做　功課　。
　　　　　　　I don't have to do homework today.

(positive)　　Wǒ jīntiān bùdébù zuò hǎoxiē gōngkè
　　　　　　　我　今天　不得不　做　好些　功課　。
　　　　　　　I have no choice but to do a lot of homework.

(negative)　　Wǒ jīntiān bú yòng zuò nàxiē gōngkè
　　　　　　　我　今天　不　用　做　那些　功課　。
　　　　　　　I don't need to do that homework.

9

評議行爲

Evaluating

Actions

評議行爲是表述一個主觀的看法，不是描述一個客觀的事實，所用的句型一般帶程度補語。主觀的看法可以有感情的成分在内，用不同的副詞和形容詞來表示强調。

本節介紹評議行爲時程度補語的使用、所涉及的副詞和形容詞，并指出和注釋中英文對副詞和形容詞使用的一些不同點。

Evaluating, judging or commenting on actions and events is stating opinions from personal or suggestive point of views. It is not about giving a factual report. It requires sentences with complement of degree that employ adverbs and adjectives to emphasize opinions.

This chapter introduces the patterns and functional uses of the complement of degree and related adverbs and adjectives. It also pinpoints some differences between Chinese and English in terms of the usage of adverbs and adjectives.

教 學 重 點　Content of Teaching and Learning

程度補語　　　　　　　　Complement of Degree

教 學 難 點　Cruxes of Teaching and Learning

程度補語句型　　　　　　Structure of the Complement of Degree
程度補語功用　　　　　　Function of the Complement of Degree
"一點" vs. "有一點"
動詞組 vs. 雙音節動詞　　Verbal Phrases vs. Two-word Verbs
漢語的副詞與英語的副詞　Chinese Adverbs vs. English Adverbs
難以翻譯的形容詞　　　　Adjectives Difficult to Translate

詞 彙 表　Glossary

常用副詞表　　　　　　　List of Commonly Used Adverbs
常用簡易形容詞表　　　　List of Commonly Used Simple Adjectives

教學重點

Content of Teaching and Learning

程度補語   Complement of Degree

功用 Function：評論、評估、判斷行爲事件。

Give a subjective view of an action, and evaluate, judge, comment on an action.

句型   Sentence Pattern：

Subject + VO		V + de (Adverb)		+ Adjective
我	看書	看 得		快。
我，	書	看 得		快。
書，	我	看 得		快。

Complement of Degrees Shown with Adverbs：

kuài jí le
快 極 了

tèbié kuài
特別 快

fēicháng kuài
非常　快

zhēn kuài
真　快

tài kuài le
太　快　了

hěn kuài
很　快

yǒudiǎnr kuài
有點兒　快

我看書看得

bú tài kuài
不 太　快

hěn màn
很　慢

tài màn le
太　慢　了

zhēn màn
真　慢

fēicháng màn
非常　　慢

tèbié màn
特別　慢

màn jí le
慢　極了

教學難點

Cruxes of Teaching and Learning

難點一　程度補語句型 Structure of the Complement of Degree

In structure, the action verb must be followed by "de" immediately. For two-word verbal phrases, the verb must be repeated.

wrong	correct		
我看書　得快。	我看書　看得　　很快。		
	我　　　看得　　特別快。		

難點二　程度補語功能 Function of the Complement of Degree

"He plays hard."這句話有兩個可能的意思，翻譯時酌情用不同的句型表達。

一個是說話人對當事人行為的評論和看法。（主觀）

一個是說話人描述當事人的行為。（儘量客觀）

In English, if you want to say "He plays hard". It could mean two things:

1) You are commenting on/judging his attitude about his playing. (Subjective)

2) You are describing his action/effort. (Objective)

Since different perspectives are reflected, different sentence patterns must be used.

比較對比　Contrast

(Opinion/comment: subject view)

Wǒ juéde tā dǎ pīngpāngqiú dǎ de fēicháng rènzhēn

我　覺得 他 打　乒乓球　打 得　非常　認真 。

In my opinion, he plays ping-pong with great seriousness.

(Manner of action: objective description)

他總是非常認真地打球。

He always plays ball very seriously.

難點三　"（一）點" vs. "有（一）點"

"A little bit" 可以是"一點"或"有一點"，對學生來說是一個大問題。參看例句，對比不同和用法。簡單地說："（一）點"是量。"有（一）點"是程度。

In English, "a little bit" can be translated into "一點" or "有一點". In other words, "一點" and "有一點" are the same in English. But they are not the same in Chinese. Thus these "little" expressions often pose "big" difficulties to learners. To make it simple: "（一）點" refers to quantity. "有（一）點" refers to a degree or an extent.

"（一）點": After a verb/Before a noun (quantify nouns: some)

Wǒ xiǎng hē (yì) diǎn shuǐ

我　想　喝（一）點 水 。

I want to drink some (a little amount of) water.

Tā zhǐ huì shuō yìdiǎn Zhōngwén

他 只 會　說　一點　中文 。

He can only speak some (a little) Chinese.

"（一）點"：After an adjective (quantify description)

Tā bǐ nǐ gāo yìdiǎn

他 比 你 高 一點 。

He is taller than you by a little (he is a little bit taller than you.)

"（一）點"：After an adjective/Before a verb (quantify the speed)

Kuài (yì) diǎn zǒu

快 （一）點 走 。

Walk a little faster (hurry up).

Màn diǎn pǎo

慢 點 跑 。

Run a little slower (slow down).

"有（一）點"：Before an adjective to modify a description

wrong	correct
我一點渴。	Wǒ yǒu yìdiǎn kě 我 有 一點 渴 。 I am a little thirsty.
今天的天氣一點冷。	Jīntiān de tiānqì yǒu diǎn lěng 今天 的 天氣 有 點 冷 。 Today's weather is a little bit cold.

難點四　動詞組 vs. 雙音節動詞
Verbal Phrases vs. Two-word Verbs

Many simple daily life action verbs in English are verbal phrases (verb-noun) in Chinese.

English (verb)	Chinese (verb + noun)
eat	吃飯

drink	喝水
sleep	睡覺
get up	起床
swim	游泳
sing	唱歌
dance	跳舞

When in sentence patterns showing complements, such as 程度補語 or 時量補語, only the verb should be repeated.

Some Chinese verbs are two-word verbs, e. g.:

study	學習	rest	休息
participate	參加	prepare	準備

When in sentence patterns showing complements such as 程度補語 or 時量補語, no part of the two word (two syllables) verb needs to be repeated.

Learners tend to, when translate from English to Chinese, make mistakes.

1) Not to repeat the verb when must: (in patterns for complements)

wrong	**correct**
我游泳得好。	我游泳游得好。
我跳舞了一個鐘頭。	我跳舞跳了一個鐘頭。

2) Repeat word when not necessary:

wrong	**correct**
我學習得很好。	我學習學得很好。

難點五　漢語的副詞與英語的副詞
Chinese Adverbs vs. English Adverbs

漢語的副詞與英語的副詞的概念和用法不同。見例句。

In English, many adjectives can become adverbs when describing actions, simply by adding "ly," e. g. "beautiful-beautifully."

　　A. She is beautiful.　　　　　　她真漂亮。
　　B. She did it beautifully.　　　　她幹得真漂亮。

In Chinese, adverbs are adverbs and adjectives are adjectives. They don't change. "漂亮" in Sentence A is an adjective used to describe (as predicate of the sentence) and in Sentence B it is still an adjective but used as a complement of the sentence.

難點六　難以翻譯的形容詞 Adjectives Difficult to Translate

1) Age

"大" and "小"：are used to refer to age, not size, when used to describe people.

"老" and "小／少 shào young"：are also used for age.

年輕 niánqīng young (of people, often of teenagers) is another word used for "young".

However, for most K-12 learners, when they want to say："when I was young ..." , they really should say：

　　"我小時候"。(They are too young to say "我年輕的時候".)

2) Old

Both "舊" and "老" are translated as "old" in English, but：

　　"新舊" is used for objects.

　　"新老" is used for people.

3) Short：

"矮"，"低"，and "短" are all translated as "short" in English, but：

Though "高矮" and "高低" are all used for height, "高矮" is for the height people and objects. "高低" is used for temperature or height in a more abstract sense. "長短" is used for length.

4) Cheap and mean：

In English, youngsters like to use the expression "cheap" and "mean" to describe people.

"便宜 piányi cheap" is only used to describe price of an object, it cannot be used to describe people. The correct expression for describing a person being cheap is "小氣/小器 xiǎoqi stingy". While "小氣" can also be translated into "mean", it refers to being "stingy/thrifty", not being cruel to others. What exactly is being "mean-cruel" in Chinese? This is a good question.

5) Smartness and stupidity

"聰明, 靈巧, 機靈" all mean smart, but:

(of intelligence)	聰明　cōngming	intelligent, bright
(of bodily function)	靈巧　língqiǎo	nimble, clever, graceful
(of street smartness)	機靈　jīling	clever, smart

"笨, 傻, 糊塗" are all used for stupidness, but:

(of slow mindedness)

笨　bèn　awkward, clumsy, cumbersome

(of simple mindedness)

傻　shǎ　silly, simple-minded, naive, foolhardy, unimaginative

(of muddle-headedness)

糊塗　hútu　confused, chaotic, in a mess, blurred, indistinct

6) Thinness

"瘦, 薄, 稀, 淡, 細" can all be translated as "thin" in English. But there are differences in use:

(of body shape)	胖	pàng	fat, stout
	瘦	shòu	thin
(of volume)	厚	hòu	thick
	薄	báo	thin
(of solutions, population)	稠	chóu	dense, thick
	稀	xī	sparse; thin
(of liquids, taste, color)	濃	nóng	thick, dense

	淡	dàn	thin
（of particles, voice, quality）	粗	cū	thick, coarse
	細	xì	thin, fine

詞彙表

常用副詞表　List of Commonly Used Adverbs（by intensity）

Adverb as prefix

有（一）點　yǒu（yì）diǎn　a bit, a little

　　　　　　　有一點餓　　　　a bit hungry

不太　　　　bú tài　　　not too, not very; without much

　　　　　　　不太高　　　　　not too tall

很　　　　　hěn　　　very

（Though meaning "very", "很" is not as strong as "very" in English.

It is often used as a rhetorical prefix to an adjective, especially a one syllable adjective with little or no intensification of the adjective's meaning.）

　　　　　　　很好　　　　　　pretty good
　　　　　　　很多　　　　　　a lot

太……了　　tài……le　　too, excessively

（With positive adjectives, it emphasizes greatness. However, with negative ones, it takes the tone of complaining.）

　　　　　　　太棒了　　　　　wonderful
　　　　　　　太貴了　　　　　too expensive

真　　　　　zhēn　　　really

　　　　　　　真便宜　　　　　really cheap

非常　　　　fēicháng　　extraordinarily, unusually

　　　　　　　非常好看　　　　awfully good looking

| 特別 | tèbié | especially, particularly, specially |
| | | 特別好吃　　extraordinarily tasty |

Adverb as suffix

……極了	jíle	extremely (adjectival or adverbial suffix)
		好極了　　　extremely well
……死了	sǐle	to death (adjectival or adverbial suffix; colloquial: usually for expressions negative in meaning)
		渴死了　　　　thirsty to death

常用簡易形容詞表　List of Commonly Used Simple Adjectives

分類便於記憶: Categorized for Easy Memorization

形容詞 (1)　　　　Pairs/Anonyms

大	dà	big	小	xiǎo	small, little
多	duō	many, much	少	shǎo	few, little, less
早	zǎo	early	晚	wǎn	late
快	kuài	fast	慢	màn	slow
好	hǎo	good, well	壞	huài	bad (差 chà poorly)
容易	róngyì	simple, easy	難	nán	difficult
貴	guì	expensive	便宜	piányi	cheap
新	xīn	new	舊	jiù	old
長	cháng	long	短	duǎn	short (of length; duration)
高	gāo	high	矮	ǎi	short (of height)
輕	qīng	light	重	zhòng	heavy, serious
胖	pàng	fat, stout	瘦	shòu	thin (of body shape)
厚	hòu	thick	薄	báo	thin (of volume)

遠	yuǎn	far	近	jìn	near
對	duì	correct	錯	cuò	wrong
冷	lěng	cold	熱	rè	hot
深	shēn	deep, dark	淺	qiǎn	shallow, light
聰明	cōngming	intelligent, smart	笨	bèn	clumsy, slow in wit
大方	dàfang	generous	小氣	xiǎoqi	stingy, narrow-minded
乾凈	gānjìng	clean, neat	髒	zāng	dirty, filthy
香	xiāng	fragrant, delicious	臭	chòu	stinky, disgusting odor

形容詞（2）　　Paired Adjectives Used Together as Nouns

大小	dàxiǎo	big or small (size)
多少	duōshǎo	number, amount, more or less (quantity)
早晚	zǎowǎn	sooner or later (time)
快慢	kuàimàn	(rate of) speed
好壞	hǎohuài	good and bad (quality)
難易	nányì	degree of difficulty
貴賤	guìjiàn	noble and base
長短	chángduǎn	length, accident, mishap
高矮	gāo'ǎi	height (high, low)
輕重	qīngzhòng	weight, seriousness, importance, propriety
胖瘦	pàngshòu	stout or thin, degree of stoutness (of body shape)
厚薄	hòubáo	(degree of) thickness, (degree of) generosity, favor
遠近	yuǎnjìn	far and near (distance)
對錯	duìcuò	correct or wrong
深淺	shēnqiǎn	depth, sense of propriety, shade (of color)
香臭	xiāngchòu	sweet-smelling and foul-smelling, good and bad

形容詞 （3）　Simple Verbs Used to Form Adjectives

看	kàn	look
吃	chī	eat
喝	hē	drink
聽	tīng	hear
玩	wán	play；have fun
唱	chàng	sing
寫	xiě	write
用	yòng	use

好（good）	不好（not good）	難（bad）
好看	不好看	難看
好吃	不好吃	難吃
好喝	不好喝	難喝
好聽	不好聽	難聽
好玩	不好玩	

or

好（easy）	不好（not easy）	難（difficult）
好唱	不好唱	難唱
好寫	不好寫	難寫
好用	不好用	難用

有	沒（有）
有意思　yǒu yìsi　interesting	沒意思　méi yìsi　boring
有用　yǒuyòng　be useful	沒用　méiyòng　useless
有錢　yǒuqián　rich, wealthy	
有名　yǒumíng 　　　famous, well-known	

形容詞（4） Physical Conditions

餓	è	be hungry
飽	bǎo	be full（after eating）
渴	kě	thirsty
忙	máng	busy
累	lèi	tired
懶	lǎn	lazy, sluggish

Sensory Comfort：

漂亮	piàoliang	good-looking, pretty
可愛	kě'ài	lovable, likeable, charming
方便	fāngbiàn	convenient
舒服	shūfu	comfortable
痛快	tòngkuai	happy, delighted; to one's heart's content
高興	gāoxìng	happy, glad; be happy to, be glad to
滿意	mǎnyì	satisfied, pleased; determined, resolved
合適	héshì	be suitable, fit
自然	zìrán	natural, at ease
正常	zhèngcháng	normal
難過	nánguò	have a difficult life; feel bad（about something）
興奮	xīngfèn	be excited
緊張	jǐnzhāng	anxious, nervous

Colloquial:

棒	bàng	fine, strong, excellent
酷	kù	"cool" (borrowed from English)
帥	shuài	handsome; elegant
醜	chǒu	ugly
討厭	tǎoyàn	annoying, bothersome
惡心	ěxin	disgusting

10

顔色　　　　　　　Color

談顏色是學習詞彙。可顏色也可用來形容/描繪和確認。把顏色另立一節一是强調顏色本身的重要語用功能，二是爲了方便教與學時可以和其他內容有多種的組合。例如、衣服、水果、用具、動物等。

Discussing colors is good for learning vocabulary. But colors can also be used to describe and identify objects. The purpose of making color a topic is two-fold. First, it emphasizes the function of color in language use; second it is convenient to combine color with other topics. Colors can be used to describe and identify clothing, food, animals and many other objects.

教 學 重 點　Content of Teaching and Learning

顏色	Color
基本顏色	Basic Colors
顏色的深淺	Description of Shades of Color
顏色形容顏色	Color on Color
彩色的/花的	Multicolors/Mixed Colors
描述性的顏色	Descriptive Colors（Nature and Color）
"是……的"結構	"是……的" Structure

教 學 難 點　Cruxes of Teaching and Learning

顏色作爲形容詞	Colors as Adjectives
顏色的使用	Description vs. Identification
形狀和顏色	Shape and Color

教學重點

Content of Teaching and Learning

顏色　yánsè　Color

基本顏色　Basic Colors

紅	hóng	red
黃	huáng	yellow
藍	lán	blue
綠	lǜ	green
棕	zōng	brown（褐 hè brown；咖啡 kāfēi coffee）
黑	hēi	black
白	bái	white
灰	huī	gray
紫	zǐ	purple，violet
粉	fěn	pink
金	jīn	golden
銀	yín	silver

顏色的深淺　Description of Shades of Color

Add 深 or 淺 before the color.

深	shēn	dark（of colour），deep
		深藍／深綠／深灰
淺	qiǎn	light（of color），shallow
		淺紅／淺綠／淺粉

顏色形容顏色　Color on Color

金黃	jīnhuáng	golden yellow，golden
銀灰	yínhuī	silver gray

銀白	yínbái	silver white
粉紅	fěnhóng	pink
紫紅	zǐhóng	purplish red, maroon
灰白	huībái	grayish white, pale
黑灰	hēihuī	blackish gray

彩色的/花的　MultiColors/Mixed Colors

彩色	cǎisè	multicolored; colored (e. g. television, film)
花的	huāde	floral, colorful

Transparent:

透明	tòumíng	transparent
無色	wúsè	colorless

描述性的顔色　Descriptive Colors (Nature and Color)

紅

橘紅	júhóng	tangerine red
血紅	xuèhóng	blood red
火紅	huǒhóng	fiery red
海棠紅	hǎitánghóng	light pink (crabapple red)

黃

杏黃	xìnghuáng	apricot yellow
橘黃	júhuáng	orange yellow
土黃	tǔhuáng	yellowish brown, khaki
鵝黃	éhuáng	light-soft yellow (as a goose)

藍

天藍	tiānlán	azure, sky blue
碧藍	bìlán	blue green (green jade blue)
海藍	hǎilán	dark blue (deep sea blue)
海軍藍	hǎijūnlán	navy blue

綠

草綠	cǎolǜ	grass-green
墨綠	mòlǜ	blackish green, forest green
軍綠	jūnlǜ	army green
祖母綠	zǔmǔlǜ	deep blue-green

白

| 雪白 | xuěbái | snow white |
| 乳白 | rǔbái | milky white, cream |

黑

| 墨黑 | mòhēi | jet black |

"是……的" 結構　　"是……的" Structure

功用　Function：

The "是……的" pattern is used to identify some characteristic of an object.

句型　Structure：

> Subject　是　characteristic　的（object）.

（color）

Wǒ de máoyī shì hóng de Hóng de shì wǒ de fěn de bú shì wǒ de
我 的 毛衣 是 紅 的。紅 的 是我的，粉 的 不 是 我 的。
My sweater is a red one. The red is mine; the pink is not mine.

Wǒ de máoyī shì hóng yánsè de
我 的 毛衣 是 紅 顏色 的。
My sweater is the red one.

（condition）

Tā de máoyī shì xīn de bú shì jiù de
他 的 毛衣 是 新 的，不 是 舊 的。
His sweater is a new one, not an old one.

（possession）

Xīn de shì tā de jiù de shì wǒ de
新 的 是 他 的，舊 的 是 我 的。
The new one is his, the old one is mine.

(nature)

Zhè běn shū shì Yīngwén de bú shì Zhōngwén de
這 本 書 是 英文 的，不 是 中文 的。
This book is an English book, not a Chinese book.

問答　Questions and Answers

Zhè yǒu yí jiàn shàngyī shì bu shì nǐ de
這 有 一 件 上 衣，是 不 是 你 的？
There is a jacket here; is it yours?

Wǒ de shàngyī shì xīn de (shàngyī) bú shì jiù de
我 的 上衣 是 新 的 （上衣），不 是 舊 的。
My jacket is a new one, not an old one.

Nà jiàn huáng yùndòngyī shì tā de ma
那 件 黃 運動衣 是 他 的 嗎？
Is that yellow sports shirt his?

Bù nà bú shì tā de shì wǒ de
不，那 不 是 他 的，是 我 的。
No, that is not his, it is mine.

Tā de shì hóng de bú shì huáng de
他 的 是 紅 的，不 是 黃 的。
His is (a) red (one), not (a) yellow (one).

Zhè shì shénme shū Yīngwén de háishi Zhōngwén de
這 是 什麼 書？英文 的 還是 中文 的？
What kind of book is this? English or Chinese?

Zhè běn shì Yīngwén de Nà běn shì Zhōngwén de
這 本 是 英文 的。那 本 是 中文 的。
This is an English book, that one is Chinese.

Zhè běn Yīngwén de shì jìsuànjī zázhì nà běn Zhōngwén de shì
這 本 英文 的 是 計算機 雜誌，那 本 中文 的 是
kèběn
課本 。
The English one is a computer magazine; that Chinese one is a textbook.

教學難點

Cruxes of Teaching and Learning

難點一　顏色作爲形容詞 Colors as Adjectives

"紅", when used by itself, is a description. When talking about a color, you say：

　　　　紅色　紅的/紅色的　紅顏色的

Adjectives have these characteristics in functional use：

1) Position：Adjective can be used to modify a noun, and the position of an adjective is before the noun it defines.

2) However, if the modifier is a one-syllable word, it does not require "的"：

　　　　　紅毛衣，黑筆

3) If the modifier is more than one syllable, we must use "的"：

　　　　　很紅的毛衣，深藍的毛衣，粉紅的毛衣，雪白的毛衣

難點二　顏色的使用 Description vs. Identification

顏色可以直接用來描述。

顏色也可以和"是……的"結構一起用來定義。請參照例句比較用法。

An adjective can be used to modify a noun as part of the object's identification. In this case, the sentence pattern to use is "是……的". An adjective can also be used to describe an object directly without use of a verb.

　　　　毛衣很紅。

See the contrast：

Description：

　　　　我的毛衣白，她的不白。

我的毛衣太白了，她的一點也不白。(with adverbs)

Identification：

我的毛衣是白的（毛衣）；她的毛衣不是白的，是紅的。

Both are in a sentence：

我的紅毛衣不是深紅的，是淺紅的。

難點三　形狀與顏色 Shape and Color

When describing a piece of clothing, shapes are often used with colors, e. g. :

blue and white stripes：藍白條的（條 tiáo string, stripe）

mixed color pattern：　花格的　（花格 huāgé checkered pattern）

11

服裝與學習用具

Clothing and
Study Tools

服裝和學習用具都是名詞。談服裝和學習用具就要用到數字和量詞以及相應的動詞。這一節的重點和難點就在於此。

Clothing and study tools are all nouns. Discussing clothing and study tools often requires using numbers and measure words along with verbs. This chapter's teaching and learning foci and cruxes are as such.

教 學 重 點　Content of Teaching and Learning

量詞	Measure Words
服裝	Clothing
服飾	Accessories
學習用具	Study Tools

教 學 難 點　Cruxes of Teaching and Learning

量詞的使用	Usage of Measure Words
"Wear" in Chinese	
動詞與名詞搭配	Matching Verbs with Nouns
複雜定語（名詞組）	Complex Attributes（Noun Phrases）

教學重點

Content of Teaching and Learning

量詞　Measure Words

（See Measure Words in Chapter 1：Numbers in Life）

Rules：

Different objects take different measure words

Measure words connect quantity／"這"／"那" with nouns.

Quantity	measure word	noun
兩	本	書

（這）	measure word	noun
這	本	書

（那）	measure word	noun
那	本	書

服裝　fúzhuāng　Clothing

衣服　yīfu　clothes，clothing

穿　chuān　wear，put on（clothing）

脫　tuō　take off，remove（clothing）

一套　yí tào　measure word：a set，a suit

　衣服　yīfu　clothes，clothing

　西服　xīfú　suit（Western-style）

一件　yí jiàn　measure word：one piece（for upper body clothing）

　上衣　shàngyī　upper outer garment（e. g. coat，jacket）

　外衣　wàiyī　outerwear，coat，outer garment

　夾克　jiākè　jacket

　大衣　dàyī　overcoat

　毛衣　máoyī　wool sweater

雨衣	yǔyī	raincoat
游泳衣	yóuyǒng yī	swimsuit, bathing suit
運動衣(衫)	yùndòng yī (shān)	sports shirt
襯衫	chènshān	shirt
T-恤衫	T-xùshān	T-shirt
背心	bèixīn	sleeveless garment (waistcoat, vest)

內衣　nèiyī　underwear (especially undershirt)

胸罩	xiōngzhào	bra, brassiere

一條　yì tiáo　measure word: a piece (for lower body clothing)

褲子	kùzi	pants, trousers
長褲	chángkù	long pants
短褲	duǎnkù	short pants
半長褲	bànchángkù	capris
運動褲	yùndòngkù	sports pants
游泳褲	yóuyǒngkù	swimming trunks
牛仔褲	niúzǎikù	jeans
咔嘰褲	kǎjīkù	khaki pants
西服褲	xīfúkù	formal/dressy pants

內褲　nèikù　underpants

褲衩	kùchǎ	underpants, shorts, briefs

裙子　qúnzi　skirt, dress

長裙	chángqún	long dress/skirt
短裙	duǎnqún	short dress/skirt
迷你裙	mínǐqún	miniskirt
西服裙	xīfúqún	formal/career skirt

一雙　yì shuāng　measure word: a pair (for paired objects: shoes, socks, gloves, etc.)

一隻　yì zhī　a measure word for the single of a pair (like ears, hands, shoes, etc.)

鞋	xié	shoes
皮鞋	píxié	leather shoes
布鞋	bùxié	shoes made of（cotton）fabric
運動鞋	yùndòngxié	athletic shoes, sneakers
球鞋	qiúxié	athletic shoes, sneakers
涼鞋	liángxié	sandals
拖鞋	tuōxié	slippers
靴子	xuēzi	boots
襪子	wàzi	socks, stockings
手套	shǒutào	gloves, mittens, baseball glove

but：

一副	yí fù	measure word：a pair, a set
眼鏡	yǎnjìng	eyeglasses
耳環	ěrhuán	earrings

服飾 fúshì Accessories

戴	dài	wear, put on（accessories）
一條	yì tiáo	measure word for something long and skinny
圍巾	wéijīn	scarf, muffler
頭巾	tóujīn	kerchief；head wrap
領帶	lǐngdài	necktie
手鏈	shǒuliàn	bracelet
項鏈	xiàngliàn	necklace
皮帶	pídài	belt, leather belt
腰帶	yāodài	waistband, girdle, belt
一個	yí ge	a general measure word
手錶	shǒubiǎo	wrist watch

戒指	jièzhi	ring（for finger）	
手鐲	shǒuzhuó	bracelet	
扣子	kòuzi	button，knot	
一副 yí fù		measure word for a set of something	
耳環	ěrhuán	earrings	
眼鏡	yǎnjìng	eyeglasses	
鞋帶	xiédài	shoelaces	
一頂 yì dǐng		measure word for hat	
帽子	màozi	cap，hat	

學習用具　Study Tools

一支 yì zhī		measure word：for songs；for long, narrow things（e. g. rifle, candle）	
筆	bǐ	pen	一支筆
一張 yì zhāng		measure word for flat things like a sheet of paper, a table, etc.	
紙	zhǐ	paper	一張紙
報紙	bàozhǐ	newspaper	一張報紙
畫	huà	painting，picture，drawing	一張畫
照片	zhàopiàn	photograph，picture，print	一張照片
一個 yí ge		a general measure word	
計算機	jìsuànjī	computer	一個計算機
計算器	jìsuànqì	calculator	一個計算器
本子	běnzi	notebook	一個本子
書包	shūbāo	school bag	一個書包
廣告	guǎnggào	advertisement	一個廣告
一本 yì běn		measure word：for books	
書	shū	book	一本書
字典 zìdiǎn（詞典 cídiǎn）		dictionary	一本字典

雜誌	zázhì	（news，etc.）magazine	一本雜誌
課本	kèběn	textbook	一本課本
漫畫	mànhuà	cartoon	一本（張）漫畫
畫報	huàbào	pictorial（magazine）	一本畫報
一篇 yì piān		measure word：article，essay	
文章	wénzhāng	article，essay，literary works	

（For more，see the List of Commonly Used Measure Words in Chapter 1：Numbers in Life.）

教學難點
Cruxes of Teaching and Learning

難點一　量詞的使用 Usage of Measure Words

學生不愛或不習慣用量詞。不同的物件要用不同的量詞。量詞還有其他的用途。

請參閱第一章的量詞表。

Learners often do not like to or are not accustomed to using measure words. Different objects require the use of different measure words.

Measure words also have other functions.

To quantify： | Quantity + Measure Word + Noun |

一	個	人
兩	個	學生
三	本	書
四	件	上衣

To specify： | "這" / "那" + Measure Word + Noun |

To ask： | "幾" / "哪" + Measure Word + Noun |

To order：一個個地 + Verb

To emphasize：個個（每個）Noun

（See Chapter 1：Numbers in Life – List of Commonly Used Measure Words for more information.）

難點二　"Wear" in Chinese

"Wear"這個詞在英文里可以指很多活動。中文要用很多不同的詞。參見例句。

In English，we use the verb "to wear" for many things：

  wear clothes

  wear accessories

  wear makeup

  wear a hairdo（certain hair style）

  wear a scar

  wear a disguise

  wear a smile

In Chinese，in order to say all the above，different verbs are required.

wear clothes	穿衣服
wear accessories	戴帽子
wear makeup	化妝
wear a disguise	化妝/偽裝
wear a hairdo（certain hair style）	梳（髮型）
wear a scar	有傷疤
wear a smile	（面帶）笑容

難點三　複雜定語（名詞組）Complex Attributes（Noun Phrases）

（See the same topic in Chapter 18：Noun Phrases.）

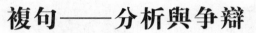

12

複句——分析與爭辯

Complex Sentence Patterns —Reasoning and Arguing

給理由和原因是分析和爭辯的起步。本節就通過例句介紹一些與此相關的句型和用法。

Reasoning is the beginning phase of analyzing and arguing. This chapter uses examples to introduce the patterns and usages of some common complex sentences needed for this language function.

教 學 重 點 Content of Teaching and Learning

複句句型	Complex Sentence Patterns
通過連詞構成	Use Conjunction（s）
通過副詞構成	Use Adverb（s）
通過疑問詞構成	Use Interrogative Pronoun（s）

教 學 難 點 Cruxes of Teaching and Learning

主語與副詞	Subjects and Adverbs
主語在句中的位置	Position of Subjects in the Sentences
"除了……以外" and "疑問詞＋都"	
"再" vs. "又"	
"不管" 與疑問	Interrogative Form in "不管" Sentence
"正在" vs. "剛"	

教學重點

Content of Teaching and Learning

複句句型 Complex Sentence Patterns

通過連詞構成 Use Conjunction（s）

1）因爲……所以…… yīnwèi suǒyǐ because...（therefore）...

Yīnwèi wǒ xǐhuan dǎ qiú suǒyǐ cháng dǎ
因爲 我 喜歡 打 球，所以 常 打。
Because I like to play a ball game,（therefore）I often play.

Yīnwèi jīntiān de tiānqì hǎo suǒyǐ wǒmen xiǎng chūqu wánr
因爲 今天 的 天氣 好，所以 我們 想 出去 玩兒。
Because today's weather is good,（therefore）we want to go out and play.

Note："Therefore" can be often omitted in English, but is required in Chinese.

2）yàoshi rúguǒ jiǎrú jiǎshǐ jiǎshè jiù
要是 （ 如果 ／假如／假使／ 假設 ）……就…… if... then...

Yàoshi wǒ yǒu shíjiān wǒ jiù qù kàn diànyǐng
要是 我 有 時間，我 就 去 看 電影 。
If I have time,（then）I will go to see a movie.

Rúguǒ nǐ jīntiān bù néng qù jiù míngtiān qù ba
如果 你 今天 不 能 去，就 明天 去 吧。
If you cannot go today,（then）go tomorrow.

Note："Then" can be often omitted in English, but is required in Chinese.

3）雖然 suīrán（儘管 jǐnguǎn＊）……

可是 kěshì（但是 dànshì＊）……

though/although...（nevertheless/still）...

Suīrán wǒ hěn máng kěshì wǒ chángcháng kàn diànshì
雖然 我 很 忙，可是 我 常常 看 電視 。
Though I am busy,（still）I often watch TV.

Jǐnguǎn tā yǒu hěn duō shì dànshì háishi měitiān duànliàn
儘管 他 有 很 多 事，但是 還是 每天 鍛煉 。

Although he has many things to do, he (still) works out daily.

Suīrán tā huì shuō Hànyǔ kě shì tā bù cháng shuō
雖然 他 會 説 漢語，可是 他 不 常 説。
Although he knows how to speak Chinese, he (still) does not often use it.

Jǐnguǎn tā hěn gāo dànshì tā bú pàng
儘管 他 很 高，但是 他 不 胖 (fat)。
Although he is tall, he is (nevertheless) not fat.

Note："Nevertheless/still" can be often omitted in English, but is required in Chinese.

4) 不但 bùdàn（不僅 bùjǐn）……而且 érqiě……

not only... but also...

(Subject)

Bùjǐn wǒmen yǒu shì érqiě tāmen yě yǒu shì
不僅 我們 有 事，而且 他們 也 有 事。
Not only do we have things to do, but they do, too.

(VP)

Tā búdàn pǎo de kuài érqiě yóuyǒng yě yóu de hǎo
他 不但 跑 得 快，而且 游泳 也 游 得 好。
Not only does he run fast, but he also swims well.

(Model Verb)

Wǒ búdàn xǐhuan kàn shū érqiě xiǎng kàn hěn duō shū
我 不但 喜歡 看 書，而且 想 看 很 多 書。
Not only do I like to read, but I also want to read many books.

(Adjective)

Zhège dōngxi búdàn guì érqiě nánkàn
這個 東西 不但 貴，而且 難看。
These things are not only expensive, but also ugly.

5) 又 yòu……又 yòu……

(a. Same as yibianr... yibianr...; b. not only... but also...; both...
and...)

Tā fēicháng máng yīnwèi tā yòu xué Hànyǔ yòu xué Fǎyǔ
a. 她 非常 忙，因爲 她 又 學 漢語 又 學 法语。
She is very busy because she is studying Chinese and French at the
same time.

Māma bú ràng wǒ yòu wán diànnǎo yòu dǎ diànhuà
媽媽　不　讓　我　又　玩　電腦　又　打　電話 。
My mom does not want me to play computer game while talking on the phone.

Bú yào yòu chī yòu shuō
不要　又　吃　又　説 。
Don't eat and talk at the same time.

Tā yòu cōngming yòu piāoliang
b.　她　又　聰明　又　漂亮 。
She is not only smart but also pretty.

Nàge rén yòu yǒu míng yòu yǒu qián
那個　人　又　有　名　又　有　錢 。
That person is rich and famous.

Tā yòu huì shuō Yīngyǔ yòu huì shuō Xībānyáyǔ
他　又　會　説　英語　又　會　説　西班牙語 。
He speaks both English and Spanish.

6）一邊 yìbiān……一邊 yìbiān……

（doing two things at the same time）

Tā chángcháng yìbiān chī fàn yìbiān kàn shū
他　常常　一邊　吃飯　一邊　看　書。
He often eats and reads at the same time.

Wǒ xǐhuan yìbiān tīng yīnyuè yìbiān zuò gōngkè
我　喜歡　一邊　聽　音樂　一邊　做　功課 。
I like to listen to music and do homework at the same time.

Bié yìbiān chī yìbiān shuō
別　一邊　吃　一邊　説 。
Don't eat and talk at the same time. (Don't talk with your mouth full.)

7）不論 búlùn（不管 bùguǎn/無論 wúlùn）……都 dōu（還 hái）……

no matter, regardless, still...

（Subject）

Zhè běn shū búlùn shì dàrén háishi xiǎohái dōu xǐhuan kàn
這　本　書，不論　是　大人　還是　小孩 ，都　喜歡　看 。
As for this book, whether by adults or children, it is well liked.

（Time）

Búlùn shì jīntiān háishi míngtiān wǒmen dōu néng qù
不論　是　今天　還是　明天 ，我們　都　能　去 。
No matter it is today or tomorrow, We can still go.

（Attributive）

Tā xǐhuan kàn diànyǐng bùguǎn shì nǎr de dōu xǐhuan kàn

他 喜歡 看 電影 ， 不管 是 哪兒 的 都 喜歡 看 。

He likes to watch movies, regardless where they come from.

（Adjective）

Wúlùn lèi bu lèi wǒ dōu hái děi zuò gōngkè

無論 累 不 累 , 我 都 還 得 做 功課 。

No matter how tired I am, I have to do my homework.

8）除了 chúleVP／NP 以外 yǐwài, 還 hái（也 yě）……

besides. . . also. . .（inclusive）

（Subject）

Chúle tā yǐwài wǒmen yě qù

除了 他 以外 , 我們 也 去 。

Besides him, we will also go.

（VP）

Chúle pǎobù yǐwài tā hái xǐhuan chàng gē

除了 跑步 以外 , 他 還 喜歡 唱 歌 。

Besides running, he also likes singing.

9）除了 chúleVP/NP 以外 yǐwài, 都 dōu……

except for. . . all. . .（exclusive）

（Subject）

Chúle tā yǐwài wǒmen dōu bú qù

除了 他 以外 , 我們 都 不·去 。

Except for him, none of us is going.

（Object）

Chúle pǎobù yǐwài shénme yùndòng tā dōu xǐhuan

除了 跑步 以外 , 什麼 運動 他 都 喜歡 。

Except for running, he likes all sports.

通過副詞構成　Use Adverb（s）

1）正在 zhèngzài……呢 ne　just now（ongoing situation）

（action）

Wǒ huíjiā de shíhou wǒ māma zhèngzài zuò fàn
我 回家 的 時候，我 媽媽 正在 做 飯。
When I arrived home, my mom was cooking.

（time）

Wǒ māma zhèngzài zuò fàn de shíhou wǒ dào jiā le
我 媽媽 正在 做 飯的 時候，我 到 家了。
When my mom was cooking, I arrived home.

（both）

Wǒ zhèng zuò fàn de shíhou tā zhèng kàn shū ne
我 正 做 飯的 時候，他 正 看 書呢。
When I was cooking, he was reading.

Nǐmen（zhèngzài）wán jìsuànjī de shíhou wǒmen yě zhèngzài
你們 （正在） 玩 計算機的 時候，我們 也 正在

wán
玩 。
When you were playing computer games, we were playing, too.

2）先 xiān……再 zài……然後 ránhòu（再 zài）……

（sequence：plan）first... then... next...

Wǒmen xiān qù Běijīng zài qù Nánjīng ránhòu zài qù Shànghǎi
我們 先去北京，再去 南京 然後 再去 上海。
First, we go to Beijing, then go to Nanjing, next to Shanghai.

3）先 xiān……又 yòu……後來 hòulái（又 yòu）……

（sequence：done）first... then... finally...

Wǒmen xiān qù le Běijīng yòu qù Nánjīng hòulái yòu qùle
我們 先 去 了北京， 又 去 南京 後來 又 去了
Shànghǎi
上海 。
First, we went to Beijing, then went to Nanjing, and finally to Shanghai.

通過疑問詞構成 Use Interrogative Pronoun （s）

"疑問詞＋都" 表示強調無一例外：Interrogative Pronoun Plus "Dou"
Emphasizing "No Exception"

功用 Function： Emphasizing "No Exception" 表強調

句型　Sentence Pattern：「疑問詞＋都」——賓語前置

rènhé　shénme
任何：什麼

　　Nǐ juéde nǐ shénme dōu dǒng
　　你 覺得 你 什麼 都 懂。
　　You think you know everything!

rènhé rén shénme rén shuí
任何 人：什麼 人／誰

　　Wǒ shuí shénme rén dōu bú rènshi
　　我 誰（什麼 人）都 不 認識。
　　I don't know anyone.

rènhé shì shénme shì
任何 事：什麼 事

　　Tā yì tiān dào wǎn shénme shì dōu méiyǒu
　　他 一 天 到 晚 什麼 事 都 没有。
　　He has nothing to do all day long.

rènhé dìdiǎn shénme dìfang nǎr
任何 地點：什麼 地方／哪兒

　　Wǒ nǎr dōu xiǎng qù
　　我 哪兒 都 想 去。
　　I want to go everywhere.

rènhé shíjiān shénme shíhou jǐ diǎn nǎ tiān
任何 時間：什麼 時候／幾 點／哪 天

　　Nǐ shénme shíhou lái wǒ dōu huānyíng
　　你 什麼 時候 来 我 都 歡迎。
　　I welcome you anytime.

rènhé zhuàngtài zěnme (yàng)
任何 狀態：怎麼 （樣）

　　zěnme shuō dōu kěyǐ
　　怎麼 説 都 可以。
　　Say (it) however you want.

教學難點

Cruxes of Teaching and Learning

難點一　主語與副詞 Subjects and Adverbs

漢語與英語不同。副詞都應在動詞前，不能放在主語前。

All adverbs are before the verb. They are not to appear before a subject.

In English, we say:

If you cannot go, then I will. （"then" is placed before "I".）

In Chinese, we say:

Yàoshi nǐ bù néng qù wǒ jiù qù

要是　你不能　去，我就去。

If you cannot go, then I will go. （"就" is never to be placed before "我"）

This is the same with words like "都"，"還"，and "也"。

難點二　主語在句中的位置 Position of Subjects in the Sentences

在用複句時，應注意主語的位置。

1）Flexible：Most of the time, the position of the subject is flexible：

（Wǒ）yīnwèi（wǒ）xǐhuan dǎ qiú suǒyǐ cháng dǎ

（我）因爲（我）喜歡　打　球所以　常　打。

Because I like to play a ballgame, therefore I often play.

2）Subject First：

Tā yìbiān kàn shū yìbiān hē kāfēi

他一邊看書，一邊喝咖啡。

He reads a book and drinks coffee at the same time.

Tā yòu chī yòu hē

他又吃又喝。

He not only eats, but also drinks（at the same time.）

3）Depends on number of doer：

4）Singular Subject：

Tā búdàn pǎo de kuài érqiě yóuyǒng yě yóu de hǎo
他 不但 跑 得 快，而且 游泳 也 游 得 好。
Not only does he run fast, but he also swims well.

5）Plural Subject：

Bùjǐn wǒmen yǒu shì érqiě tāmen yě yǒu shì
不僅 我們 有 事，而且 他們 也 有 事。
Not only do we have things to do, but they do, too.

難點三 "除了……以外……" and "疑問詞＋都"

"除了……以外" 與 "疑問詞＋都" 配用表强調。

When "除了……以外……都…… " singles out exceptions, meaning "other than…, " we often use "疑問詞＋都" to emphasize the part of the object/VP that is not the exception.

Chúle zhège yǐwài shénme (biéde) wǒ dōu xǐhuan chī
除了 這個 以外， 什麼 （別的） 我 都 喜歡 吃。
(positive)
Except for this one, I like all other ones.
(meaning：This one is the only one that I don't like)

Chúle Zhōngguócài yǐwài shénme biéde cài wǒ dōu bù xǐhuan
除了 中國菜 以外， 什麼 （別的） 菜 我 都 不 喜歡
chī
吃 。(negative)
I don't like any kind of food except for Chinese.
(meaning：Chinese is the only food that I like.)

難點四 "再" vs. "又"

"再" 和 "又" 都表示重復。但 "再" 計劃期待重復，"又" 表示重復已發生。

"再" and "又" both are adverbs meaning "again or repeat the action".
"再 zài again, once more, time and again or repeatedly" indicates a repetition of

a plan; "又 yòu again or also" is for action that has already occurred.

Wǒ xǐhuan zhège diànyǐng suǒyǐ xiǎng zài kàn yí biàn
我　喜歡　這個　　電影　所以　想　再　看　一　遍 。

I like this movie and want to see it again.

　　（Wanting to see it again but has not yet done so. ）

Wǒ xǐhuan zhège diànyǐng suǒyǐ yòu kànle yí biàn
我　喜歡　這個　　電影　所以　又　看了　一　遍 。

I like this movie, so I saw it once more.

　　（Already repeated the action. ）

難點五　　"不管" 與疑問 Interrogative Form in "不管" Sentences

不論（不管，無論）……都……no matter. . .

"不論（不管，無論）"句用疑問形式。

"不論（不管，無論）" sentences have an interrogative form embedded within them, e. g. :

1) Yes/No question：

Búlùn míngtiān tiānqì hǎo bu hǎo wǒmen dōu qù
不論　明天　天氣　好 不 好 ,我們　都　去。

Regardless of the weather condition（good or bad,）we are going.

2) WH-question：

Búlùn shénme shíhou dōu kěyǐ。
不論　什麼　時候　都 可以

It will be fine no matter when.

3) Choice "還是"

Búlùn shì Zhōngwén háishi Yīngwén tā dōu huì shuō
不論　是　中文　　還是　英文 ,他　都　會　說 。

No matter whether in English or Chinese, he knows how to speak.

難點六　　"正在" vs. "剛"

It should be noted that "正在" can be confused with "剛" because both can be translated as "just as" in English.

1) "正在" emphasizes an "ongoing situation"

Tā lái de shíhou wǒmen zhèngzài chī fàn
他 來 的 時候 ，我們 　正在 　吃 飯。

When he came, we were just (during the process of) having a meal.

2) "剛" emphasizes the immediate situation that has happened before the actual action.

Tā lái de shíhou wǒmen gāng yào chī fàn
他 來 的 時候 ，我們 　剛 要 吃 飯。
When he came, we were just about to have dinner.

Tā lái de shíhou wǒmen gāng (gāng) chīle fàn
他 來 的 時候 ，我們 　剛 （剛） 吃了 飯。
When he came, we just finished eating dinner.

13

叙述與詢問

Telling Stories
—Narration
and Inquiry

從方便叙述的角度講，行爲和事件分兩類。一類是日常的活動和行爲，即反復發生的習慣性行爲；一類是特定的事件與行爲，即一次性的行爲。在叙述和詢問這兩類事件和行爲時，使用的語言句型有所不同。這是本節介紹和討論的重點和難點，并附疑問句表。

本節將兩類行爲放在一起是爲了讓讀者有一個明確的概念和對比。教學時可分開，逐步掌握使用。同時，不要忘記，談事件和行爲總是要和事件行爲發生的時間、地點和方式聯繫起來。

We divide narration of actions into two categories because they require different sentence patterns. The first category of action is defined as general activities. They refer to repeated, habitual, routine, or planned actions. The second category of action is defined as specific events. They refer to one-time behaviors. In this section, we list sentence patterns and illustrate functional usage. There is also a list of questions attached.

This chapter compares the concepts and uses of the above-mentioned categories. Mastery of narration and inquiry of actions can be developed gradually. It must be remembered that an event or an action always happens at a time, at a location and in a given manner or by certain means.

教 學 重 點　Content of Teaching and Learning

日常活動行爲	General Actions
特殊疑問句	WH – Questions
特定事件	Specific Events
"了" Sentences	
詢問特定事件行爲	Inquring of Specifil Events

教 學 難 點　Cruxes of Teaching and Learning

日常與特定	General Actions vs. Specific Events
比較否定詞 "不" 和 "没"	Comparing Negatives："不" vs. "没"
"了" 的各種用法	When/How to Use "了"

教學重點

日常活動行爲　General Actions

定義　Definition of General Actions：

日常的活動和行爲，即反復發生的習慣性行爲。

Everyday activities, habitual actions, repeated occurrences, routine schedule and plans

句型　Sentence Patterns for General Actions

S	T	P	M	VO.
Wǒ 我				chī fàn 吃 飯。
	I eat.			
Wǒ 我	měitiān 每天			chī fàn 吃 飯。
	I eat everyday.			
Wǒ 我		zài jiā 在 家		chī zǎofàn 吃 早飯。
	I eat breakfast at home.			
Wǒ 我			gēn jiārén yìqǐ 跟 家人 一起	chī zǎofàn 吃 早飯。
	I eat with my family.			
Wǒ 我	měitiān 每天	zài jiā gēn jiārén yìqǐ 在 家 跟 家人 一起		chī zǎofàn 吃 早飯。
	I eat everyday at home with my family.			

特殊疑問句　WH-Questions

(subject)	Shuí 誰			chī fàn 吃 飯？

		Nǐ		chī shénme
(object)		你		吃 什麼 ？
		Nǐ		chī shénme fàn
(definition)		你		吃 什麼 飯？
		Nǐ		chī jǐ ge
(quantity)		你		吃 幾 個pizza？
		Nǐ		chī duōshao
		你		吃 多少 pizza？
		Nǐ		chī shénme
(VO)		你		吃 什麼 ？
	Nǐ jǐ diǎn			chī zǎofàn
(time)	你 幾 點			吃 早飯
	Nǐ shénme shíhou			chī wǎnfàn
	你 什麼 時候			吃 晚飯 ？
		Nǐ	zài nǎr	chī fàn
(place)		你	在 哪兒	吃 飯
		Nǐ	cóng nǎr	qù chī fàn
		你	從 哪兒	去 吃 飯
		Nǐ	qù nǎr	chī fàn
		你	去 哪兒	吃 飯
		Nǐ	zěnme	chī
(how)		你	怎麼	吃？
		Nǐ	yòng shénme	chī
		你	用 什麼	吃？
		Nǐ	gēn shuí	chī
		你	跟 誰	吃？

特定事件　Specific Events

定義　Definition of a Specific Event

特定的事件與行爲，即一次性的行爲。

"A Specific Event" refers to one-time behavior that has been completed at the time of narration.

"了"　　Sentences

強調特定的事件與行爲，即一次性的行爲發生或完成，在句尾用"了"。

了 at the end indicates that the whole event has occurred or been completed.

S	T	P	M			VO	了
Wǒ						chī fàn	le
我						吃 飯	了。
Wǒ	jīntiān					chī fàn	le
我	今天					吃 飯	了。
Wǒ		zài jiā				chī fàn	le
我		在 家				吃 飯	了。
Wǒ			gēn péngyou yìqǐ			chī fàn	le
我			跟 朋友 一起			吃 飯	了。
Wǒ	jīntiān	zài jiā gēn	péngyou yìqǐ			chī fàn	le
我	今天	在 家 跟	朋友 一起			吃 飯	了。

當賓語有數量或其他（複雜）定語時，"了"放在動詞後。

Use right after the verb when a quantity or a complicated modification of the object is involved.

Wǒ　jīntiān zài jiā gēn péngyou chīle yí piàn pǐsà
我 （今天 在 家 跟　朋友 ）吃了 一 片 匹薩。
I (today, at home with friends) ate a slice of pizza.

Wǒ　jīntiān zài jiā gēn péngyou chī le māma zuò de pǐsà
我 （今天 在 家 跟　朋友 ）吃了 媽媽 做 的 匹薩。
I (today, at home with friends) ate the pizza my mom made.

Double emphasis 強調：I have already eaten.

Wǒ yǐjing chī le
我 已經 吃 了。

Negative 否定：I have not eaten yet.

méiyǒu
沒有 （when using"沒有"，no need for "了"）
Wǒ méi (yǒu) chī fàn
我 沒 （有）吃 飯。

Wǒ hái méiyǒu chī ne
我　還　沒有　吃　呢。

詢問特定事件行爲　Inquiry of Specific Events

問具體事件的發生 Questions for Specific Events：

Subject	+	(T P M)	+	Verb	+	Object

Nǐ　　　　　　　　　　　　　chī méi chī wǎnfàn
你　　　　　　　　　　　　　吃 沒 吃　晚飯 ？

Nǐ　　　　　　　　　　　　　chīle méiyǒu
你　　　　　　　　　　　　　吃了　沒有 ？

提供有關一次性事件具體發生的條件用"是……的"結構。

To further provide information on time, place, or means that are related to one specific event, use "是……的" structure.

Statement：

Wǒ měitiān dōu bù chī zǎofàn kěshì jīntiān chī zǎofàn le
我　每天　都 不 吃　早飯，可是　今天　吃　早飯　了。

詢問以上動作具體發生的條件：

Inquiry of time/place/manner that is related to the specific actions stated above：

是	+	(T P M)	+	Verb + 的

Time：

Nǐ　　shì　　shénme shíhou　　chī de (fàn)
你　　是　　什麼　時候　　吃 的 （飯）？

Wǒ　　shì　　zǎoshang bā diǎn　　chī de
我　　是　　早上　八　點　　吃 的。

Place：

Nǐ　　shì　　zài nǎr　　chī de
你　　是　　在 哪兒　　吃 的？

Wǒ　　shì　　zài jiā　　chī de
我　　是　　在 家　　吃 的。

How (means or manner)：

Nǐ　　shì　　zěnme　　chī de
你　　是　　怎麼　　吃 的？

Wǒ	shì	gēn péngyou yìqǐ	chī de
我	是	跟　朋友　一起	吃　的。
Wǒ	shì	yòng kuàizi	chī de
我	是	用　筷子（chopsticks）	吃　的。

"是……的" 結構　Function of the "是……的……" Structure

追問有關一次性事件具體發生的條件，包括時間、地點和方式。

When referring to a specific action that has been done and wishing the need to add or further inquire about the conditions（time，place，how）under which the action has occurred，we use the "shi... de..." structure.

That is to say that this structure supplies further information to a "le" sentence，e. g. :

Wǒ chī zǎofàn le　wǒ shì zǎoshang bā diǎn zài xuéxiào gēn
我　吃　早飯　了。我　是　早上　八　點　在　學校　跟
péngyou yìqǐ chī de
朋友　　一起　吃　的。

教學難點

Cruxes of Teaching and Learning

難點一　日常與特定 General Actions vs. Specific Events

對比　Compare

Statement of a General Action	Narration of a Specific Event
我每天都吃早飯。	我今天吃早飯了
I eat breakfast everyday.	I ate breakfast this morning.
我每天八點在家吃早飯。	我是八點在家吃的。
I eat breakfast daily at 8 o'clock.	I ate at home at 8 o'clock.
	（If we talk about the meal this morning.）
他不愛吃早飯。	他今天也沒吃早飯。
He does like to eat breakfast.	He did not eat breakfast today.

(As preference.) (He skipped a meal.)

Comparing a General Situation with a Specific Action

(every breakfast)

Wǒ měitiān dōu chī zǎofàn

我 每天 都 吃 早飯 。

I eat breafast everyday.

Wǒ měitiān zǎoshang bā diǎn zài xuéxiào gēn péngyou chī

我 每天 早上 八 點 在 學校 跟 朋友 吃 。

I eat every morning at 8 o'clock at school with my friends.

(today's breakfast)

Wǒ jīntiān zǎoshang chī zǎofàn le

我 今天 早上 吃 早飯 了。

I had breakfast this morning.

Wǒ shì zǎoshang bā diǎn zài xuéxiào gēn péngyou chī de

我 是 早上 八 點 在 學校 跟 朋友 吃 的。

I ate this morning at 8 o'clock with my friends at school.

難點二 比較否定詞"不"和"没"

Comparing Negatives：不 vs. 没

"不"和"没"都是否定。否定行爲時，"不"否定經常性的行爲和意願，"没"否定所有，也否定一次性的事件的發生。

Both "不" and "没" are both negatives. But："不" is used to deny a general situation or willingness to perform an action. "没" is used to deny possession or the completion of a specific event.

不：

1) Negative used for general situations：

    a：Description/ Adjectives as Predicate

        Tā bù hǎo

        他 不 好 。

    b：Identification/ "是" as Predicate

        Nǐ bú shì lǎoshī

        你 不 是 老師 。

    c：Everyday, habitual, repeated, planned actions/Action Verbs as

Predicates

> Wǒ měitiān dōu bù chī zǎofàn Wǒ bú ài chī zǎofàn yě bù
> 我　每天　都　不　吃　早飯。我　不　愛　吃　早飯，也　不
> xiǎng chī
> 想　吃。

> I never eat breakfast. I don't like to eat breakfast, and I don't want
> to do it.

2) Negative indicating unwillingness：purposefully not do（did not do）

> Zuótiān tā māma gěi tā zuòle zǎofàn kěshì tā bù chī
> 昨天　他　媽媽　給他　做了　早飯，可是　他　不　吃。

> Yesterday, his mom made breakfast for him but he did not eat it
> （decline/refuse）.

没：

1) Negative for possession：（没有）

> Wǒ méiyǒu gēge
> 我　沒有　哥哥。

> I don't have any older brother.

2) Negative for a specific action（one time occurrence）

> Jīntiān wǒ méi zuò gōngkè
> 今天　我　没　做　功課。

> I did not do my homework today.

Examine the following sentences carefully. Note the differences：

1) Jīntiān wǒ méi zuò gōngkè yīnwèi lǎoshī méi liú zuòyè bú yòng
今天　我　没　做　功課，因爲　老師　没　留　作業，不　用
zuò
做。

I did not do my homework today because the teacher did not give any,
and I don't need to do it.

2) Zuótiān tā méi chī zǎofàn yīnwèi nà shíhou tā bú è suǒyǐ bù
昨天　他　没　吃　早飯，因爲（那　時候）他　不　餓，所以　不
xiǎng chī
想　吃。

He did not eat breakfast yesterday, because he wasn't hungry and did
not want to eat.

難點三　"了"的各種用法 When/How to Use "了"

"了" at the end of the sentence

1) "了" at the end of a sentence indicates that occurrence has been completed at one time.

> Wǒ měitiān dōu bù chī zǎofàn　kěshì jīntiān zài xuéxiào chī
> 我　每天　都　不　吃　早飯，可是　今天　在　學校　吃
> zǎofàn　le
> （早飯　）了。

> I don't normally eat breakfast, but I did today at school.

2) "了" at the end of a sentence with time duration indicates that the action is ongoing.

> Wǒ xuéxí Hànyǔ xué le yì nián bàn le　Wǒ xuéle yì nián bàn
> 我　學習　漢語　學了一　年　半　了。/ 我　學了一　年　半
> de Hànyǔ le
> 的　漢語　了。

> I have been learning Chinese for a year and a half (now).

3) "了" at the end of a sentence indicates a change：

Note："了" is always used with the current status of a situation, and not the previous one.

> Tāmen yǐqián hěn bèn　xiànzài dōu cōngming le
> Adjective：他們　以前　很　笨，現在　都　聰明　了。
> They used to be stupid but have become smart now.

> Wǒ bú shì zhōngxuéshēng le　wǒ shì dàxuéshēng le
> "be"：我　不　是　中學生　了，我　是　大學生　了。
> I am not a high school student anymore, I am in college now.

> Bàba māma yǒu sān ge háizi le
> "have"：爸爸　媽媽　有　三　個孩子了。
> Daddy and Mumy have 3 children. (There must be a new addition.)

> Tā shíliù suì le
> Noun：他 十六 歲了。
> He is (turned) 16.

> Zuótiān tā xiǎng qù kěshì jīntiān bù xiǎng qù le
> Plan：昨天　她　想　去，可是　今天　不　想　去了。

She wanted to go yesterday but today she no longer wants to go.

　　　　　　　　Nǐ yǐqián bù xǐhuan hē Kěkǒukělè xiàn zài xǐhuan le
Preference：　你 以前 不 喜歡 喝 可口可樂，現 在 喜歡 了。
　　　　　　　　You did not like Coca-cola before but you like it now.

　　　　　　　　Wǒ yǐqián chángcháng chī pǐsà xiànzài bù cháng chī le
Habit：　　我 以前 常常 吃 匹薩，現在 不 常 吃 了。
　　　　　　　　I used to eat pizza often, but not too often now.

"了" Right after the Verb

Important Notes：

不要把"了"看做是過去時，很多用"了"的情況無法作如此解釋。

It cannot be emphasized enough that "了" is not to be seen as an indicator of past tense. In many cases, "了" simply implies the completion of an action. There are situations when "了" appears directly after a verb：

1)　"了" is used directly after the verb when quantity or complex modification of the object is involved.

　　　　Wǒ jīntiān zài jiā gēn péngyou chīle yí piàn pǐsà
　　　　我 (今天 在 家 跟 朋友)吃了一 片 匹薩。
　　　　I (today at home with my friends) ate a slice of pizza.

　　　　Wǒ jīntiān zài jiā gēn péngyou chīle māma zuò de pǐsà
　　　　我 (今天 在 家 跟 朋友)吃了 媽媽 做 的 匹薩。
　　　　I (today at home with my freinds) ate the pizza my mom made.

2)　"了" is used right after the verb when a series of actions is listd.

　　　　Xīngqītiān wǒ zuòle gōngkè kànle diànyǐng dǎle qiú hái
　　　　星期天 我 做了 功課，看了 電影 ，打了 球，還
　　　　wánle jìsuànjī
　　　　玩了 計算機。

　　　　Last Sunday, I did my homework, watched a movie, played a ball-game, and also played computer games.

3)　"了" is used right after the first verb to emphasize the immediate connection with the second.

　　　　Wǒ xiàle kè jiù huí jiā
　　　　我 下了 課就 回 家。

　　　　(This is a plan. The action has not happened yet.)

　　　　As soon as the class is over, I am going home.

(If the first action is completed, then the second will follow in no time.)

Compare：

Wǒ xiàle kè jiù huí jiā le
我　下了課就回家了。

("了" at the end indicates both actions were done.)

As soon as class was over, I went home.

4）"了" is used right after a verb when a time duration is indicated.

Wǒ xuéxí Hànyǔ xuéle yì nián bàn　　Wǒ xuéle yì nián bàn
我　學習　漢語　學了一　年　半 。/我　學了一　年　半

de Hànyǔ
的　漢語 。

I learned Chinese for a year and half (during a certain period of my life).

"了" Patterns

1）"太 adjective 了!" is used to emphasize an extreme status of a situation, good or bad.

Tài hǎo le
太　好　了!（Great! Wonderful!）

Tài guì le
太　貴　了!（Too expensive!）

2）"快……了" or "（就）要/快……了" is used to predict that something is about to happen soon.

Qìchē kuài lái le
汽車　快　來　了。
The bus is coming!

Kuài yào kāi xué le
快　要　開　學　了。
The school is going to be in session!

14

疑問句

Questions

　　提問是索取信息情報的重要手段，是人際交流的重要方式。學會和掌握提問是國家外語教學標準（ACTFL Foreign Language Learning Standards，http：//www. actfl. org）規定的內容之一，也是 AP 中文考試等測試的重要內容之一。

　　本書各章節均就討論的話題提供有關的疑問句型及使用，而本節就疑問形式作一簡要歸納。

　　Asking questions is an essential way to obtain information. It is an indispensable means for interpersonal communication. According to National Foreign Language Standards（ACTFL Foreign Language Learning Standards，http：//www. actfl. org）, commanding inquiry is highly important as well. It is also included in any proficiency testing such as the AP Chinese Test.

　　Every chapter of this book provides question patterns and uses related to the topic. This chapter puts together a general summary of all discussions on questions.

教 學 重 點　Content of Teaching and Learning

疑問句	Questions
是非/正反疑問句	Yes/No questions
特殊疑問句	Special Questions：WH-Questions
選擇疑問句	Alternative Questions

教 學 難 點　Cruxes of Teaching and Learning

形容詞做謂語:"是"和"好"　　Adjective as Predicate："是" vs. "好"

"or" 在疑問句和陳述句中　　"Or" in Questions vs. "Or" in Statements

"To ask" vs. "問"

"I don't know ..." vs. "我不知道"

複合句　　　　　　　　　　Complex Sentences

詞 彙 表　Glossary

疑問詞表　　　　　　　　　　List of the Interrogatives

教學重點

Content of Teaching and Learning

疑問句　Questions

功能　Functions：Inquiring and Exchanging Information

句型　Structures：最基本的提問方式分三種

There are 3 basic groups of questions.

是非/正反疑問句　Yes/No Questions

Yes/No Questions：There are 2 basic forms of Yes/No Questions.

Ma Question：．……嗎？ Add "ma" at the end of a sentence to form a Yes/No Question.

Nǐ lèi ma
你 累 嗎？

Tā shì nǐ de péngyǒu ma
他 是 你 的 朋友 嗎？

Nǐ yǒu jiějiě ma
你 有 姐姐 嗎？

Nǐ ài wán jìsuànjī ma
你 愛 玩 計算機 嗎？

Use positive or negative form of adjective or verb to form a Yes/No Question.

Positive / Negative：動詞/形容詞＋不/沒動詞/形容詞

| V / Adjective ＋ Negative /Verb/Adjective |

Nǐ máng bù máng
你 忙 不 忙？

Tā qù méi qù
他 去 沒 去？

Nǐ shì bu shì zhōngxuéshēng
你 是 不 是 中學生 ？

Nǐ yǒu méiyǒu gēgē
你 有 沒有 哥哥？

Nǐ xǐhuān bu xǐhuān kàn shū
你 喜歡 不 喜歡 看 書？

Nǐ xiǎng bu xiǎng chī Zhōngguócài
你 想 不 想 吃 中國菜 ？

特殊疑問句　Special Questions：WH-Questions

重點提示：漢語特殊疑問句的特點是提問時詞序不變。

In Chinese, when asking a question, the words order remains the same as in a statement. To form a question, use a "WH-word" to replace the part that is being asked at its original position in the sentence.

WH-words

Who/whom	誰	shuí
Whose	誰的	shuíde
What	什麼	shénme
Which	什麼/哪（個）	shénme/nǎ（ge）
When	什麼時候	shénme shíhou
At what time	幾點	jǐ diǎn
Where	哪（裏）	nǎ（li）
How	怎麼	zěnme
With whom	跟誰（一起）	gēn shuí（yīqǐ）
How much/How many	多少/幾（個）	duōshao/jǐ（ge）
How about it	怎麼樣	zěnmeyàng
Why	爲什麼	wèishénme
How long	多長時間/多久	duōcháng shǐjiān/duō jiǔ

陳述句與疑問句對比：

Subject + Time	+ Place + Manner	+ Verb + Object

Statement 我　　每天　　在學校 跟同學一起　看　　很多書。

Questions

Subject	Time	Place	Manner	Verb	Object
誰				看	書?
那				是	誰的書?
你				看	什麼?
你				看	什麼書?
你				看	哪本書?
你	什麼時候			看	書?
你	幾點			看	書?
你		在哪		看	書?
你			怎麼	看?	
你			跟誰一起	看?	
你				看	多少（本）書?
你				看	幾本書?
你			為什麼	看	這本書?
這本書					怎麼樣?
你				看	書看得怎麼樣?
你				看	書看了多長時間?

選擇疑問句　Alternative Questions

原則上，可用“還是”提供各項選擇。

實際應用時，多與特殊疑問句結合使用。

Grammatically speaking, “還是” may be used to form a question.

Functionally, it is often used in combination with “WH-Questions”.

Subject	Time	Place	Manner	Verb	Object

Subject	Time	Place	Manner	Verb	Object
你還是他				看	書?
那本書				是	你的還是他的?
你				看	中文書還是英文書?
你	上午還是下午			看	書?
你		在家還是在學校		看	書?
你			自己看還是跟我一起看?		

你　　　　　　　　　　　　　看一本還是兩本書？

誰看書，你還是他？

那是誰的書，是你的還是他的？

你看哪本書，這本還是那本？

你幾點看書，八點還是九點？

你在哪兒看書，在家還是在學校？

你跟誰一起看，我還是他？

你看幾本書，一本還是兩本？

難點提示 Attention：

應對學生強調：英語的"or"在漢語中分陳述形式"或者"和疑問形式"還是"，不可混淆。

"Or" in English can be used in either a statement or a question, while in Chinese, "還是" is used only in questions, and "或者" is used only in statements.

Question：　你想看一本還是兩本？

Statement：　我想看一本或（者）兩本。

教學難點
Cruxes of Teaching and Learning

難點一　形容詞做謂語："是"和"好"
Adjective as Predicate："是" vs. "好"

Two key words for differentiation：Identification vs. Description.

Identification：中文的"是"的功用一般只限於認定。

The verb "to be" has limited function in Chinese. It is used only to identify what is what and who is whom.

我是學生，不是老師。

I am a student, I am not a teacher.

這是書，不是雜誌。

This is a book, it is not a magazine.

Description：中文的形容詞具有動詞的功用，可直接用來描述。

Adjectives can be used independently to describe situations and conditions.

我很好。　I am fine.

Therefore, when asking "Yes/No Questions" for description, use adjectives without the verb "to be".

positive adjective + negative adjective

你好不好？　How are you doing?

難點二　"or" 在疑問句和陳述句中
"Or" in Questions vs. "Or" in Statements

英語的 "or" 在漢語中分陳述形式 "或者" 和疑問形式 "還是"，二者不可混淆。

Attention："Or" in English can be used in either a statement or a question, while in Chinese, "還是" is used only in questions, and "或者" is used only in statements.

Question：　你想看一本還是兩本？

Do you want to read one or two books?

Statement：　我想看一本或（者）兩本。

I want to read one or two books.

難點三　"To ask" vs. "問"

英文的 "to ask" 可以提問也可以請人做事。

The English word "to ask" can be used for two major purposes：

To ask a question

To ask someone to do something

中文的"問"只可以提問，請人做事要用兼語句。

In Chinese, these are two different expressions.

English	Chinese
He asked you a question. （A）	他問你一個問題。
He asked me, "what is this?" （B）	他問我"這是什麼?"
He asked me where the bathroom was. （C）	他問我廁所在哪兒?
He asked you to have some tea. （D）	他請（讓，叫）你喝茶。

"問" can be followed by direct or indirect objects as shown in A, B and C.

"問" must be followed by a question word or a question form as in A, B and C.

The sentence used "問" can be a direct quote or an indirect quote as in B and C.

When asking someone to do something, we cannot use "問" as shown in D.

難點四 "I don't know . . ." vs. "我不知道"

"我不知道"後要用疑問形式。

In English "I don't know. . ." is followed by "if . . ." or "whether or not. . ." or some other "wh. . . + statement":

I don't know if he is coming.

I don't know whether or not he has a sister.

I don't know where he lives.

In Chinese, "我不知道" must be followed by a question form:

我不知道他來不來。

我不知道他有沒有姐姐嘛。

我不知道他住在哪兒。

It is easy for students to make the mistakes by saying:

（×）我不知道要是他來。

難點五　複合句 Complex Sentences

不論（不管，無論）……都…… no matter what...

"不論（不管，無論）"包含疑問形式。

"不論（不管，無論）" sentences have a question form embedded within them.

Yes/No question form：

> Búlùn míngtiān tiānqì hǎo bu hǎo wǒmen dōu qù
> 不論　明天　天氣　好不好，我們　都　去。
> We are going tomorrow regardless of the weather.

WH-question form：

> Búlùn shénme shíhou dōu kěyǐ
> 不論　什麼　時候　都　可以。
> Any time is fine.

"還是"（Or/Whether）

> Búlùn shì Zhōngwén háishi Yīngwén tā dōu huì shuō
> 不論　是　中文　還是　英文，他　都　會　說。
> No matter whether in English or Chinese, he speaks well.

15

方位

**Direction and
Position**

　　談方位是人際交流的一個重要話題。這一節爲這個話題的展開提供所需的詞彙和句型，並解釋可能出現的教學難點。因爲這個話題可談國家、地區、社區，甚至學校、家庭、室內外，我們在本節還包括了相關的詞彙表和其他語法，供教學使用。

　　Direction and position is an important communication topic and may include country, region, even community, school and family, inside and outside. This chapter provides the necessary vocabulary and sentence patterns for this topic. It also pinpoints some of the possible difficulties for English-speaking learners.

教 學 重 點　Content of Teaching and Learning

方位詞	Words Indicating Position/Location
方位詞尾	Suffixes Indicating Position/Location
方位詞組	Phrases Indicating Position/Location
有用句型	Sentence Patterns for Describing Position/Location

教 學 難 點　Cruxes of Teaching and Learning

"Northeast" vs. "東北"

複雜名詞組　　　　Complex Noun Phrases

"部""邊""面""方"的用法　Use of "部", "邊", "面" and "方"

文 化 聯 繫　Cultural Relations

說漢語的國家與地區　Chinese-Speaking Countries and Regions

詞 彙 表　Glossary

建築	Structure
居家	Home
學校	School

教學重點

Content of Teaching and Learning

方位詞　Words Indicating Position/Location

方向　fāngxiàng　direction, orientation

東	dōng	east	南	nán	south
西	xī	west	北	běi	north

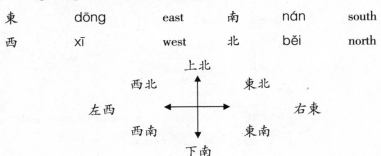

方位詞尾　Suffixes Indicating Position/Location

部	bù	part, section
邊	biān	side, border, edge, fringe
面	miàn	face (toward), surface, a whole area
方	fāng	direction, side, party, place, region

dōngbù	xībù	zhōngbù	zhōngxībù
東部	西部	中部	中西部

dōngfāng	xīfāng	nánfāng	běifāng
東方	西方	南方	北方

dōngbian mian	xībian mian	nánbian mian	běibian mian
東邊　（面）	西邊（面）	南邊　（面）	北邊　（面）

方位詞組　Phrases Indicating Position/Location：

前（邊/面）	qián	in front, front
後（邊/面）	hòu	after, behind
左（邊/面）	zuǒ	left
右（邊/面）	yòu	right
上（邊/面）	shàng	on, on top of ...
下（邊/面）	xià	under, below
裏（邊/面）	lǐ	in, inside
外（邊/面）	wài	outside
對面	duìmiàn	opposite; across from, face to face
旁邊	pángbiān	beside, next to
中間	zhōngjiān	between, in the middle
兩邊	liǎngbiān	both sides
附近	fùjìn	adjacent, in the vicinity
周圍	zhōuwéi	around, surrounding
四周	sìzhōu	all around

A Complex Noun Phrase：

Modifier always goes before the noun.

1) Description of a location using an object as definition：

　　　xuéxiào de yòubian

　　　學校　　的　　右邊

the right side of the school, to the right of the school

2) Description of an object using a position as definition：

　　　yòubian de xuéxiào

　　　右邊　　的　　學校　　the school on the right

有用句型　Sentence Patterns for Describing Position/Location：

以下句型是描述方位地理必不可少的。

Here are three sentence patterns needed to describe position and direction.

陳述　Statements

1）在　Something 在 somewhere

Zhījiāgē zài Měiguó de zhōngxībù
芝加哥 在 美國 的 中西部 。

Chicago is (located) in the midwest (area) of the U. S.

2）是　Somewhere 是 something (specific)

Xuéxiào hé shāngdiàn de zhōngjiān shì Zhījiāgē Túshūguǎn
學校 和 商店 的 中間 是 芝加哥 圖書館 。
In between the school and the store is the Chicago Library.

3）有　Somewhere 有 something

（a non specific place or a list of places/things）

Xuéxiào hé shāngdiàn de zhōngjiān shì yí ge túshūguǎn
學校 和 商店 的 中間 是 一 個 圖書館 。
In between the school and the store, there is a library.

Zhījiāgē túshūguǎn de pángbiān yǒu xuéxiào shāngdiàn hé
芝加哥 圖書館 的 旁邊 有 學校 、 商店 和

yínháng
銀行 。
Next to the Chicago Library, there are schools, stores, and banks.

問句　Questions

1）在　Something 在 somewhere

Zhījiāgē zài nǎr
芝加哥 在 哪兒?
Where Chicago is (located)?

2）是　Somewhere 是 something (specific)

Xuéxiào hé shāngdiàn de zhōngjiān shì shénme
學校 和 商店 的 中間 是 什麼 ?

What is in between the school and the store?

3) 有　Somewhere 有（list of things）

Zhījiāgē Túshūguǎn de pángbiān yǒu shénme
芝加哥　圖書館　的　旁邊　有　什麼？
What（institutions）are there next to the Chicago Library?

教學難點

Crnxes of Teaching and Learning

難點一　"Northeast" vs. "東北"

對比中英的不同說法。

In English, locations and directions start with "North" and "South".

Northeast　　　Northwest　　　Southeast　　　Southwest

In Chinese, locations and directions start with "東" and "西".

東北　　　　東南　　　　西北　　　　西南

難點二　複雜名詞組 Complex Noun Phrases

（Please also see Chapter 18：Noun Phrases）

複雜名詞組 Compound/Complex Noun Phrases 對學生來說比較難。英文的名詞的構成有幾種方式，而漢語的定語要放在名詞前。不然意思就會錯了。請看下列例句對比。

複雜名詞組 Compound/Complex Noun Phrases can be confusing to English speakers.

In English：There are three ways to form a noun phrase：

　　（noun with 's）　　　　　David's left

　　（of）　　　　　　　　the left side of David

　　（that/which clause）　　the side that is on the left of David

In Chinese：There is only one way to form a noun phrase：

the modification/definition goes before the noun：大衛的左邊

If the positions of the modifier and the noun are switched，meaning changes：

A. 大衛的左邊 David's left

（Uses a person to define a location）

B. 左邊的大衛 David who is on the left

（Uses a location to identify a person）

（There must be another person who is on the right.）

Compare：

我們的老師在大衛的左邊。

Our teacher is on David's left side.

大衛的左邊是我們的老師。

The person to David's left is our teacher.

左邊的大衛是我的朋友，右邊的我不認識。

David who is on the left is my friend. I don't know who the one on the right is.

難點三　"部""邊""面""方"的用法
Use of "部"，"邊"，"面" and "方"

"部" indicates part of a whole area

Huáshèngdùn zài Měiguó de dōngbù Jiāzhōu zài xībù
華盛頓　　　在 美國 的 東部，加州 在 西部。
Washington D. C. is located in the East of the U. S.，while California is in the West.

Zhījiāgē shì Měiguó zhōngxībù de yí ge dà chéngshì
芝加哥 是 美國　中西部 的 一 個 大　城市 。
Chicago is a large city in the Midwest of the U. S.

"邊" and "面" are interchangeable

1）Northern dialects usually use "邊"，while Southern dialects often use

"面".

東邊（面）　　西邊（面）　　南邊（面）　　北邊（面）

2) "邊" and "面" may refer to an area within a region or outside the region but usually in the vicinity.

Huáshèngdùn zài Měiguó de dōngbiān Jiāzhōu zài xībiān
華盛頓　　在　美國　的　東邊　，加州　在　西邊。
Washington D. C. is on the east coast of the U. S., and California is on the west coast.

Jiānádà zài Měiguó de běibiān
加拿大　在　美國　的　北邊　。
Canada is located in the north of the U. S..

"方" points out direction. However, its usage is a little tricky

1) "南方" and "北方" are usually related to climatic regions or zones, such as "the South" and "the North" of a country.

Běijīng shì Zhōngguó běifāng de yí ge chéngshì Nánjīng shì
北京　是　中國　　北方　的　一　個　城市　，南京　是

Zhōngguó nánfāng de yí ge chéngshì
中國　　南方　的　一　個　城市　。
Beijing is a city in the north of China, while Nanjing is a city in the south of China.

2) In contrast, "東方" and "西方" almost exclusively refer to the "Eastern Hemisphere" and the "Western Hemisphere" of the globe rather than within a country.

Zhōngguó shì yí ge dōngfāng guójiā Měiguó shì xīfāng guójiā
中國　　是　一　個　東方　國家，美國　是　西方　國家。
China is a country in the East, while the U. S. is a country in the West.

3) In order to refer to the east and west part of the country, we use "東部" and "西部".

Huáshèngdùn zài Měiguó de dōngbù Jiāzhōu zài xībù
華盛頓　　在　美國　的　東部　，加州　在　西部。
Washington D. C. is on the east coast of the U. S., and California is on the west coast.

█ 文化聯繫

說漢語的國家與地區 Chinese-Speaking Countries and Regions

中國（大陸、臺灣、香港、澳門），新加坡，美國的中國城等

█ 詞彙表

建築 jiànzhù construct, build；building, structure, architecture

房子	fángzi		house, building, room（of a house, etc.）
	樓房	lóufáng	multi-storied building
	大樓	dàlóu	multi-storied building
	高樓	gāolóu	tall building
	摩天大樓	mótiān dàlóu	skyscraper
	大廈	dàshà	mansion, large building（often used in names of such buildings）
家	jiā		family, household, home, residence
	院子	yuànzi	courtyard, yard
	花園	huāyuán	flower garden
	菜園	càiyuán	vegetable garden, vegetable plot
	庭院	tíngyuàn	front courtyard of a Chinese-style house
	陽臺	yángtái	balcony, veranda
	平臺	píngtái	platform, terrace

大門	dàmén	front door, front gate, main gate
柵欄	zhàlan	railings, fence

居家　jūjiā　Related Home

房間	fángjiān	room（within a house, etc.）
門	mén	door, gate
窗戶	chuānghu	window
牆	qiáng	wall
牆角	qiángjiǎo	corner of a wall
樓上	lóushàng	upper floor, upstairs
樓下	lóuxià	lower floor, downstairs
樓梯	lóutī	stairs, staircase, ladder
臺階	táijiē	steps, staircase
地下室	dìxiàshì	basement
閣樓	gélóu	attic, garret
走廊	zǒuláng	corridor, porch, passage
門庭	méntíng	entrance and courtyard
門廳	méntīng	vestibule, entrance hall
客廳	kètīng	drawing room, parlor
餐廳	cāntīng	dining room, restaurant
廚房	chúfáng	kitchen
書房	shūfáng	study, studio
臥室	wòshì	bedroom
工作間	gōngzuòjiān	workshop, shop（production division of a factory）
游戲室	yóuxìshì	recreation room, game room
廁所	cèsuǒ	bathroom, lavatory
洗澡間	xǐzǎojiān	bathroom

	壁爐	bìlú	fireplace
家具	jiājù	furniture	
	桌子	zhuōzi	table, desk
	書桌	shūzhuō	desk
	辦公桌	bàngōngzhuō	
			desk (especially in an office)
	飯桌	fànzhuō	dining table
	咖啡桌	kāfēi zhuō	coffee table
	茶几	chájī	tea table
	椅子	yǐzi	chair
	沙發	shāfā	sofa
	床	chuáng	bed
	櫃子	guìzi	cabinet, cupboard
	衣櫃	yīguì	wardrobe, chest of drawers
	櫃櫥	guìchú	cupboard, sideboard
	床頭櫃	chuángtóuguì	bedside cupboard
	書架	shūjià	bookshelf

設施用具　shèshī yòngjù　facilities, installation, utensil, appliance

家用電器　jiāyòng diànqì　Facilities/Household Appliances

	照片	zhàopiàn	photo (graph), picture, print
	畫像	huàxiàng	paint a portrait; portrait
	挂圖	guàtú	wall map, wall chart
	黑板	hēibǎn	blackboard
	鏡子	jìngzi	mirror, eyeglasses, plate glass
	投影機	tóuyǐngjī	projector
	錄放機	lùfàngjī	VCR/DVD
	電腦	diànnǎo	computer
	電視	diànshì	television, TV

燈	dēng	lantern, lamp, light
電燈	diàndēng	electric lamp, electric light
臺燈	táidēng	table lamp, desk lamp
洗衣機	xǐyījī	washing machine
烘乾機	hōnggānjī	drier
洗碗機	xǐwǎnjī	dishwasher
冰箱	bīngxiāng	icebox, refrigerator, freezer
烤箱	kǎoxiāng	oven
微波爐	wēibōlú	microwave oven
空調	kōngtiáo	air conditioning

學校　School

設施	shèshī	facilities
教室	jiàoshì	classroom
辦公室	bàngōngshì	office (the room itself)
校長辦公室		Principal's Office
圖書館	túshūguǎn	library
體育館	tǐyùguǎn	gym
禮堂	lǐtáng	auditorium, assembly hall
實驗室	shíyànshì	laboratory
語言實驗室		language lab
會議室	huìyìshì	conference room, meeting room
停車場	tíngchēchǎng	parking lot, parking area
操場	cāochǎng	drill ground, sports ground
游泳池	yóuyǒngchí	swimming pool
洗手間	xǐshǒujiān	bathroom, washroom
餐廳	cāntīng	dining room
警衛	jǐngwèi	security guard

課程設置與服務　　　Curricula and Academic Services

系	xì	department
年級	niánjí	grade, year (in school)
英文	Yīngwén	English, the English language (especially written)
外文	wàiwén	foreign language (written or spoken)
數學	shùxué	mathematics (as a subject)
社會科學	shèhuì kēxué	social sciences
科學	kēxué	science
體育	tǐyù	physical education, physical culture; sports
音樂藝術	yīnyuè yìshù	music and art
計算機	jìsuànjī	computer, calculating machine
特殊教育	tèshū jiàoyù	special education
咨詢	zīxún	counseling
課外活動	kèwài huódòng	extracurricular activities

16

地點表

List of
Places

地點是事件行爲發生的所在。地點表爲擴展學習提供方便。

本表的排列一是按詞尾拼音的前後順序，二是分類。

Places are locations where actions occur. This list provides the convenience of expanded learning. The arrangement of vocabulary by suffix in alphabetical order and by category.

按詞尾拼音的前後順序　By Suffix in Alphabetical Order

吧	bā	bar
	酒吧	jiǔbā	bar (especially Western-style)
	網吧	wǎngbā	Internet cafe
場	chǎng	open space, field, market
	操場	cāochǎng	drill ground, sport ground
	廣場	guǎngchǎng	(public) square
	機場	jīchǎng	airport
	籃球場	lánqiúchǎng	basketball court
	商場	shāngchǎng	market, marketplace, department store
	市場	shìchǎng	market, marketplace
	停車場	tíngchēchǎng	parking lot, parking area
	體育場	tǐyùchǎng	stadium
	網球場	wǎngqiúchǎng	tennis court
	足球場	zúqiúchǎng	football (soccer) field
店	diàn	shop, store, inn
	飯店	fàndiàn	hotel, restaurant
	商店	shāngdiàn	shop, store
	書店	shūdiàn	bookstore
	小吃店	xiǎochīdiàn	snack shop, snack bar
	專賣店	zhuānmàidiàn	store exclusively for goods of a name

		brand
館	guǎn	mansion, building
博物館	bówùguǎn	museum
茶館	cháguǎn	teahouse
飯館	fànguǎn	restaurant
咖啡館	kāfēiguǎn	coffee shop
理髮館	lǐfàguǎn	barber shop, hairdresser's
美髮館	měifàguǎn	beauty salon
美術館	měishùguǎn	art gallery
體育館	tǐyùguǎn	gym
天文館	tiānwénguǎn	planetarium
圖書館	túshūguǎn	library
局	jú	office, bureau, department, classifier for sports events
警察局	jǐngchájú	police station
郵局	yóujú	post office
所	suǒ	place, location; a suffix indicating an office, institute, etc.
廁所	cèsuǒ	bathroom, lavatory
派出所	pàichūsuǒ	local police station
堂	táng	main room, main hall
教堂	jiàotáng	church, chapel, cathedral, abbey
禮堂	lǐtáng	auditorium, assembly hall
廳	tīng	hall
餐廳	cāntīng	dining room, restaurant
大廳	dàtīng	hall (often used for gatherings)
客廳	kètīng	drawing room, parlor
門廳	méntīng	vestibule, entrance hall
市政廳	shìzhèngtīng	municipal administration hall, city hall

舞廳	wǔtīng	ballroom, dance hall
音樂廳	yīnyuètīng	concert hall, music hall
園	yuán	garden, park, orchard
菜園	càiyuán	vegetable garden, vegetable plot
動物園	dòngwùyuán	zoo
公園	gōngyuán	public park, public garden
花園	huāyuán	flower garden
游樂園	yóulèyuán	amusement park; pleasure ground (or garden)
植物園	zhíwùyuán	botanical garden
院	yuàn	courtyard, yard
電影院	diànyǐngyuàn	movie theater
劇院	jùyuàn	theater
老人院	lǎorényuàn	nursing home for the elderly
學院	xuéyuàn	academy, college, institute, school
醫院	yīyuàn	hospital
院子	yuànzi	courtyard, yard
站	zhàn	stop, station, service center, service station
車站	chēzhàn	station, depot, stop (for bus, train, etc.)
火車站	huǒchēzhàn	train station
加油站	jiāyóuzhàn	gas station, service station
汽車站	qìchēzhàn	(automobile) service station
網站	wǎngzhàn	website

分類地點 By Category

買東西   Shopping

| 商店 | shāngdiàn | shop, store |

商場	shāngchǎng	market, marketplace, department store
超市	chāoshì	supermarket
書店	shūdiàn	bookstore

外出旅游　　Outing/Travel

飯店	fàndiàn	hotel, restaurant
酒店	jiǔdiàn	wineshop
旅館	lǚguǎn	hotel
旅店	lǚdiàn	inn, hotel
飯館	fànguǎn	restaurant
茶館	cháguǎn	teahouse
咖啡館	kāfēiguǎn	coffee shop
餐廳	cāntīng	dining room, restaurant
酒吧	jiǔbā	bar (especially Western-style)
小吃店	xiǎochīdiàn	snack shop, snack bar
車站	chēzhàn	station, depot, stop (for bus, train, etc.)
火車站	huǒchēzhàn	train station
加油站	jiāyóuzhàn	gas station, service station
飛機場	fēijīchǎng	airport, airfield
停車場	tíngchēchǎng	parking lot, parking area

服務　　Service

市政廳	shìzhèngtīng	municipal administration hall, city hall
警察局	jǐngchájú	police station
派出所	pàichūsuǒ	local police station
消防隊	xiāofángduì	fire brigade
圖書館	túshūguǎn	library
天文館	tiānwénguǎn	planetarium

博物館	bówùguǎn	museum
體育館	tǐyùguǎn	gym
公園	gōngyuán	public park, public garden
銀行	yínháng	bank
郵局	yóujú	post office
醫院	yīyuàn	hospital
教堂	jiàotáng	church, chapel, cathedral, abbey

娛樂　yúlè　Recreation, amusement, entertainment

電影院	diànyǐngyuàn	movie theater
劇院	jùyuàn	theater
舞廳	wǔtīng	ballroom, dance hall
游樂場	yóulèchǎng	amusement park, recreation groud

17

怎麼做？

How Is It Done?
—Methods,
Manners,
Means of Action

　　談論事件和行爲往往與行爲發生的方式和途徑分不開。這一節列舉出五類這樣的方式和途徑供教與學使用。

Events and actions are associated with methods, manners and means. This chapter lists five categories of such ways and means of action.

教 學 重 點　Content of Teaching and Learning

行爲方式與工具表　　　List of Methods, Manners and Means

　與人　　　　　　　　With People

　工具　　　　　　　　Tools

　交通工具　　　　　　Means of Transportation

　描述性狀態　　　　　Descriptive Manners

　伴隨狀態　　　　　　Companion Action

教 學 難 點　Cruxes of Teaching and Learning

狀語在句中的位置　　　Positions of Adverbial Phrases in the Sentences

描述性狀態 vs. 伴隨狀態 Descriptive Manners vs. Companion Action

詞 彙 表　Glossary

方式狀語表　　　　　　List of Adverbial Phrases by Category

教學重點

Content of Teaching and Learning

行爲方式與工具表 List of Methods, Manners and Means

與人 With People

跟 gēn／和 hé（一起 yìqǐ）   together with someone

> Wǒ gēn péngyou yìqǐ wán
> 我 跟 朋友 一起 玩。
> I play with my friends.

自己 zìjǐ   oneself; on one's own; alone
一個人 yí ge rén   by oneself; alone

> Wǒ zìjǐ   yí ge rén wán
> 我 自己（一 個 人）玩。
> I play alone.

To people 給 gěi . . .   give; to, toward someone

> Wǒ gěi péngyou dǎ diànhuà
> 我 給 朋友 打 電話。
> I give my friend a phone call.

For people/purpose 爲 wèi . . . for someone

> Wèi biéren zuò shì
> 爲 別人 做 事。
> Do things for others.

Replace, substitute for; in place of 替 tì for someone（replace, substitute）

> Qǐng tì wǒ bǎ zhège gěi tā
> 請 替 我 把 這個 給 他。
> Please give this to him for me.

工具 Tools

> yòng bǐ
Use tools 用 筆   use a pen

　　　　yòng diànnǎo　jìsuànjī
　　　　用　　　電腦　（計算機）　　　use a computer
　　　　yòng Hànyǔ
Use language 用　　漢語　　　　　　use Chinese language
　　　　qǐng yòng Hànyǔ shuō
　　　　請　用　　漢語　　說　。　Please speak in Chinese.

交通工具　Means of Transportation

Take：坐 zuò　　sit, travel by, go by (a vehicle)

　　　Wǒ měitiān zuò chē qù shàng xué
　　　我　每天　坐　車　去　上　學。
　　　I go to school everyday by bus.

On foot：走 zǒu　　walk, travel on foot

　　　Tā zǒu lù lái shàng xué
　　　他　走　路　來　上　學。
　　　He walks to school.

描寫性狀態　Descriptive Manners

"－地"is like "-ly" suffix in English.

　　　Tā gāoxìng de pǎo lái pǎo qù
　　　她　高興　地　跑　來　跑　去。
　　　She runs around happily.

In order

　　　Qǐng nǐ yì bǐ yì bǐ de xiě
　　　請　你 一 筆 一 筆 地 寫。
　　　Please write one stroke after another.

伴隨狀態　Companion Action

Active manners：

　　　Tā xiàozhe shuō
　　　他　笑着　說。
　　　He said with a smile.

教學難點

Cruxes of Teaching and Learning

難點一　狀語在句中的位置
Positions of Adverbial Phrases in the Sentences

英文的狀語的位置靈活，可在動詞前，可在動詞後。漢語在動詞前。

In English, the position of adverbial phrases (phrases of methods, manners, means) in a sentence is flexible. Adverbial phrases may go before or after verbal phrases. In Chinese, there is no such flexibility. All phrases, as listed in this chapter, must go before the verbs. This cannot be emphasized enough.

難點二　描述性狀態 vs. 伴隨狀態
Descriptive Manners vs. Companion Action

請看例句的對比。

This is an area where mistakes often occur in use. A comparative demonstration may explain more clearly for learners.

Comparison One：

V 着 V：companion action to show manner

　　　A. 他笑着說。　　　　　　　　He said with a smile/while smiling.

　　　（Adverb）Adjective ＋ V to show manner

　　　B. 我們高興地說："太好了。" We said "Great!" happily.

As we see, in (A), "with a smile" is a companion action. In (B), "happily" is a description of the action. "With a smile" does not necessarily mean "happily". "Happily" does not necessarily mean with a smile.

Comparison Two：

V 着 V：companion action to show manner

　　　A. 他笑着說。　　　　　　　　He said with a smile.

Use the "一邊……一邊……" pattern to show two actions happening at the same time.

　　　　　B. 他一邊説一邊笑。　　　　　He is talking and laughing.

Comparison Three：Subtleness of Emphasis
　　"V 着" Manner of being　　Function：vivid description of scenes
　　桌子上放着一本書。　　　　　There is a book on the table.
　　"V 了" Completion of an Action
　　我在桌子上放了一本書。　　　I put a book on the table.
　　"V 在" Location of the result of an action
　　書放在桌子上了。　　　　　　The book was put on the table.

詞彙表

方式狀語表　List of Adverbial Phrases by Category

與人　With people

跟 gēn／和 hé …… (一起 yìqǐ)　　　together with somone
　　Wǒ gēn péngyou yìqǐ wán
　　我　跟　朋友　一起　玩 。　I play with my friends.

自己　　zìjǐ　　　　　　　　　oneself; one's own; alone
一個人　yí ge rén　　　　　　by oneself; alone
　　Wǒ zìjǐ　yí ge rén wán
　　我　自己(一　個　人)玩 。　I play alone.

To people
給 gěi …… give; to, toward someone
　　Wǒ gěi péngyou dǎ diànhuà
　　我　給　朋友　打　電話 。　I give my friend a phone call.

For people／purpose
爲 wèi …… for someone

Wèi biérén zuò shì
爲　別人　做　事。　　　　　　Do things for others.

Replace, substitute for; in place of
替 tì for someone（replace, substitute）

Qǐng tì wǒ bǎ zhè ge gěi tā
請　替　我　把　這　個　給　他。　Please give this to him for me.

工具　Tools

用 yòng use, employ, apply

Tools

yòng bǐ
用　筆　　　　　　　　　　　use a pen

yòng diànnǎo jìsuànjī
用　　電腦　（計算機）　use a computer

Language

yòng Hànyǔ
用　　漢語　　　　　　　　use Chinese language

Qǐng yòng Hànyǔ shuō
請　用　漢語　說。Please speak in Chinese.

交通工具　Means of Transportation

Verb

開	kāi	operate/drive（a vehicle）
駕駛	jiàshǐ	operate（a vehicle, plane, boat, etc.）
坐	zuò	sit, travel by, go by（a vehicle）
乘	chéng	ride on/take a vehicle
打	dǎ	take（get, hire）（e. g. a taxi）

Noun

車	chē	vehicle
汽車	qìchē	motor vehicle, automobile, car
小汽車	xiǎoqìchē	small automobile

公共汽車	gōnggòng qìchē	bus
出租車	chūzūchē	taxicab
計程車	jìchéngchē	taxicab
面包車	miànbāochē	minibus, van (so called for its oblong shape)
面的	miàndí	minibus, taxicab
救護車	jiùhùchē	ambulance
救火車	jiùhuǒchē	fire engine
校車	xiàochē	school bus
旅遊車	lǚyóuchē	tourist coach, sightseeing bus
卡車	kǎchē	truck
火車	huǒchē	train
地鐵	dìtiě	subway
飛機	fēijī	airplane
船	chuán	boat, ship, vessel
馬車	mǎchē	horse-drawn carriage, mule (or horse) cart
牛車	niúchē	ox cart

Wǒ měitiān zuò chē qù shàng xué

我 每天 坐 車 去 上 學 。

I go to school everyday by bus.

Wǒ bàba kāi chē qù shàng bān

我 爸爸 開 車 去 上 班 。

My dad drives to work.

騎	qí	ride (astride, like on a bicycle, horse)
馬	mǎ	horse
摩托車	mótuōchē	motorbike, motorcycle
自行車	zìxíngchē	bicycle
脚踏車	jiǎotàchē	bicycle

Wǒ qí chē qù shàng xué

我 騎 車 去 上 學 。

I ride a bike to school.

走　　zǒu　　　　　　　　　　　　walk，travel on foot

　　走路　　zǒu lù　　　　　　　　walk，travel on foot

　　　　Tā zǒu lù lái shàng xué
　　　　他　走　路　來　上　學　。
　　　　He walks to school.

跑　　pǎo　　　　　　　　　　　　run，walk

　　跑步　　pǎobù　　　　　　　　run；jogging（a form of physical exercise）

　　　　Tā pǎo bù lái shàng xué
　　　　她　跑　步　來　上　學　。
　　　　She runs to school.

描述性狀語　Descriptive Manner

1）adjective + "地" Use of "地"："-地" is like "-ly" suffix in English

　　高興地　　gāoxìng de　　　happily

　　着急地　　zháojí de　　　　anxiously，hurriedly

　　緊張地　　jǐnzhāng de　　　nervously

　　興奮地　　xīngfèn de　　　　excitedly

　　努力地　　nǔlì de　　　　　with extra effort；earnestly

　　　　Tā gāoxìng de pǎo lái pǎo qù
　　　　她　高興　地跑　來　跑　去。　She runs around happily.

2）duplicative adjective + "地"

　　好好地　　　　hǎohāo de　　　　　　properly，thoroughly；to one's heart's content

　　快快地　　　　kuàikuài de　　　　　in a big hurry

　　慢慢地　　　　mànmān de　　　　　slowly

　　高高興興地　　gāogāoxìngxìng de　　gladly，with great joy

　　　　Qǐng mànmān de shuō
　　　　請　　慢慢　地　説。　Please speak slowly.

　　Exception：A one-word（mono-syllablic）adjective can modify a verb directly：

　　　　Màn zǒu
　　　　慢　走！Walk slowly！（Watch your steps！）

3）Order：Duplicated Number + Measure Word + 地

一個一個地　one by one

一筆一筆地　one stroke after another

Qǐng nǐ yì bǐ yì bǐ de xiě

請　你一筆一筆地寫。

Please write one stroke after another.

伴隨狀語　Companion Actions：Active Manner

1）Use of "着"：Manner of Action

笑　xiào　smile, laugh

Tā xiàozhe shuō　　Nà tài hǎo le

他　笑着　說："那太好了!"

He smiled while saying, "Great!"

哭　kū　cry, weep

Tā kūzhe shuō　　Wǒ tài nánguò le

他　哭着　說："我太難過了."

He cried while saying, "I'm so sad."

站　zhàn　stand

坐　zuò　sit

Lǎoshī zhànzhe jiǎng kè wǒmen zuòzhe tīng

老師　站着　講課,我們　坐着　聽。

Our teacher is standing while giving instructions, and we are sitting while listening.

Other verbs：commonly used with "着"：唱 chàng sing, 跑 pǎo run, 跳 tiào jump, etl.

2）Other Uses of "V 着"

Used like the "-ly" suffix or "is done" in English

Manner of Being：We may also use this pattern to indicate the manner of being of an object.

On people：

帶　dài　carry, bring, take to

Tā shēnshang dàizhe yìxiē qián

他　身上　帶着　一些　錢。

He is carrying money on his person.

Tā cháng dàizhe péngyou qù nǎr
他　常　帶着　朋友　去　那兒。
He is often found taking his friends there.

拿　ná　hold, grasp, take, capture

Tā shǒuli názhe yì zhī bǐ
他　手裏　拿着　一　支　筆。
He is holding a pen in his hand.

穿　chuān　put on (clothing)

Tā chuānzhe yí jiàn chángxiù de chènshān
他　穿着　一　件　長袖　的　襯衫　。
He is wearing a long sleeve shirt.

戴　dài　wear, put on (like hat, eyeglasses, etc.)

Wǒ dàizhe yí fù mòjìng
我　戴着　一　副　墨鏡　。
I am wearing a pair of sunglasses.

About an object：

放　fàng　release, set free, put

Shūjià shang fàngzhe hěn duō shū
書架　上　放着　很　多　書。
There are some books (put) on the table.

擺　bǎi　arrange with care, placed as decoration

Chájī shàng bǎizhe zhàopiàn
茶幾　上　擺着　照片　。
There are picture photos (put) on the tea stand.

裝　zhuāng　pack, load, assemble, install

Shūbāo li zhuāngzhe hěn duō shū
書包　裏　裝着　很　多　書。
There are many books (packed) in the bag.

掛　guà　hang, suspend

Qiángshang guàzhe liǎng zhāng huà
牆上　挂着　兩　張　畫。
There are two paintings hanging on the wall.

Compare the following two sentences：

"V 着" is a more descriptive way to indicate there is something is some place.

Qiángshang yǒu liǎng zhāng huà

牆上　　　　有　兩　張　畫 。

The wall (on it) has two paintings.

Qiángshang guàzhe liǎng zhāng huà

牆上　　　掛着　兩　張　畫 。

There are two paintings hanging on the wall.

18

名詞組

Noun Phrases

漢語的名詞的構成與英語有不同處。本節就此展開例舉漢語名詞組的構成及其在句中的位置。

The structures of the Chinese noun phrases are different in many ways from English. This chapter is devoted to list Chinese noun phrases, their structures and positions in sentences compared with English.

教學重點 Content of Teaching and Learning

名詞組的構成	Formation of Noun Phrases
"的" 的使用	"的" and Noun Phrases
其他定語	Other Modifiers
複雜定語	Compound Modifiers
複合名詞組在句中	Complex Noun Phrases in the Sentences

教學難點 Cruxes of Teaching and Learning

名詞組	Noun Phrases
形容詞修飾名詞	Adjective as Modification
定語（修飾詞）的順序	Order of Modifiers

教學重點

名詞組的構成　Formation of Noun Phrases

所有的修飾成分都放在被修飾的名詞前。

All definitions go before the noun that is being modified/defined.

"的"的使用　　"的"and Noun Phrases

"的"的作用是連接修飾成分和名詞。

Usually, a Chinese noun phrase is formed with the help "的". "的" connects a definition to a noun.

代詞修飾名詞　Pronoun + Noun

		tā de chē	
(singular pronoun)		他 的 車	his car
		wǒmen de péngyou	
(plural pronoun)		我們 的 朋友	our friend

名詞修飾名詞　Noun + Noun

		xuéxiào de diànnǎo	
(general noun)		學校 的 電腦	the school's computer
		Wáng Míng de diànnǎo	
(proper noun)		王 明 的 電腦	Wang Ming's computer
		Rìběn chē	
(abstract noun)		日本 車	Japanese car

形容詞修飾名詞　Adjective + Noun

(one-word/charcter adjective)

	hǎo shū	
	好 書	a good book

(two-word/charcter adjective)

	hǎokàn de shū	
	好 看 的 書	a very interesting book

（adverb ＋ adjective）

hěn guì de shū
很　貴　的　書　　　　an expensive book

動詞修飾名詞　Verb ＋ Noun

wǒ　mǎi de shū
（verb）　　　　（我）買　的　書　　the book I bought

主謂結構修飾名詞　Subject-predicate ＋ Noun

（subject ＋ verb）＋ Noun

wǒ mǎi de shū
我　買　的　書　the book I bought

（subject ＋ time ＋ verb）＋ Noun

wǒ zuótiān mǎi de shū
我　昨天　買　的　書　the book I bought yesterday

（subject ＋ place ＋ verb）＋ Noun

wǒ zài shū diàn mǎi de shū
我　在　書　店　買　的　書　the book I bought at bookstore

（subject ＋ manner ＋ verb）＋ Noun

wǒ gēn péngyou yìqǐ mǎi de shū
我　跟　朋友　一起　買　的　書
the book I bought with my friend

wǒ zuò chē qù mǎi de shū
我　坐　車　去　買　的　書　the book I bought going by bus

wǒ yòng wǒ zìjǐ de qián mǎi de shū
我　用　我　自己　的　錢　買　的　書
the book I bought with my own money

例外　Exceptions：

三種不用 "的" 的情況 There are 3 exceptions without "的"

1）單數人稱代詞修飾家庭成員時 A singular personal pronoun modifies a family member：

wǒ māma　　　　　nǐ bàba
我　媽媽　my mom　　你　爸爸　your dad

Compare：

wǒ de chē
我　的　車　　　　my car（ "Car" is not a family member. ）

wǒmen de māma
我們　　的　媽媽 our mom（ "Our" is a plural pronoun. ）

2）單音節形容詞修飾名詞

A one-word/character adjective modifies a noun：

　　hǎo shū　　　　　　　　huàirén
　　好　書　a good book　　壞人　a bad person

Compare：

　　hǎokàn de shū
　　好看　的　書　　　　a very interesting book

　　hěn huài de rén
　　很　壞　的　人　　　a very bad person

3）抽象名詞 The definitive noun is an abstract one：

　　Zhōngguórén
　　中國人　　　　Chinese（a person of Chinese origin）

　　Zhījiāgē Dàxué
　　芝加哥　大學
　　（the）University of Chicago（the one particular school）

Compare

　　Zhōngguó de chéngshì
　　中國　　　的　城市　a city in China

　　Zhījiāgē de dàxué
　　芝加哥　的　大學
　　a university in Chicago（one of the universities in Chicago）

其他定語　Other Modifiers

　　數量＋量詞　　Number ＋ Measure Word

　　　　yí ge péngyou
　　　　一　個　朋友　　　　　　　a friend

　　　　liǎng ge xuésheng
　　　　兩　個　學生　　　　　　　two students

　　"這"與"那"＋量詞　　"This/That" ＋ Measure Word

　　　　zhège péngyou
　　　　這個　朋友　　　　　　　this friend

　　　　nàge xuésheng
　　　　那個　學生　　　　　　　that student

複雜定語　Compound Modifiers

wǒ de nàge péngyou
我 的 那個　朋友

　　　　　　　　　　　　　　that friend of mine

wǒ de nà sān ge péngyou
我 的 那 三 個　朋友

　　　　　　　　　　　　　　those three friends of mine

wǒ de nàge Zhōngguó péngyou
我 的 那個　　中國　　　朋友

　　　　　　　　　　　　　　that Chinese friend of mine

wǒ de nà sān ge Zhōngguó péngyou
我 的 那 三 個　　中國　　　朋友

　　　　　　　　　　　　　　those three Chinese friends of mine

複合名詞組在句中　Complex Noun Phrases in the Sentences

Verbal Phrase (Subject (Time, Place, Manner) Verb) as Compound Noun Phrase:

Wǒ mǎi shū
我 買 書。　　S V O

　　Wǒ mǎi de shū hěn guì
　　我 買 的 書 很 貴。
　　The book I bought is very expensive.

　　Nà běn shū shì wǒ mǎi de
　　那 本 書 是 我 買 的。
　　That book is the one I bought.

Tā měitiān kàn shū
他 每天 看 書。　　S (T) VO

　　Tā měitiān kàn de shū dōu shì Yīngwén shū
　　他 每 天 看 的 書 都 是 英文 書。
　　The books that he reads everyday are all English books.

　　Zhè běn shū shì tā měitiān dōu yào kàn de
　　這 本 書 是 他 每天 都 要 看 的。
　　This book is the one he has been reading everyday.

Nǐ zài Zhōngguó mǎi shū
你 在 中國 買 書。　　S (P) VO

Nǐ zài Zhōngguó mǎi de shū shì Zhōngwén de
你 在 中國 買 的 書 是 中文 的。
The book that you bought in China is Chinese.

Nǐ jiějie kàn de shū shì bu shì nǐ zài Zhōngguó mǎi de
你 姐姐 看 的 書 是 不 是 你 在 中國 買 的？
Is the book that your sister is reading the one you bought in China?

Tāmen yòng jìsuànjī xiě wénzhāng
他們 用 計算機 寫 文章 。　　S (M) VO

Tāmen yòng jìsuànjī xiě de wénzhāng zhēn cháng
他們 用 計算機 寫 的 文章 真 長 。
The article they are writing on the computer is really long.

Bào shang de wénzhāng shì tāmen yòng xuéxiào de jìsuànjī
報 上 的 文章 是 他們 用 學校 的 計算機
xiě de ma
寫 的 嗎？
Is the article in the paper the one they wrote on the school computer?

Dàmíng zuótiān zài jiā gēn péngyou wánr jìsuànjī le
大明 昨天 在 家 跟 朋友 玩兒 計算機 了。

S (T, P, M) VO

Dàmíng zuótiān zài jiā wánr de jìsuànjī bú shì xīn de
大明 昨天 在 家 玩兒 的 計算機 不 是 新 的。
The computer Daming played at home yesterday is not new.

Zhège jìsuànjī jiù shì zuótiān Dàmíng zài jiā gēn péngyou wánr
這個 計算機 就 是 昨天 大明 在 家 跟 朋友 玩兒
de nàge
的 那個。
This is the computer that Daming played yesterday at home with his
friends.

Complex Noun Phrase as Subject：

Zuótiān lái wǒmen xuéxiào de rén shì cóng Zhōngguó lái de
昨天 來 我們 學校 的 人 是 從 中國 來 的。
The person who visited our school yesterday came from China.

Tā bú huì xiě de zì tài duō le
他 不 會 寫 的 字 太 多 了。
The wordx he can't write are too many.

Comples Noun Phrase as Object：

Nǐ rènshi nàge chuān hóng shàngyī de rén ma

你 認識 那個 穿 紅 上衣 的 人 嗎？

Do you know that person wearing a red jacket?

Tā xǐhuan wǒ zuótiān zài shāngdiàn mǎi de zázhì

他 喜歡 我 昨天 在 商店 買 的 雜誌。

He likes the magazine I bought at the store yesterday.

教學難點

Cruxes of Teaching and Learning

難點一　名詞組 Noun Phrases

英文名詞與中文名詞的構成不同，對初學者是難點。特別是複合詞，尤其需要不斷地練習和強調。

Noun phrases are difficult for English speakers who are beginning learners.

In Chinese, all noun modifiers, no matter how long or how complex, go before the noun.

In English, the noun is often said before the modifier. Therefore translating or using a noun phrase correctly in Chinese often requires some thinking for English speakers.

與英文對比 Compare with English：

In English, there are 3 ways of forming a noun phrase：

1）with "'s"（possession）：my car, my mom's car

2）with "of"：that car of mine

3）with a "that/which, who, etc." clause：

　　the car that I bought yesterday

In Chinese, there is only one way：

All modifications go before the noun to be defined.

English：　　　　　　　　　　　　　　Chinese：

1）with "'s"（possession）：

my car：	我的車

2）with "of"：

that car of mine：	我的車

3）with a "that/which, who, etc." clause：

the car that I bought yesterday：	我昨天買的車

難點二　形容詞修飾名詞 Adjective as Modification

并非所有的單音節形容詞都能直接修飾名詞，"多""少""貴"就是這樣的例外。

In theory, when a one-word/character adjective modifies a noun, "的" can be omitted. But it is not always so. Some one-word adjectives cannot be used alone without an adverb when modifying a noun, and therefore require "的", for example：

	wrong	**correct**
多	多書	很多的書；特別多的書
少	少書	很少的書；非常少的書
貴	貴書	很貴的書；非常貴的書

難點三　定語（修飾詞）的順序 Order of Modifiers

When using multiple modifiers, the order of the modification is decided by their closeness to the nature of the object.

The closer to the nature of the noun, the closer the modifier is placed to the noun. See below and compare with the English translations：

wǒ de péngyou	
我　的　朋友	friend of mine/my friend
nàge péngyou	
那個　朋友	that friend
sān ge péngyou	
三　個　朋友	three friends

Zhōngguó péngyou

中國　　　　朋友　　　　　　a Chinese friend

but, when combined:

wǒ de nàge péngyou

我 的 那個　朋友　　　　　that friend of mine

wǒ de nà sān ge péngyou

我 的 那 三 個　朋友　　　those three friends of mine

wǒ de nàge Zhōngguó péngyou

我 的 那個　　中國　　　朋友 that Chinese friend of mine

wǒ de nà sān ge Zhōngguó péngyou

我 的 那 三 個　中國　　朋友
those three Chinese friends of mine

19

度量衡

Measurements

長度　chángdù　　Length

（Decimal System）

公里	gōnglǐ	kilometer
米	mǐ	meter（linear measurement）
厘米	límǐ	centimeter
毫米	háomǐ	millimeter

（English System）

英里	yīnglǐ	mile
英尺	yīngchǐ	foot（twelve inches）
英寸	yīngcùn	inch

重量　zhòngliàng　Weight

（Decimal System）

公斤	gōngjīn	kilogram
克	kè	gram

（English System）

磅	bàng	pound（unit of weight）
盎司	àngsī	ounce

面積　miànjī　　Area, surface area

（Decimal System）

平方（米）	píngfāng（mǐ）	square（meter）

（English System）

平方（英尺）	píngfāng（yīngchǐ）	square（foot）

容積　róngjī　　Volume, bulk, content

（Decimal System）

升	shēng	liter

（English System）

加侖	jiālún	gallon

錢	qián	Cash，money
人民幣	rénmínbì	Renminbi（unit of currency in the PRC）
美元	měiyuán	United States dollar, American dollar
元	yuán	*yuan*（unit of Chinese currency）
（塊）	kuài	colloquial expression：same as "*yuan*"（unit of Chinese currency）
角	jiǎo	unit of Chinese currency, one-tenth of a *yuan*
（毛）	máo	colloquial expression：same as "*jiao*", one-tenth of a *yuan*）
分	fēn	unit of Chinese currency, one-tenth of a *jiao*

句型 jùxíng Sentence Patterns

……等於……

……一共是……

等於	děngyú	be equal to，be equivalent to，be tantamount to……
一共	yígòng	altogether

20

比較

Comparison

比較是高級思考的一個方面。可以比人、比東西、比行為事件。比較可以與其他話題交叉教學。本節按照語法的特點把比較分為五種。

Comparison is a higher level of thinking. In daily life, we can compare people, objects and behavior/activity. Comparison can be used with other topics in teaching and learning, such as number, object, activity, weather, etc. This chapter can be placed into five categories according to grammatical characteristics.

教 學 重 點　Content of Teaching and Learning

三級比較	Three-levels of Comparison
比較不同	Comparing Difference
比較相同	Comparing Similarity
比較所有	Comparing Possession
比較喜好	Comparing Preferences

教 學 難 點　Cruxes of Teaching and Learning

"很"和"much"在比較句中	"很" vs. "Much" in Comparison
比較句中數量的位置	Position of Quantity in Comparative Sentences
中英文比較所有的不同	"有" vs. "to Have" in Comparison
喜好的比較	Preferences in Comparison
比較句的否定式	Negatives in Comparison
"比" vs. "跟"	

教學重點

Content of Teaching and Learning

三級比較　Three-levels of Comparison

功用 Function：用形容詞把比較分成比較級、更高級和最高級。

句型　　Structures：

Level I：　　Use an adjective itself to establish the difference

Level II：　　Use "更/還" before an adjective

Level III：　　Use "最" before an adjective

比人　Comparing People

| Wǒ | | gāo |
| 我 | | 高 。|

I am tall.

| Tā | gèng hái | gāo |
| 他 | 更 （還） | 高 。|

He is (even) taller.

| Nǐ | zuì | gāo |
| 你 | 最 | 高 。|

You are the tallest.

比東西　Comparing Objects

Zhège diànnǎo hǎoyòng
這個　電腦　好用　。
This computer is easy to use.

| Wǒ de | gèng | hǎoyòng |
| 我 的 | 更 | 好用 。|

Mine is easier to use.

| Nǐ de | zuì | hǎoyòng |
| 你 的 | 最 | 好用 。|

Yours is the easiest to use.

比行為　Comparing Actions

Wǒ yóuyǒng yóu de　　　　　　　　kuài
我　游泳　游　得　　　　　　　　快 。
I swim fast.

Nǐ yóuyǒng yóu de　　　gèng　　　kuài
你　游泳　游　得　　　更　　　　快 。
You swim faster.

Tā yóuyǒng yóu de　　　zuì　　　kuài
她　游泳　游　得　　　最　　　　快 。
She swims the fastest.

比較不同　Comparing Difference

功用 Function：找出人、物、行為的不同

句型　Structure：

A 比 B	Adjective	(Quantity)

比人　Comparing People

I, compared to you, am　　taller　　　by this much.

Wǒ bǐ nǐ　　　　　gāo
我　比　你　　　　高 。

Wǒ bǐ nǐ　　　　　gāo　　　yì diǎn
我　比　你　　　　高　　　一　點 。

Wǒ bǐ nǐ　　　　　gāo　　　hěn duō
我　比　你　　　　高　　　很　多 。

Wǒ bǐ nǐ　　　　　gāo　　　de duō de duō
我　比　你　　　　高　　　得　多（得　多）。

比東西　Comparing Objects

This/My computer, compared to that one, is easier to use by this much.

Zhège diànnǎo bǐ nàge　hǎoyòng
這個　電腦　比　那個　好用 。

Wǒ de　　　　bǐ nàge　gèng hǎoyòng
我　的　　　　比　那個　更　好用 。

Wǒ de	bǐ nàge	hǎoyòng	yì diǎn
我 的	比 那個	好用	一 點 。
Wǒ de	bǐ nàge	hǎoyòng	hěn duō de duō
我 的	比 那個	好用	很 多（得 多）。

比行爲　Comparing Actions

I swim, compared to you,		faster	by this much.
Wǒ yóuyǒng	bǐ nǐ yóuyǒng	yóu de kuài	
我 游泳	比 你 游泳	游 得 快 。	
Wǒ	bǐ nǐ yóuyǒng	yóu de kuài	
我	比 你 游泳	游 得 快 。	
Wǒ yóuyǒng	bǐ nǐ	yóu de kuài	
我 游泳	比 你	游 得 快 。	
Wǒ yóuyǒng	bǐ nǐ	yóu de kuài	yìdiǎn
我 游泳	比 你	游 得 快	一點 。
Wǒ yóuyǒng	bǐ nǐ	yóu de kuài	de duō
我 游泳	比 你	游 得 快	得 多 。

否定　Negatives

没有：（True negative）

Wǒ méiyǒu nǐ dà Wǒ bǐ nǐ xiǎo
我 没有 你大，我 比 你 小 。
I am not as old as you are. I am younger than you.

Wǒ de diànnǎo méiyǒu nǐ de hǎoyòng
我 的 電腦 没有 你 的 好用 。
My computer is not as useful as yours/ Yours is better than mine.

Wǒ méiyǒu nǐ yóuyǒng yóu de kuài
我 没有 你 游泳 游 得 快 。
I don't swim as fast as you do/You swim faster than I do.

不比：（not necessarily negative, could mean the same）

Wǒ shíliù suì nǐ yě shíliù suì nǐ bù bǐ wǒ dà
我 十六 歲，你 也 十六 歲，你 不 比 我 大。
I am 16, you are also 16. You are not older than I.

Wǒ de diànnǎo bù bǐ nǐ de hǎoyòng
我 的 電腦 不 比 你 的 好用 。
My computer is no better than yours.

Wǒ bù bǐ nǐ yóuyǒng yóu de kuài
我 不 比 你 游泳 游 得 快 。
I don't swim faster than you do.

問句　Questions

Yes/No Question：e. g.

Nǐ bǐ tā yóu de kuài ma
你 比 他 游 得 快 嗎？
Do you swim faster than he does?

WH-Question：e. g.

Shuí bǐ nǐ yóu de kuài
誰 比 你 游 得 快 ？
Who swims faster than you do?

Choices：e. g.

Nǐ bǐ tā yóu de kuài háishi màn
你 比 他 游 得 快 還是 慢 ？
Do you swim faster or slower than he does?

比較相同　Comparing Similarity

功用 Function：認同相似處。

句型　Structure：

A 跟 B　　+　　一樣　+　　Adjective (specify similarity).

比人　Comparing People

Wǒ gēn nǐ　　　yíyàng
Positive 我 跟 你 　　一樣 。
I am the same as you are.

Wǒ gēn nǐ　　　yíyàng　　　dà
我 跟 你 　　一樣 　　大 。
I am as old as you are.

Wǒ gēn nǐ　　　bù yíyàng　　　dà
Negative：我 跟 你 　　不 一樣 　（大）。
I am no of the same (age) as you are.

Wǒ bù gēn nǐ　　yíyàng
我 不 跟 你 　一樣 。
I am not the same as you are.

比東西　Comparing Objects

Positive	Nàge diànyǐng gēn zhège 那個　電影　跟　這個　　　　　一樣　。 That movie is the same as this one.	yíyàng
Negative	Nàge diànyǐng gēn zhège 那個　電影　跟　這個　　　　　不　一樣　。 That movie is not the same as this one.	bù yíyàng

Positive

Nàge diànyǐng gēn zhège　　　　yíyàng　yǒu yìsi
那個　電影　跟　這個　　　　一樣　有 意思。
That movie is as interesting as this one.

Negative

Nàge diànyǐng bù gēn zhège　　　yíyàng　yǒu yìsi
那個　電影　不　跟　這個　　　一樣　有 意思。
That movie is not as interesting as this one.

比行為　Comparing Actions

Positive

Wǒ pǎobù pǎo de gēn nǐ　　　　　yíyàng　kuài
我　跑步　跑　得　跟　你　　　　一樣　快　。

Wǒ pǎobù gēn nǐ pǎobù pǎo de　　yíyàng　kuài
我（跑步）跟　你（跑步）跑　得　一樣　快　。
I run as fast as you do.

Negative

Wǒ pǎobù bù gēn nǐ pǎo de　　　yíyàng　kuài
我　跑步　不　跟　你　跑　得　　一樣　快　。

Wǒ pǎobù gēn nǐ pǎo de　　　bù yíyàng　kuài
我　跑步　跟　你　跑　得　　不　一樣　快　。
I don't run as fast as you do.

問句　Questions

Yes/No Question：.

Nǐ gēn tā yíyàng dà ma
你　跟　他　一樣　大　嗎？
Are you and he the same age?

Zhège gēn nàge yíyàng ma
這個　跟　那個　一樣　嗎？
Are this one and that one the same？

Nǐ gēn tā yóu de yíyàng kuài ma
你　跟　他　游　得　一樣　快　嗎？
Do you swim as fast as he does？

WH-Question：

Nǎge gēn zhège yíyàng dà
哪個　跟　這個　一樣　大？
Which one is as big as this one?

Shénme gēn zhège yíyàng
什麼　　跟　這個　一樣？
What is the same as this?

Shuí gēn nǐ yóu de yíyàng kuài
誰　跟　你　游　得　一樣　快？
Who swims as fast as you do？

Choices：

Nǐ gēn wǒ yíyàng dà háishi gēn tā yíyàng dà
你　跟　我　一樣　大　還是　跟　他　一樣　大？
Are you the same age as I am or as he is?

Zhège gēn nàge yíyàng dà háishi yíyàng guì
這個　跟　那個　一樣　大　還是　一樣　貴？
Is this one as big or as expensive as that one?

Nǐ gēn tā yóu de yíyàng kuài háishi pǎo de yíyàng kuài
你　跟　他　游　得　一樣　快　還是　跑　得　一樣　快？
Do you swim as fast or run as fast as he does?

（which one？）

比較所有　Comparing Possession

　　與英文不同，中文不能用動詞"有"比較所有，只能比較所有的數量。

In English, we say, "I have more sisters than you do." In Chinese, never use the verb "有" when comparing the number of things two parties have. Compare the number/of objects only.

比不同　Comparing Difference

Structure：A's possession　　比　　B's possession　多/少　quantity.

I have (two) more sisters than you do.

	Wǒ de mèimei	bǐ nǐ(de mèimei)	duō
Positive	我　的　妹妹	比你（的　妹妹）	多。
	Wǒ	bǐ nǐ de mèimei	duō
	我	比你的　妹妹	多。

```
Wǒ de mèimei   bǐ nǐ(de)           duō   liǎng ge
我 的 妹妹   比 你(的)           多   兩 個 。
```

比相同　Comparing Similarity

Structure：　A's possession　跟/和　B's possession　一樣多/少.

I have (don't) the same number of sisters as you do.

```
              Wǒ de mèimei gēn nǐ  de mèimei   yíyàng duō
Positive      我 的 妹妹 跟 你( 的 妹妹 )   一 樣 多 。
              Wǒ de mèimei gēn nǐ           bù yíyàng duō
Negative      我 的 妹妹 跟 你           不 一 樣 多 。
```

問句　Questions

Do you have more (fewer) sisters than he does?

```
Nǐ de mèimei bǐ tā de duō  shǎo  ma
你 的 妹妹 比 他 的 多 ( 少 ) 嗎 ?
```

Do you have the same number of sisters as he does?

```
Nǐ de mèimei gēn tā de yíyàng duō(shǎo)ma
你 的 妹妹 跟 他 的 一 樣 多 ( 少 ) 嗎 ?
```

Who has more (fewer) sisters?

```
Shuí de mèimei duō(shǎo)
誰 的 妹妹 多 ( 少 )?
```

比較喜好　Comparing Preferences

喜歡/愛是一個特別的動詞，比較喜好的用法與其他動詞不同。

In Chinese，喜歡/愛 "like" is a special verb. It is not an action but indicates a preference.

比不同　Comparing Difference

```
          Wǒ bǐ tā                xǐhuan chàng gē
Positive  我 比 他                喜 歡 唱 歌 。
          I like singing more than he does.

          Nǐ bǐ wǒ gèng hái        xǐhuan chàng gē
          你 比 我 更 ( 還 )        喜 歡 唱 歌 。
          You like singing more than I do.
```

Negative
Wǒ méiyǒu tā nàme   xǐhuan chàng gē
我 沒有 他（那麼）   喜歡 唱 歌。
I don't like singing as much as he does.

Wǒ bù bǐ tā   xǐhuan chàng gē
我 不比他   喜歡 唱 歌。
I don't like singing as much as he does.

比相同　Comparing Similarity

Positive
Wǒ gēn nǐ yíyàng   xǐhuan   chàng gē
我 跟 你 一樣   喜歡   唱 歌。
I like singing as much as you do.

Negative
Wǒ gēn tā yíyàng   bù xǐhuan   chàng gē
我 跟 他 一樣   不 喜歡   唱 歌。
I dislike singing as much as he does.

問句　Questions

Nǐ bǐ tā xǐhuan chàng gē ma
你 比他 喜歡 唱 歌 嗎？
Do you like singing more than he does?

Nǐ yǒu tā（nàme）xǐhuan chàng gē ma
你 有 他（那麼）喜歡 唱 歌 嗎？
Do you like singing as much as he does?

Nǐ gēn tā yíyàng（nàme）xǐhuan chàng gē ma
你 跟 他 一樣（那麼）喜歡 唱 歌 嗎？
Do you like singing as much as he does?

教學難點

Cruxes of Teaching and Learning

難點一　"很"和 "Much" 在比較句中
"很" vs. "Much" in Comparison

"很" 跟英語的 "much"，"a lot" 用法不同。在比較句中，"很" 只能跟 "多" 在一起作爲比較的數量補語，不能在形容詞前修飾形容詞。

In English, "much/a lot" appears before an adjective to show a difference:

I am much (a lot) taller than you are.

In Chinese, "很" is part of the quantity. It must appear after adjective.

我比你高很多。This cannot be emphasized enough.

wrong	correct
我比你很高。	我比你高很多。

難點二　比較句中數量的位置
Position of Quantity in Comparative Sentences

在比較句中，形容詞指示差別，數量補語得放在形容詞的後邊用來指明差別的多少。

In English, a difference of quantity goes before the adjective:

I am a little bit (two inches) taller than you are.

In Chinese, a difference of quantity must appear after the adjective that it refers to.

我比你高一點（兩寸）。

難點三　中英文比較所有的不同
"有" vs. "to Have" in Comparison

與英文不同，中文不能用動詞"有"比較所有。要比只能比要比的人與物，只能比所有的數量。

In English, when comparing possession, we use the verb "to have":

I have more sisters than you do.

In Chinese, never use the verb "有" to compare the number of objects being possessed.

我的書比你（的）多三本。

難點四　喜好的比較 Preferences in Comparison

喜歡/愛是一個特別的動詞，比較喜好的用法與其他動詞不同。

In Chinese, the verb "喜歡/愛" "to like" is a special word. It is different from other action verbs.

難點五　比較句的否定式 Negatives in Comparison

Negative：

沒有：（true negative）

　　我沒有你大，我比你小。

　　I am not as old as you are, I am younger.

不比：（not necessarily negative. It could mean "the same".）

　　我不比你大。

　　I am not as old as you are. （I may be younger or the same age.）

　　我十六歲，你也十六歲，你不比我大。

　　I am16, you are also 16, you are not older than Iam. （We are the same age.）

難點六　"比" vs. "跟"

"比" 用來表示不同，"跟" 表示相同。

"比" is used to compare differences. "跟/和/與/同" are used to identify similarties.

21

指路

Asking and
Giving Directions

　　問路和指路在我們的日常生活中經常發生，本章介紹了結果補語、可能補語、相關句型、有用詞彙及可能的指示順序。最後附有有關交通詞彙表。

Asking and giving directions are done daily. This chapter supports that topic with introductions to resultant complements and potential complements, related sentence patterns, useful vocabularies, and a recommended sequence of coherent direction giving. Vocabulary lists of road signs and expressions related to traffic are also provided.

教 學 重 點　Content of Teaching and Learning

認識路標	Identifying Landmarks
結果補語	Resultant Complement
計劃路綫和預測時間	Plan the Route and Predict the Time
可能補語	Potential Complement
指方向	Giving Directions
往……	Toward . . .
指路——有用的句型	Giving Directions—Useful Sentence Patterns

教 學 難 點　Cruxes of Teaching and Learning

結果補語	Resultant Complement
"在"作爲結果	"在" as A Result
可能補語 vs. 結果補語	Potential Complements vs. Resultant Complement
"能"與"可能"	Potentials and Abilities
可能補語 vs. 程度補語	Potential Complement vs. Complement of Degree

詞 彙 表　Glossary

常用結果補語	Frequently Used Resultant Complements
常用可能補語	Frequently Used Potential Complements

| 路標 | Road Signs |
| 交通用語 | Related Traffic Expressions |

補充語法點 Supplementary Notes

| 趨向補語 | Directional Complement |

教學重點

Content of Teaching and Learning

指路最常用到的句型有以下的 3 個：

1）認證路標要用結果補語。

2）計劃、預測路綫和時間要用可能補語。

3）指方向要用"往……"等。

Asking and Giving Directions is an essential life task. The most useful patterns to carry out this task are：

1）Identify landmarks by using "看見（when you see ...）" and "走到 when you walk to...";

2）Identify possibilities in time, accessibility, etc. by using "到得了/到不了";

3）Identify direction by using "往 go toward ..." or "turn to this or that way".

認識路標　Identifying Landmarks

In order to identify landmarks, we use a pattern like：

Kànjian lùkǒu de shāngdiàn yǐhòu wǎng yòu guǎi
看見　路口的　商店　以後　往　右　拐 。
When you see the store at the corner, turn right.

Zǒudào dì èr ge hónglǜdēng wǎng dōng kāi
走到　第二個　紅綠燈　往　東　開 。
Drive up to the second traffic lights and turn towards the east.

The patterns used here are called "結果補語 Resultant Complement".

結果補語　Resultant Complement

1）功用　Function：

英文的動詞自身指企圖的有些包括結果，例如："I looked and I saw."（我看了，并看見了。）可以說 "looked" 是努力，"saw" 是結果。中文的"看"差不多包括眼的所有功能，相當於英文的 "look/see/watch/observe/

read" 至更多，可并不暗示動作的程度或結果。需要其他的成分，比如補語，補充需要説明的情況。結果補語是用動詞或形容詞來説明動作達到或取得什麼成果。

In English, when we say "I looked and I saw", we mean that we took the action of "look" and we received the sight with our eyes: "looked" implies the effort while "saw" implies the result.

In Chinese, "看" is to look/see/watch/observe/read, covering almost everything you do with your eyes. But the verb itself gives no implication as to how far the action is carried and what result is achieved. We need another verb or an adjective to be attached directly to the verb to indicate the result.

2）句型　Sentence Pattern：

Wǒ　　　kàn
我　　　　看 。(Action)
I look/see/watch/read.

But to show result of an action, we use：

Subject	Verb + Verb/Adjective

動詞做結果：A verb indicates the result of the action：

Wǒ　　　　　kàndǒng　　le
我　　　　　　看懂　　　了。
I comprehended (through observing).

形容詞做結果：An adjective indicates the result of the action：

Wǒ　　　　　kàncuò　　le
我　　　　　　看錯　　　了。
I saw it wrong.

3）否定　Negative："没" denies the result not the action.

（我看了，可是……）

Wǒ　méi　　　kàndǒng
我　没　　　　看懂　。
I did not understand (through observing.)

Wǒ　méi　　　kàncuò
我　没　　　　看錯　。
I did not see it wrong.

4）賓語在句中的位置　Position of object in sentence：

結果必須緊挨着動作。賓語次之，除非將賓語前置。

The result must follow the action immediately. The object of the sentence usually has to go after the action and result. Unless the object is put before the verb for emphasize：

Wǒ kànjiàn tā le
我　看見　他了。
I saw him.

Wǒ hái méi kànwán nà běn shū
我 還 沒　看完　那 本 書。
I have not yet finished reading that book.

5）帶結果補語的副詞　Adverbs with resultative complement：

已經……了　　　yǐjing……le　　　already

還沒有……呢　　hái méiyǒu……ne not yet

Wǒ yǐjing kànwán liǎng běn shū le
我 已經　看完　兩　本　書了。
I have already finished reading two books.

Wǒ yì běn hái méi kànwán ne
我 一 本 還 沒　看完　呢。
I have not yet finished even one.

6）問句　Questions：

Nǐ kànjian wǒ gēge le ma
你 看見　我 哥哥 了 嗎？
Have you seen my brother?

Nǐ kànjiàn méi kànjian wǒ gēge
你 看見 沒　看見　我 哥哥？
Have you seen my brother?

Nǐ kànjian wǒ gēge méiyǒu
你 看見　我 哥哥　沒有 ？
Have you seem my brother?

7）常用結果補語 Frequently Used Result ant Complements

形容詞 Adjectives（To the extend）

好	hǎo	well, properly
做好	zuòhǎo	finished, did nicely and thoroughly
坐好	zuòhǎo	sat still, sat well
對	duì	correct

	看對	kànduì	saw correctly, saw through to the point
錯	cuò	wrong	
	説錯	shuōcuò	spoke incorrectly
清楚	qīngchǔ		clear, distinct
	看清楚	kàn qīngchǔ	saw clearly, saw distinctly

動詞 Verbs (Pay attention: you may achieve the same result through different actions.)

見	jiàn	perceive through senses	
	看見	kànjian	saw
	聽見	tīngjian	heard
	聞見	wénjian	smelled
	遇見	yùjian	came across, encountered
會	huì	know how	
	看會	kànhuì	mastered(know how)through observing
	聽會	tīnghuì	mastered (know how) through listening
	學會	xuéhuì	mastered (know how) through learning
懂	dǒng	comprehend	
	看懂	kàndǒng	comprehended through watching/reading
	聽懂	tīngdǒng	comprehended through listening
完	wán	finish	
	看完	kànwán	finished reading/watching
	聽完	tīngwán	finished listening
	學完	xuéwán	finished studying
到	dào	arrive	
	看到	kàndào	saw
	聽到	tīngdào	heard
	學到	xuédào	learned up to
	走到	zǒudào	arrived at
走	zǒu	depart, walk	

開走	kāizǒu	drove away
拿走	názǒu	took away
帶走	dàizǒu	carried off

計劃路綫和預測時間　Plan the Route and Predict the Time

可能補語　Potential Complement

功用　Function：Potential complement is used to predict the potential result of an action. It is intended to be more objective than subjective in perspective.

句型　Sentence Pattern：

Subject　　　Verb ＋得 Verb/Adjective

Wǒ　　　kàn　de　jiàn
我　　　看　得　見　。
I can see it. (I will achieve seeing (it).)

A verb indicates the potential result of the action：

Wǒ　　　kàn　de　dǒng
我　　　看　得　懂　。
I can comprehend through observing/reading.

(It is a possibility that I can achieve comprehension.)

An adjective indicates the potential result of the action：

Wǒ　　　kàn　de　qīngchu
我　　　看　得　清楚　。
I can see it clearly.

(I will achieve seeing (it) with clarity.)

否定　Negative："不" denies the potential result not the action.

（要是我看，可能……）

Wǒ kàn bu dǒng
我 看 不 懂 。
I cannot understand.

Wǒ kàn bu qīngchu
我 看 不 清楚 。
I cannot see clearly.

賓語在句中的位置　Position of object in sentence：

The result must follow the action immediately. The object of the sentence usually has to go after the action and result.

> Wǒ kàn de jiàn tā
> 我　看　得　見　他。
> I can see him (I can receive the sight of him)

> Wǒ kàn bu wán nà běn shū
> 我　看　不　完　那　本　書。
> I cannot finish reading that book.

鑒別、預測可能性　Identify Possibilities：

若對旅行的時間、路面的情況作鑒定和推測，需要用可能補語。

In order to predict possibilities, such as traveling time, accessibility of the road or transportation, etc., we use "可能補語 Potential Complement."

> Jīntiān de tiānqì bù hǎo, tā kěnéng lái bu liǎo le
> 今天　的天氣不　好，他　可能　來不了了。
> Today's weather is not good, I don't think he can make it here.

> Qù nàr de lù bú tài yuǎn, shí fēnzhōng kāi de dào dào de liǎo
> 去那兒的路不太遠，十　分鐘　開得到／到得了。
> It is not far, we will get there in 10 minutes.

其他的可能　Other Possibilities：

> lái de liǎo lái bu liǎo
> 來得了／來不了
>
> qù de liǎo qù bu liǎo
> 去得了／去不了
>
> zǒu de liǎo zǒu bu liǎo
> 走得了／走不了
>
> dào de liǎo dào bu liǎo
> 到得了／到不了
>
> huí de liǎo huí bu liǎo
> 回得了／回不了

問句　Questions：

> Nǐ kàn de jiàn tā ma
> 你看得見他嗎？
> Can you see him?

Nǐ kàn de jiàn kàn bu jiàn tā
你　看　得　見　看　不　見　他？
Can you see him, or not?

常用可能補語　Frequently Used Potential Complements

形容詞 Adjectives

好	hǎo	well, properly
做得好	zuò de hǎo	can finish, do nicely and thoroughly
清楚	qīngchu	clear, distinct
看得清楚	kàn de qīngchu	can see clearly/distinctly
說得清楚	shuō de qīngchu	can communicate/explain clearly

動詞 Verbs (Pay attention: you may achieve the same result through different actions.)

見	jiàn	perceive through senses
看得見	kàn de jiàn	can see
聽得見	tīng de jiàn	can hear
會	huì	know how
看得會	kàn de huì	can master (know how) through observing/reading
學得會	xué de huì	can master (know how) through learning
懂	dǒng	comprehend
看得懂	kàn de dǒng	can comprehend through watching/reading
聽得懂	tīng de dǒng	can comprehend through listening
完	wán	finish
看得完	kàn de wán	can finish reading/watching
聽得完	tīng de wán	can finish listening
到	dào	arrive
看得到	kàn de dào	can see

聽得到	tīng de dào	can hear
走得到	zǒu de dào	can arrive at
走　　zǒu	depart, walk	
開得走	kāi de zǒu	can drive away
拿得走	ná de zǒu	can take away

指方向　Giving Directions

往……　Toward...

"往……V" 可能是用得最多的一個句子

In order to identify a direction to travel, we use the pattern "往... V".

In English, when giving directions, we simply say, "go south, turn left."

In Chinese, we usually specify the direction first, then the action：

	wǎng nán zǒu
Go south：	往　南　走
	wǎng zuǒ guǎi
Turn left：	往　左　拐

1) 其他相似的介詞 Other Prepositions Similar to "往..." to Show Directions：

往	wǎng	toward; go to
朝	cháo	towards; facing ...
向	xiàng	face; turn toward
冲	chòng	towards; in the direction of

2) 方向 Possible Directions：

	dōng xī nán běi
east/west/south/north	東　/西/　南　/北
	shàng xià zuǒ yòu
up/down/left/right	上　/下/　左　/右
	qián hòu lǐ wài
front/back/in/out	前　/後/裏/外

3) 可能用的動詞 Possible Action Verbs Used to Show Directions：

拐	guǎi	turn, change direction

走	zǒu	walk, travel on foot
開	kāi	drive
跑	pǎo	run

Note

有人說"拐左"，但不是標準說法。漢語的介詞結構/狀語應置於動詞前。

Some people say "拐左," but, this is not a standard (grammatically correct) expression. In Chinese, habitually, all prepositional phrases go before verbs. "往" is such a phrase.

指路——有用的句型　Giving Directions — Useful Sentence Patterns

問路 wènlù Asking the way

Qǐngwèn qù　　　zěnme zǒu
請問，　去 ××× 怎麼　走 ?
Excuse me, how do I get to xxx (place)?

回答 huídá Reply, answer

1) 從 cóng……到 dào…… from... to...

Cóng zhè zǒu dào nàr
從　這　走　到　那兒。
Go from here to there.

2) 從 cóng……往 wǎng…… from ... towards ...

Cóng nàr wǎng yòu guǎi
從　那兒　往　右　拐
From there turn right.

3) 過…… guò Cross, pass; across; over

Zài nàr guò mǎlù
在　那兒　過　馬路。
Cross the street there.

Guò liǎng tiáo jiē
過　　兩　　條　街。
Over two blocks.

4) 走 zǒu　(period of time)　　go/walk (a period of time)

Zǒu wǔ fēnzhōng
走 五 分鐘
Walk for 5 minutes

5）沿着 yánzhe……（一直 yìzhí）往 wǎng……

… along … （go straight）towards …

yánzhe zhè tiáo jiē yìzhí wǎng qián zǒu
沿着 這 條 街 一直 往 前 走。
Go straight ahead along this road.

6）走 zǒu 到 dào（看見 kànjian）……往 wǎng

……until you get to（see）…

Zǒudào lùkǒu kànjian hónglǜdēng wǎng yòu guǎi
走到 路口 看見 紅綠燈 往 右 拐。
Walk to the corner, after seeing the traffic lights, turn right.

7）先 xiān……然後 ránhòu（再 zài）…… first … then …

Nǐ xiān yánzhe zhè tiáo jiē yìzhí wǎng qián zǒu zǒudào lùkǒu
你 先 沿着 這 條 街 一直 往 前 走，走到 路口
wǎng yòu guǎi kànjian hónglǜdēng ránhòu zài wǎng yòu guǎi
往 右 拐，看見 紅綠燈 然後 再 往 右 拐，
jiù dào le
就 到 了。
First go straight ahead along this road, come to the corner and turn
right, then when you see the traffic lights, make another right turn.
Then you will be there.

教學難點

Cruxes of Teaching and Learning

難點一　結果補語 Resultant Complement

結果補語比較難。有的容易掌握，有的相對難懂。常出錯的有幾個。

Resultant Complement itself is a difficult learning point. Some results of actions are easier for learners, some are more difficult to understand. Here we list a few that are easy to misuse.

看見 kànjiàn see/saw

“看見”用得最多也最難掌握。“看 kàn look”是做的事，“見 jiàn perceive”是做到的事。“看”不一定“見”，“見”不一定在“看”。相似的還有“聽見、聞見、遇見”。

This is perhaps the most frequently used but the most confusing for learners. But once understood, it may be helpful in understanding other resultant complements.

“看 kàn look” is the effort while “見 jiàn perceive” is to receive the sight. The logic here is that you may try to look, but you may or may not see anything. Also you may accidentally see something even though you have not actively looked. The same applies to “聽見，聞見，遇見”. e. g. :

看見	kànjiàn	saw

Nǐmen kàn kànjian shénme le
你們　看，看見　什麼　了？
(Look, what did you see?)

聽見	tīngjiàn	heard

Wǒ zhùyì tīng le kěshì shénme dōu méi tīngjiàn
我　注意　聽　了，可是　什麼　都　沒　聽見　。
(I listened carefully but did not hear anything.)

聞見	wénjiàn	smelled

Tā wénjian le yì gǔ xiāngwèi
他　聞見　了一股　香味　。
(He smelled some delicious aroma.)

遇見	yùjiàn	come across, encounter

Wǒ zài lùshang yùjian le tā
我　在　路上　遇見　了他。
I met with (bumped into) him on the way.

做完 zuòwán finish doing

英文說“finish doing”，中文說“做完 zuòwán finish doing”。“做”是行爲，“完”是結果。

In English, we say “finished doing” something when it is completed.

In Chinese, “做” or other verbs are actions; “完” is one of the results you achieve through actions, thus “完” appears after the action verb, e. g. :

Wǒ chīwán le
我　吃完　了。
I have finished eating.

拿走 názǒu take away

學生一般先學了"走 zǒu walk"，不太習慣用"走"做補語。若把"走"當做"move away, leave"就容易了。教學中，創造使用的情景很重要。

For most learners who have learned "走 zǒu" "to walk" it is a little diffi-cult for them to understand it as a result of an action. But once they know "走 zǒu" also means "to move" and "to leave", it will be easier for them to get ac-customed to use "走 zǒu" to indicate the result, e. g. :

Tā bǎ nà běn shū názǒu le
他　把　那　本　書　拿走　了。
He took the book (away.)

Huǒchē kāizǒu le
火車　　　開走　了。
The train took off (drove away).

難點二　"在"作爲結果　"在" as a Result

做補語常會與"在 a place"做狀語混淆；做狀語出現在動詞前；做補語放在動詞後。

"在 a place" as a result also causes confusion at times. Most learners learn-ed "在" as the location of an action and it has to be put before the action verbs in a sentence：

Wǒ bàba zài zhōngxué gōngzuò
我　爸爸在　中學　　工作　。
My dad works in a high school.

However, "在 a place" can also be the result as an action and be used after the verb.

Wǒ bàba zhàn zài nàr
我　爸爸　站　在　那兒。
My dad stood there.

Don't panic! Please note: the emphases are not the same.

If the "在 a place" phrase is needed before the verb, it refers to the location where the action is/has been conducted.

Wǒ jiā zài Zhījiāgē zhù
我　家　在　芝加哥　住 。
My family lives in Chicago.

Emphasis: It is at Chicago where my family lives.

Wǒ zài zhuōzi shang fàngle yì běn shū
我　在　桌子　上　放了　一　本　書 。
I put a book on the table.

Emphasis: The table is the location where I put a book.

If the "在" is needed after the verb, it refers to where the object is ended up as a result of the action.

我家住在芝加哥。　　My family lives in Chicago.

Emphasis: My family is at Chicago because we live there.

Wǒ bǎ nà běn shū fàng zài zhuōzi shang le
我　把　那　本　書　放　在　桌子　上　了 。
I put the book on the table.

Emphasis: What happened to the book? It ended up on the table.

難點三　可能補語 vs. 結果補語
Potential Complement vs. Resultant Complement

可能補語與結果補語的不同：顧名思義，一個是可能，一個是結果。

Both "可能補語" and "結果補語" are intended to be objective in perspective. While "結果補語" is meant to show result of an action, how far an action is planned or has been carried out; "可能補語" is to predict or estimate a possible result.

"結果補語" is used to show result.

"看見 kànjiàn see/saw"

"可能補語" is used to predict potential/possibility.

"看得見 kàn de jiàn can be seen"

難點四　"能"與"可能"Potentials and Abilities

"能"與"可能"的不同在看問題的角度。"能"指的是做事者的能力，"可能"指的是事情。同時使用，"能"在句中可以加強"可能"。

What is the difference? The difference is the perspective！"能 néng can . . . ; be possible" expresses a more subjective view. It emphasizes capability. "可能 kěnéng possibility, likelihood" expresses a more objective view and it meant to predict a possibility. "能" can be used to enhance "可能" in a sentence：

Wǒ néng jīntiān kànwán zhè běn shū
我　能　今天　看完　這　本　書。
I can finish reading this book today.

（ I have the capacity to finish this book today. ）

Wǒ jīntiān kàn de wán zhè běn shū
我　今天　看　得　完　這　本　書。
I can finish reading this book today.

（ It is possible that I will finish reading this today. ）

Wǒ jīntiān néng kàn de wán zhè běn shū
我　今天　能　看　得　完　這　本　書。
I can finish reading this book today.

（Double emphasis：it can be and will be done！）

難點五　可能補語 vs. 程度補語
Potential Complement vs. Complement of Degree

"可能補語" and "程度補語" obviously have different grammatical functions. However, they can be confused because they seem to be similar in structure since both use "Verb 得 Adjective". Note：they are not as similar as one may believe.

對比不同：Note the differences：

When using 程度補語, you may add adverbs to modify adjectives：

Tā tiàowǔ tiào de fēicháng hǎo
他　跳舞　跳　得　非常　好 。
He dances very well.

When using 可能補語 , you cannot add an adverb before adjective：

Tā tiào de hǎo tiào bu hǎo　　Tā tiào de hǎo
他　跳　得　好　跳　不　好 ？他　跳　得　好 。
Can he dance well? Yes, he can.

（Can he possibly deliver a quality performance?）

詞彙表

路標　Road Signs

停	tíng	stop
慢行	màn xíng	move（act, progress）slowly
出口	chūkǒu	exit
入口	rùkǒu	enter；entrance
請繞行	qǐng ràoxíng	detour
禁止通行	jìnzhǐ tōngxíng	no thoroughfare（as a posted prohibition）, road blocked
安全行駛	ānquán xíngshǐ	drive safely

交通用語　Related Traffic Expressions

交通	jiāotōng	traffic
交通工具	jiāotōng gōngjù	means of transportation
交通警	jiāotōngjǐng	traffic police
路	lù	road, path
公路	gōnglù	highway, public road
高速公路	gāosù gōnglù	expressway
馬路	mǎlù	street（the part for vehicular traffic）

路口	lùkǒu		intersection, street cornor
十字路口	shízì lùkǒu		intersection (of two
			roads in an x – shape)

街	jiē	street, road	
大街	dàjiē		main street
街道	jiēdào		street, road,
			neighborhood

紅綠燈	hónglǜdēng	traffic lights	
堵車	dǔ chē	traffic jam	
塞車	sāichē	traffic jam	

補充語法點

Supplementary Notes

趨向補語 Directional Complements

簡單趨向補語 Simple Directional Complement

功用 Function:

"來" or "去" goes after a verb to indicate the direction of the action.

"來" indicates that the action is towards the speaker;

"去" indicates that the action is away from the speaker.

句型 Sentence Patterns:

Verb	來/去

上　　　　　　　來!　　Come up!

If there is a destination for the action, then it goes in between the verb and 來/去.

Verb (Place)	來/去

　　　　上　這兒　　　來。　　　Come up here.

If there is a starting location for the action, then it goes before the verb.

> 從（place）Verb 來/去

　　　從　家　　帶　來　一本書。　　Bring a book from home.

有關動詞　Related Verbs

The basic group of verbs that implies directional movements of the body

上	shàng	get on, go up
下	xià	get off, go down
進	jìn	enter
出	chū	go out, exit
過	guò	pass by, come across, go over
回	huí	return, go back
到	dào	arrive, go to
起	qǐ	rise, stand up

Toward speaker	away from speaker
上來	上去
下來	下去
進來	進去
出來	出去
過來	過去
回來	回去
到（Place）來	到（Place）去
起來	

Other verbs that indicate moving back and forth：

走	zǒu	walk, travel on foot
跑	pǎo	run, run away
爬	pá	crawl, creep, climb
滾	gǔn	roll

開	kāi	drive, operate (a machine, etc.)
騎	qí	ride (astride, like on a bicycle, horse, etc.)

Common verbs that refer to moving objects:

搬	bān	move, take away (mostly heavy or large objects)
帶	dài	carry, bring, take to
買	mǎi	buy, purchase
拿	ná	hole, grasp, take, capture
扔	rēng	throw, toss
運	yùn	transport
裝	zhuāng	pack, load

複合趨向補語

功用　Function:

Combine a verb with a simple directional complement to enrich an expression.

句型　Sentence Pattern:

Combine a verb with a simple directional complement.

Verb	simple directional complement

跑　　上來

toward speaker	away from speaker
走上來	走上去
走下來	走下去
走進來	走進去
走出來	走出去
走過來	走過去
走回來	走回去
走到（Place）來	走到（Place）去
走上（Place）來	走上（Place）去

趨向補語的引申用法

Some simple directional complement phrases have extended meanings.　They serve as suffixes.

Extended Use：

出來	chūlái	achievement or completion of a task
想出來	xiǎng chūlai	come up with an idea
看出來	kàn chūlai	see through, understand
起來	qǐlái	arising, beginning to do, accomplishing
唱起來	chàng qǐlai	sing out, start singing
想起來	xiǎng qǐlai	remember, recall
下去	xiàqù	indicating continuation or completion
吃下去	chī xiàqu	eat（sth.）

22

指令

Giving
Instructions
（Orders,
Directions）

給指令是經常發生的事。在公共場所和服務設施等會遇到，緊急情況和日常活動都需要。在中小學課堂上就會不斷出現。

但指令所用的語法點有可能是比較複雜的。本節着重介紹下指令時必用的一些語法點和可能的學習難點。

後附的詞彙表是與食物等有關的。教與學做飯、看病、買東西等話題時，可參考。

Giving instructions (orders, directions) is a daily occurrence. It happens in public places and at home, for service and emergencies. We do it in classroom instruction all the time.

The grammatical structures used for giving instructions can vary. This chapter introduces some necessary sentence patterns and explains some common difficulties.

The attached vocabulary lists relates mostly to food. Cooking, doctor's visits, shopping and similar activities often use instruction. Use whenever necessary.

教 學 重 點　Content of Teaching and Learning

指令	Giving Instructions (Orders, Directions)
動詞句	Verb as Action
兼語句	Pivotal Sentence
"把"字句	"把" Sentence
常用的指令	Commonly Used Instructions

教 學 難 點　Cruxes of Teaching and Learning

"問" vs. "請"	Asking a Question vs. Asking Someone
"想" vs. "想讓"	Wanting Someone to Do Something
聽什麼？	Listening to "What"?
"把"字句的使用	Use of "把" Sentence
"把"字句與"被"字句的比較與使用	
	"把" Sentence vs. "被" Sentence

詞 彙 表 Glossary

食物	Food
用餐	Having a Meal
飲料	Drinks/Beverages
蔬菜	Vegetables
水果	Fruits
動物	Animals
植物	Plants

文 化 聯 繫 Cultural Relations

中國食品	Chinese Food
中國珍寶	Chinese Treasures

教學重點

Content of Teaching and Learning

指令　Giving Instructions（Orders，Directions）

給指令時可用以下三類句子。

In order to give instructions, orders or directions, we may use three kinds of sentence patterns.

動詞句　Verb as Action

功用　Function：To give an order or instruction.

句型　Sentence Pattern：

		Guòlai
Come over here.	過來 ！	
		Gěi wǒ
Give it to me.	給　我 ！	
		Chī ba
Eat（it）！	吃　吧 ！	

否定形式　Negative：　不要

		Bú yào guòlái
Don't come over here.	不　要　過來 ！	
		Bú yào gěi wǒ
Don't give it to me.	不　要　給　我 ！	
		Bú yào chī ba
Don't eat it.	不　要　吃　吧 ！	

客氣起見請用"請"。

For the sake of politeness, we may add 請—meaning "please" —at the beginning of the sentence：

		Qǐng guòlai
Please come over here.	請　　過來 ！	
		Qǐng gěi wǒ
Please give it to me.	請　　給　我 ！	

Qǐng chī ba

Please eat it.   請　吃　吧！

Note

"吧" 在句末有建議的意思。 "吧" usually indicates a tone of suggestion.

兼語句　Pivotal Sentence

Use "請", "讓", or "叫" to invite, make or allow someone to do something:

功用　Function: Give an invitation, order or permission for an action.

句型　Sentence Pattern:

請/讓/叫	Someone	Verb (Object)

Wǒ qǐng nǐ hē kāfēi

我　請　你　喝　咖啡 。

I will take you out for some coffee.

Wǒ māma ràng wǒ xiànzài jiù zuò gōngkè

我　媽媽　讓　我　現在　就　做　功課 。

My mom wants me to do homework now.

Tā jiào wǒmen kuàidiǎn zǒu

他　叫　我們　快點　走 。

He asked us to hurry up.

否定形式　Negative Form:　不 or 不想

Wǒ bù qǐng tā hē kāfēi wǒ qǐng nǐ

我　不　請　他　喝　咖啡，我　請　你 。

I am not inviting him for coffee, I am inviting you.

Wǒ bù xiǎng qǐng nǐ hē kāfēi

or 我　不　想　請　你　喝　咖啡 。

I don't feel like taking you out for coffee.

Wǒ māma bú ràng wǒ xiànzài jiù zuò gōngkè

我　媽媽　不　讓　我　現在　就　做　功課 。

My mom won't allow me to do my homework now.

Wǒ māma bù xiǎng ràng wǒ xiànzài jiù zuò gōngkè

or 我　媽媽　不　想　讓　我　現在　就　做　功課 。

My mom does not want me to do my homework now.

Tā bú jiào wǒmen nàme kuài de zǒu

他　不　叫　我們　那麼　快　地　走 。

He won't let us walk that fast.

　　　　　Tā bù xiǎng jiào wǒmen nàme kuài de zǒu
　or 他 不 想 叫 我們 那麼 快 地 走 。
　　　　　He does not want us to walk that fast.

"把" 字句　　"把" Sentence

Give instructions by focusing on the object of the action

功用　Function：Emphasize how the object of the action should be manipulated.

句型　Sentence Pattern：

把	Object	Verb	Extent of the Action

　　　Qǐng nǐ bǎ nà běn shū gěi wǒ
　　　請 你 把 那 本 書 給 我 。
　　　Please pass that book to me.

　　　Bǎ tā sòng dào yīyuàn qù
　　　把 他 送 到 醫院 去 。
　　　Take him to the hostipal.

　　　Bǎ yīfu chuānshang
　　　把 衣服 穿上 　　　。
　　　Put on your jacket.

比較　Compare：

Give me that book.
$\begin{cases} \text{Gěi wǒ nà běn shū} \\ 給 我 那 本 書 。（A） \\ \text{Bǎ nà běn shū gěi wǒ} \\ 把 那 本 書 給 我 。（B） \end{cases}$

　　顯然（A）和（B）都對。（A）和（B）會起同樣結果。

　　不同的是：（A）和（B）的注意點不同。（A）的注意點是"給我"；
（B）的注意點是"那本書"。

　　Obviously,（A）and（B）are both perfectly correct sentences.（A）and
（B）may cause the same action, producing the same result.

　　A simple way to explain：（A）and（B）differ in emphasis：（A）The emphasis is on "to me" — "給我"；（B）The emphasis is on "the book" —
"那本書".

常用的指令　Commonly used Instructions

課堂用語　Language Used in the Classroom

Qǐng ānjìng
請　安靜！
Be quiet!

Qǐng zhùyì tīng
請　注意　聽。
Please pay attention.

Qǐng jǔ shǒu
請　舉手。
Raise your hand!

Bié pǎo
別　跑！
Stop running!

Qǐng gēn wǒ shuō
請　跟　我　説。
Please say it after me.

Kuài diǎn
快　點！
Hurry up!

Qǐng dào qiánmian lái qǐng dào nàbian qù
請　到　前面　來/請　到　那邊　去。
Please come to the front/go over there.

Shàng kè de shíhou búyào chī dōngxi
上　課的　時候　不要　吃　東西。
No food in class.

Bǎ diànnǎo dǎkāi
把　電腦　打開。
Turn on your computer.

Qǐng bǎ běnzi cóng shūbāo li ná chūlai
請　把本子　從　書包　裏拿　出來。
Please take out your notebook from your bag.

Qǐng bǎ shū fàng zài zhuōshang
請　把書　放　在　桌上　。
Put the book on your desk.

在醫院裏 In Hospital

Qǐng bǎ yīfu xiézi tuō xiàlai
請　把衣服/鞋子　脫　下來。
Please take off your clothes/shoes.

Qǐng bǎ zhège sòng dào nàr qù
請　把　這個　送　到　那兒去。
Please take this over there.

做飯 Cooking

Bǎ cài xǐ gānjìng
把 菜 洗 乾净 。
Clean the greens.

Bǎ cài qiēchéng xiǎo kuài
把 菜 切成 小 塊 。
Cut the vegetables into small pieces.

Bǎ róuhǎo de miàntuán fàngjìn kǎoxiāng kǎo sìshí fēnzhōng
把 揉好 的 麵糰 放進 烤箱 烤 四十 分鐘 。
Put the dough in the oven and bake for 40 minutes.

教學難點

Cruxes of Teaching and Learning

難點一　"問" vs. "請" Asking a Question vs. Asking Someone

英文的 "ask" 有兩個功能：問問題和請人做事。

在漢語裏，這兩個功能是用不同動詞句子表示的。"問" 只能問問題，請人做事要用兼語句。

The word "ask" is commonly used. It must be used with care.

In English, the word "ask" can be used for two different functions：

　　1）To ask a question.

　　2）To ask someone to do something.

In Chinese,

　　1）To ask a question is "問/問題"

　　2）To ask someone to do something is "請/讓/叫" 某人做事.

"問"：

Wǒ wèn tā yí ge wèntí
我 問 他 一 個 問題。
I am asking him a question.

Wǒ wèn tā nǐ máng bu máng
我 問 他 "你 忙 不 忙？"

I asked him, "Are you busy?"

Wǒ wèn tā máng bu máng

我　問　他　忙　不　忙？

I asked him if he was busy.

"請／讓／叫"：

Wǒ qǐng tā gěi wǒ jiǎng yí ge gùshi

我　請　他　給　我　講　一　個　故事。

I asked him to tell me a story.

Tā ràng wǒ tīng tā shuō

他　讓　我　聽　他　説　。

He asked me to listen to him.

Qǐng nǐ jiào tā lái hǎo ma

請　你　叫　她　來，好　嗎？

Would you please ask her to come here?

對比 Compare：

Wǒ qǐng tā wèn wǒ yí ge wèntí

我　請　他　問　我　一　個　問題。

I asked (invited) him to ask me a question.

難點二　"想" vs. "想讓" Wanting Someone to Do Something

在英文裏，可以説："I want you to do this."這句話中的"want"不能直接譯成漢語的"想"。

"想"和"想讓"在漢語裏的意思是不一樣的。

In English, when we say, "I want you to do this," the word "want" refers to your desire to have someone to get something done. That is to say, you ask someone to carry out an action according to your instructions.

Therefore, in Chinese, this "want" must be translated as "（想）請／讓／叫" not just "想".

Wǒ bà bù xiǎng ràng wǒ gēn péngyou chūqu

我　爸　不（想）讓　我　跟　朋友　出去。

My dad does not want me to go out with my friends.

Tā bú jiào wǒ gàosu nǐ

她　不　叫　我　告訴　你。

She does not want me to tell you.

難點三 聽什麼? Listening to "What"?

英語的 "listen" 後可跟人："listen to me/you/him/her..."

漢語的 "聽" 後只能跟物不能跟人。

In English, we may say "listen to me/you/him/her...". One listens to "a person".

In Chinese, we don't listen to a person. We listen to "what a person says" or "a person's words".

Tā ràng wǒ tīng tā shuō
他 讓 我 聽 他 説 。
He asked me to listen to him.

Bié tīng tā de huà
別 聽 他 的（話）。
Don't listen to him.

同樣 The same applies to：

	tīng bù tīng lǎoshī de
listen/not listen to your teacher	聽 / 不 聽 老師 的
	tīng bù tīng fùmǔ de
listen/not listen to your parents	聽 / 不 聽 父母 的
	tīng bù tīng péngyou de
listen/not listen to your friends	聽 / 不 聽 朋友 的

難點四 "把"字句的使用 Use of "把" Sentence

"把"字句的功用是強調動作的對象賓語。

在句子的結構上有兩個值得注意的地方。

Functionally, the emphasis of the action is on the object of 把 sentence.

In terms of sentence structure, there are two things worth noting：

1）"把"將賓語提到動詞之前以示強調，這個賓語應是已知的。

We use "把" to move the object in front of the verb to reflect this emphasis on the object. Thus the object must be a known or designated one.

bǎ shū fàng zhuō shang

Put the book on the table：把　書　放　　桌　上　　。

　　"The book 書" is not a random one. It is the particular book that we are talking about.

2)"把"字句動詞的後邊必須有附加成分，如補語等，以示動作的程度。不可與把字句同用的只有可能補語。

There has to be an element after the verb. This element indicates to what extent the action is going to be/has been done.

In other words, it is incorrect to end a "把" sentence with a verb alone.

bǎ shū fàng

（×）　　把　書　放　。

The only linguistic element that is not suitable to go with a "把" sentence is a "potential complement." In this case, you can only use "能不能" instead.

　　　　　　Would you be able to finish reading the book today?

　　　　　　Nǐ jīntiān bǎ zhè běn shū kàn de wán kàn bu wán

（×）　　你　今　天　把　這　本　書　看　得　完　看　不　完　?(A)

　　　　　　Nǐ jīntiān néng bu néng bǎ zhè běn shū kànwán

（√）　　你　今　天　能　不　能　把　這　本　書　看　完　?(B)

（A）錯。因爲完成的可能性不是可以實際測量的行爲本身。

（B）對。因爲談的是行爲者的能力而不是書。

If you think about it, (A) does not make sense because the potential of finishing is not a tangible result of the action.

(B) is our choice because "能不能" means the doer has the capacity to achieve the goal of finishing the book. The potential is about the doer, not the action itself.

同樣，情態動詞都應該放在"把"之前。

Similarly, all modal verbs must be put before the "把" phrase.

Tā yīnggāi bǎ shū huán gěi nǐ

他　應該　把　書　還　給　你　。

He should return the book to you.

The following is a list of the linguistic elements indicating the result or extention of the action in a "把" sentence：

What will you do with your homework?

(Adjective as Result) Get it done properly.

Bǎ nǐ de gōngkè zuò hǎo
把 你 的 功課 做 好 。

(Direction of Action) Take it home.

Bǎ nǐ de gōngkè dàihuí jiā qù
把 你 的 功課 帶回 家 去 。

(Duplication of Verb) Have a look!

Bǎ nǐ de gōngkè kàn yi kàn
把 你 的 功課 看 一 看 。

(Evaluation of Action) Must do it very well!

Yídìng yào bǎ nǐ de gōngkè zuò de tèbié hǎo
一 定 要 把 你 的 功課 做 得 特別 好 。

(Frequency of Action) Should get it checked twice.

Yīnggāi bǎ gōngkè jiǎnchá liǎng biàn
應該 把 功課 檢查 兩 遍 。

(Place as Result) Put it on the table.

Bǎ nǐ de gōngkè fàng zài zhuōzi shang
把 你 的 功課 放 在 桌子 上 。

(Quantity) Did half.

Bǎ gōngkè zuòle yíbàn
把 功課 做了 一半 。

(To Indicate Completion) Get it done!

Bǎ nǐ de gōngkè zuò le
把 你 的 功課 做 了 。

(Time Duration) Only did half a hour.

Zhǐ bǎ gōngkè zuòle bàn ge zhōngtóu
只 把 功課 做了 半 個 鍾頭 。

(To a Person as Result) Hand it to the teacher.

Bǎ nǐ de gōngkè jiāo gěi lǎoshī
把 你 的 功課 交 給 老師 。

(Verb as Result) Finish it.

Bǎ gōngkè zuòwán
把 功課 做完 。

難點五 "把"字句與"被"字句的比較與使用
"把"Sentence vs. "被"Sentence

比較 Comparison

Zuòyè zuòwán le
作業 做完 了。　　Homework is done!

這個句子可以是"把"字句也可能是"被"字句。

To be more specific, this sentence could also be expressed as:

Wǒ bǎ zuòyè zuòwán le
A. 我 把 作業 做完 了。 I got my homework done!

Zuòyè ràng tā zuòwán le
B. 作業 讓 他 做完 了! The homework was done by him!

"把"字句與"被"字句的相同點 Similarities:

功用上都强調行爲的對象。句型上都要動詞後的附加成分以示動作完成的程度。

In function, both sentences focus on the object. In structure, both sentence patterns require the same kind of elements after verbs.

"把"字句與"被"字句的不同點 Differences:

簡單地説,在功用上,"把"字句是主動的被動。行爲者的動作是主動的,動作的目標是被强調的,行爲的情景是受限定的。"被"字句是真的被動。

In function, "把 Sentence" is "actively passive" in nature: The doer of the action is in an active mode but the action itself is in a given situation and the focus of the action is on the object. 被字句 is truly "passive."

從結構上説,區別見以下例句。

Structure of "把 Sentence":

Subject	"把"	Object	Verb	Complement
Wǒ	bǎ	zuòyè	zuò	wán le
我	把	作業	做	完 了。

I finished my homework.

Structure of "被 Sentence"：

Object	"被/讓/叫"	Doer	Verb	Complement
Zuòyè	ràng	tā	zuò	wán le
作業	讓	他	做	完 了。

Homework was done by him.

被字句　"被" Sentence

功用　Function：An action is/was done to an object.

句型　Sentence Pattern：

Object	"被/讓/叫"	（Doer）	Verb	Extent of the Action
Zuòyè	ràng	tā	zuò	wán le
作業	讓	他	做	完 了。

The homework has been completed by him.

Note

1）"被"字句的重點在賓語和行爲本身，行爲者是誰不重要。

In the "被" sentence the focus is on the object and the action. Who carries out the action is much less significant. Thus doers are not frequently mentioned in Chinese sentences.

Zuòyè yǐjing zuòwán le
作業　已經　做完　了。
The homework is already done.

2）引出行爲者的詞

Words that introduce the "doers" of an action in the "被" sentence：

被　bèi　by
讓　ràng　by（less formal）
叫　jiào　by（least informal）

3）用"被"時，人稱也可省略。

If "被" is used, the doer may be omitted：

Zuòyè bèi tā zuòwán le
作業　被他　做完　了。

Homework was done by him.

Zuòyè bèi zuòwán le

作業　被　做完　了。

Homewrok was done.

詞彙表

食物	shíwù	Food	
（食品	shípǐn	food, foodstuffs, provisions）	
吃	chī	eat	
餓	è	be hungry	
飽	bǎo	be full (after eating)	
中餐（中國飯）	Zhōngcān	Chinese food, Chinese cuisine	
西餐	xīcān	Western-style food (meal)	
米	mǐ	hulled rice	
米飯	mǐfàn	cooked rice	
麵	miàn	wheat flour	
麵條	miàntiáo	noodles	
麵包	miànbāo	bread	
點心	diǎnxin	snacks, refreshments, dim sum	
蛋糕	dàngāo	cake	
餅乾	bǐnggān	cracker, biscuit	
肉類	ròulèi	meats	
肉食	ròushí	meat	
家禽	jiāqín	domesticated fowl, poultry	
水產	shuǐchǎn	aquatic product	
海鮮	hǎixiān	seafood	

素食	sùshí	vegetarian diet
菜	cài	vegetables，dishes
豆類	dòulèi	legumes
豆子	dòuzi	beans，peas，legumes
豆製品	dòuzhìpǐn	bean products（beancurd，dried beancurd，etc.）
豆腐	dòufu	beancurd
豆漿	dòujiāng	soybean milk
奶製品	nǎizhìpǐn	diary products
奶酪	nǎilào	cheese
冰激凌	bīngjīlíng	icecream
營養	yíngyǎng	nutrition，nourishment
維生素	wéishēngsù	vitamin
纖維	xiānwéi	fiber

用餐　yòngcān　dine，have a meal

飯館	fànguǎn	restaurant
餐廳	cāntīng	dining room，restaurant
酒店	jiǔdiàn	wineshop
飯店	fàndiàn	hotel，restaurant
服務	fúwù	service，serve
服務員	fúwùyuán	attendant，service person
菜譜	càipǔ	menu，cookbook
菜單	càidān	menu
賬單	zhàngdān	invoice，bill，check
付錢	fù qián	pay

飲料　yǐnliào　drink，beverage

| 喝 | hē | drink |
| 渴 | kě | thirsty |

	醉	zuì	drunk, intoxicated
果汁		guǒzhī	fruit juice, syrup
	橘汁	júzhī	orange juice
	蘋果汁	píngguǒzhī	apple juice
汽水		qìshuǐ	sofe drink, soda water
	可口可樂	Kěkǒukělè	Coca-Cola
	百事可樂	Bǎishìkělè	Pepsi
	雪碧	Xuěbì	Sprite
	七喜	Qīxǐ	7-up
酒		jiǔ	alcoholic beverage, wine, liquor
	白酒	báijiǔ	white liquor
	葡萄酒	pútaojiǔ	grape wine
	米酒	mǐjiǔ	rice wine (made of glutinous rice)
	料酒	liàojiǔ	cooking wine
其他		qítā	others
	茶	chá	tea
	咖啡	kāfēi	coffee
	牛奶	niúnǎi	milk (from a cow)

蔬菜　shūcài　vegetables, greens

白菜	báicài	Chinese cabbage, celery cabbage, bok choy
扁豆	biǎndòu	hyacinth bean, green bean
葱	cōng	scallions, leeks, green onion
胡蘿卜	húluóbo	carrot
黄瓜	huángguā	cucumber
姜	jiāng	ginger
韭菜	jiǔcài	Chinese chives

辣椒	làjiāo	hot pepper
蘿卜	luóbo	radish, turnip
蘑菇	mógu	mushroom
南瓜	nánguā	pumpkin
茄子	qiézi	eggplant
芹菜	qíncài	celery
青椒	qīngjiāo	green pepper
生菜	shēngcài	(romaine) lettuce
蒜	suàn	garlic
土豆	tǔdòu	potato
西紅柿/番茄	xīhóngshì/fānqié	tomato
香菜	xiāngcài	coriander

水果　shuǐguǒ　Fruit (s)

菠蘿	bōluó	pineapple
草莓	cǎoméi	strawberry
橙子	chéngzi	orange
橘子	júzi	tangerine
梨	lí	pear
李子	lǐzi	plum
荔枝	lìzhī	litchi
蘋果	píngguǒ	apple
葡萄	pútao	grape
桃子	táozi	peach
甜瓜	tiánguā	muskmelon
西瓜	xīguā	watermelon
香蕉	xiāngjiāo	banana
杏	xìng	apricot
櫻桃	yīngtáo	cherry

椰子	yēzi	coconut

動物　dòngwù　animals

公	gōng	male（animal）
母	mǔ	female（animal）
大象	dàxiàng	elephant
長頸鹿	chángjǐnglù	giraffe
刺猬	cìwei	hedgehog
狗	gǒu	dog
猴子	hóuzi	monkey
狐狸	húli	fox
老虎	lǎohǔ	tiger
老鼠	lǎoshǔ	rat, mouse
狼	láng	wolf
鹿	lù	deer
馬	mǎ	horse
猫	māo	cat
牛	niú	ox
蛇	shé	snake
獅子	shīzi	lion
松鼠	sōngshǔ	squirrel
兔子	tùzi	rabbit, hare
熊猫	xióngmāo	panda
羊	yáng	sheep, goat
猪	zhū	pig, hog

禽　qín　birds

鶏	jī	chicken
鴨	yā	duck（the bird）
鳥	niǎo	bird

火鷄	huǒjī	turkey

海洋動物　hǎiyáng dòngwù　marine animals

魚	yú	fish
蝦	xiā	shrimp
龍蝦	lóngxiā	lobster
螃蟹	pángxie	(river) crab
烏龜	wūguī	tortoise
青蛙	qīngwā	frog

植物　zhíwù　plants, flora; vegetables

樹	shù	tree, plant
草	cǎo	grass, herbs
花	huā	flower

文化聯繫

Cultural Relations

中國食品　Zhōngguó shípǐn　Chinese Food

餃子	jiǎozi	"jiaozi", boiled stuffed dumplings (traditional food at Chinese New Year; when the boiled stuffed dumplings are fried, they are called 鍋貼 guōtiē "pot-stickers")
長壽麵	chángshòumiàn	long-life noodles (eaten at weddings and birthdays)
年糕	niángāo	lunar New Year's cake (made with glutinous rice flour)
元宵	yuánxiāo	sweet glutinous rice flour dumpling (prepared for the Lantern Festival)
月餅	yuèbing	moon cake (eaten during Mid-autumn Festival)
粽子	zòngzi	"zongzi" (pyramid-shaped glutinous rice dumpling

with various fllings, special food at the Dragon Boat Festival）

中國珍寶　Zhōngguó zhēnbǎo　Chinese Treasures

珍奇動物　zhēnqí dòngwù　（precious）rare animals

熊猫	xióngmāo	panda
金絲猴	jīnsīhóu	golden monkey
丹頂鶴	dāndǐnghè	red-crowned crane
東北虎	dōngběihǔ	Manchurian tiger
雪豹	xuěbào	snow leopard

吉祥物　jíxiángwù　lucky charms, mascots（for sports teams）

松柏	sōngbǎi	pine and cypress（as a symbol of fidelity）
壽桃	shòutáo	long-life peach（as a symbol of immortality）
鯉魚	lǐyú	carp（as a symbol of prosperity）
牡丹	mǔdan	peony（as a national flower）
福娃	fúwá	blessed baby（as a symbol of happiness/hope）
紅包	hóngbāo	red wrapping（gift of money wrapped in red paper）

23

季節與天氣

Seasons and Weather

　　季節與天氣是個經久不衰的話題。本節集中介紹跟此話題密切相關的詞彙和句型。不同的年級和不同水平的學生都可以根據學習的要求加減學習的內容。

　　Seasons and weather is a classic topic. This chapter concentrates on vocabulary and sentence patterns related to this topic. Learners of all ages and levels may choose from the content according to the needs.

教 學 重 點　Content of Teaching and Learning

季節	Seasons
四季	Four seasons
季節變化	Changing Seasons
天氣	Weather
描述天氣	Describing Weather
天氣預報	Weather Fore cast
溫度	Temperature
描述溫度	Describing Tenperature

教 學 難 點　Cruxes of Teaching and Learning

一年四季	Seasons in the Year
描述天氣	Describing Weather
溫度	Temperature

詞 彙 表　Glossary

季節	Seasons
天氣	Weather
溫度	Temperature

教學重點

Content of Teaching and Learning

季節 Seasons

四季 sìjì four seasons

Yì nián yǒu sì ge jìjié
一 年 有 四 個 季節。
In some places, there are four seasons in a year.

春季（春天）	chūnjì	spring, springtime
夏季（夏天）	xiàjì	summer
秋季（秋天）	qiūjì	fall, autumn
冬季（冬天）	dōngjì	winter

Yì nián zhǐyǒu liǎng jì
一 年 只有 兩 季。
In other places, there are only two seasons in a year.

旱季	hànjì	dry season
雨季	yǔjì	rainy season

季節變化 Changing Seasons

1）表季節或時間的變化在句末用"了"。請參看第 13 章關於"了"的用法部分。

To indicate the time/season changes, we use "了" at the end of the sentence. For more details on use of "le" and "le" indicating change, please refer to "When/How to use '了'" in Chapter 13.

Dōngtiān guòqu le chūntiān dàolái le
冬天 過去 了，春天 到來 了。
Winter passes, spring arrives.

Shù lǜ le huā kāi le xiǎocǎo zhǎng chulai le
樹 綠了，花 開 了，小草 長 出來 了。
Trees are turning green, flowers are blossoming, and the grass is growing.

2）表季節變化還可以用比較。請參看第 20 章：比較。

To indicate change, we may also use comparison. For more details on comparisons, please refer to the Chapter 20：Comparison.

Chūntiān tiānqì yì tiān bǐ yì tiān nuǎnhuo le
春天　　　天气　一　天　比一　天　暖和　了。
In spring, the weather gets warmer day by day.

Jīnnián dōngtiān méiyǒu qùnián nàme lěng
今年　　　冬天　　没有　去年　那么　冷。
This winter is not as cold as last year.

Zhījiāgē de dōngtiān gēn Běijīng chàbuduō yíyàng
芝加哥　的　冬天　　跟　北京　　差不多　一样。
The winter in Chicago is almost the same as that in Beijing.

3）表季节的时间长短，还可以用时间段。请参看第一章：时间。

To indicate duration of a season, we may use time duration. For more details on time duration, please refer to Chapter 1：Time.

Zhījiāgē de chūntiān hěn duǎn shì cóng sān yuè dào wǔ yuè
芝加哥　的　春天　　很　短，是　从　三　月　到　五　月，
zhǐyǒu liǎng ge yuè
只有　两个月。
In Chicago, spring is short. It lasts from March to May, only for two months.

天气　tiānqì　Weather

描述天气　Describing Weather

句型　Sentence Patterns：

1）又……又……　not only... but also...

Chūntiān chángcháng yòu guā fēng yòu xià yǔ
春天　　　常常　　又刮风又下雨。
It is windy and also rainy in spring.

2）不……不……　neither... nor...

Qiūtiān bù lěng yě bú rè
秋天　不冷也不热。
It is not cold nor hot in the fall.

3）有时候……有时候……　sometimes... sometimes...

Dōngtiān yǒu shíhou guā dà fēng yǒu shíhou xià dà xuě
冬天　　有时候刮大风，有时候下大雪。

In winter, sometimes it has strong wind, sometimes it has heavy snow.

兩個不同的中文句子表達同一個英文的意思：

There are two ways to say the same thing:

A. 有（颱）　　noun

Jīntiān yǒu（guā）dà fēng

今天　有（颱）大　風　。

It has strong wind today. (It is very windy today.)

B. verb　得　怎麼樣（adjective）

Jīntiān guā fēng guā de hěn dà

今天　颱　風　颳　得　很　大　。

Today's wind is blowing hard. (It is very windy today.)

問句　Question

問天氣情況

The typical way to inquire about weather is by using "怎麼樣".

Zuìjìn de tiānqì zěnmeyàng

最近 的 天氣　怎麼樣　？

How has the weather been lately?

有關詞彙　Expressions to Describe Weather

1) 形容詞（Adjectives：）

冷	lěng	cold
熱	rè	hot
暖和	nuǎnhuo	nice and warm
涼快	liángkuai	pleasantly cool
潮濕	cháoshī	moist, damp
悶熱	mēnrè	hot and stuffy
晴	qíng	sunny, clear, fine
陰	yīn	cloudy
多雲	duōyún	partially cloudy

2) 名詞（Nouns：）

晴天	qíngtiān	fine day, clear weather

陰天	yīntiān	cloudy day, overcast sky

3）成語（Idioms, Set Phrases：）　理想的天氣 Ideal Weather

四季分明	sìjì fēnmíng	four seasons are distinct
四季如春	sìjì rú chūn	like spring all year round
冬暖夏凉	dōng nuǎn xià liáng	winter is warm and summer is cool
天高氣爽	tiān gāo qì shuǎng	high sky and refreshing air of autumn

北京的四季　Four Seasons in Beijing：

Běijīng yì nián sìjì fēnmíng
北京 一 年 四季 分明 。
Beijing has four distinctive seasons.

Chūntiān tiānqì nuǎnhuo
春天　　天氣　暖和 。
The weather in spring is warm.

Xiàtiān yòu mēn yòu rè
夏天　又 悶 又 熱 。
Summer is hot and suffocating.

Qiūtiān liángkuai tiān gāo qì shuǎng bù lěng yě bú rè
秋天　　凉快 ，天 高 氣 爽　不 冷 也 不 熱 。
Fall is cool. The sky is high and the air is fresh. It is neither too hot nor too cold.

Dōngtiān lěng yǒu shíhòu guā dàfēng yǒu shíhòu xià dàxuě
冬天　　冷 ，有 時候 颳 大風 ，有 時候 下 大雪 。
Winter is cold. Sometimes, it is windy, sometimes, it is snowy.

天氣預報　tiānqì yùbào　Weather Report, Weather Forecast

What do we have today? Actions：

下	xià	(of rain, snow, etc.) fall
下雨	xià yǔ	rain
大雨	dàyǔ	heavy rain
小雨	xiǎoyǔ	light rain
毛毛雨	máomaoyǔ	drizzle
暴雨	bàoyǔ	rainstorm
暴風雨	bàofēngyǔ	storm

下雪	xià xuě	snow
	大雪	dàxuě	heavy snow
	小雪	xiǎoxuě	light snow
	暴風雪	bàofēngxuě	snowstorm，blizzard
	雨夾雪	yǔjiāxuě	sleet
下霧	xià wù	mist，fog
下霜	xià shuāng	be covered with frost
下雹子	xià báozi	hailstone

颳	guā	（of the wind）blow
	颳風	guā fēng	（of the wind）blow
	大風	dàfēng	strong wind
	小風	xiǎofēng	light breeze，slight wind
	輕風	qīngfēng	light breeze
	臺風	táifēng	typhoon
	暴風	bàofēng	storm wind
	龍卷風	lóngjuǎnfēng	tornado

打	dǎ	strike，hit
	打雷	dǎ léi	thunder
閃	shǎn	lightning，flash
	閃電	shǎndiàn	lightning
出	chū	arise，emerge，appear
	出太陽	chū tàiyáng	sun comes out，sunshine
	出彩虹	chū cǎihóng	rainbow appears

温度　Temperature

温度的度量用"度"。美國用華氏，中國用攝氏。

描述溫度　Describing Temperature

Measurement of Temperature：

Temperature is measured using "度 dù degree".

Two systems of measuring temperature are in use：

    a. 攝氏　shèshì　Celsius or centigrade

    b. 華氏　huáshì　Fahrenheit

The U. S uses Fahrenheit to measure the temperature. China uses Celsius.

Description of Temperature：

The description of temperature is "高 gāo high" or "低 dī low".

    temperature is high or low：

        溫度高　　溫度低

    high or low temperature：

        高溫　　　低溫

有關詞彙　Related Expressions

氣溫	qìwēn	atmospheric temperature，air temperature
體溫	tǐwēn	body temperature
室溫	shìwēn	indoor temperature，room temperature
攝氏	shèshì	Celsius，Centigrade
華氏	huáshì	Fahrenheit
度	dù	degree（are in temperature，angle，latitude）
最高氣溫	zuì gāo qìwēn	highest air temperature
最低氣溫	zuì dī qìwēn	lowest air temperature
平均溫度	píngjūn wēndù	average temperature
零上	língshàng	above zero（temperature）
零下	língxià	below zero（temperature）
零下 30 度	língxià dù	30 degrees below zero

教學難點

Cruxes of Teaching and Learning

難點一　一年四季 Seasons in the Year

英文說"spring 2006"。中文說"2006 年春天"。

中文的季節表達有兩點要強調：

1）中文的時間表達總是從大概念到小概念。

2）季節總是與當年的時間概念聯繫在一起。

In English, we say "spring 2006."

In Chinese, we say "2006 年春天". As with any time expressions, the broader concept goes before the smaller one. A year is longer than a season, therefore all seasons fall into a year's time frame.

This year's seasons	**Last year's seasons**
jīnnián chūntiān 今年　　春天	qùnián chūntiān 去年　　春天
jīnnián xiàtiān 今年　　夏天	qùnián xiàtiān 去年　　夏天
jīnnián qiūtian 今年　　秋天	qùnián qiūtian 去年　　秋天
jīnnián dōngtiān 今年　　冬天	qùnián dōngtiān 去年　　冬天

難點二　描述天氣 Describing Weather

請注意中英文的表達的不同：

In English, we say "It is windy/rainy today".

In Chinese, there is no literal translation. We use two patterns to say the same thing.

Jīntiān yǒu guā dà fēng
今天　有／颳大　風。
There is (blows) a strong wind today. (It is very windy today.) or

Jīntiān de fēng guā fēng guā de hěn dà
今天（的　風）颳　風　颳　得　很　大。
Today's wind is blowing hard. (It is very windy today.)

Also, in English, we say, "It is sunny today".

In Chinese, we may express the same idea in two ways:

Jīntiān hěn qíng
(Description)　　今天　很　晴。　　It is clear today.

Jīntiān shì qíngtiān
(Identification)　　今天　是　晴天。　Today is a clear day.

難點三　溫度 Temperature

請注意中英文的表達的不同：

There are three aspects relating to describing temperature that need to be stressed.

1) Since there are two systems of measuring temperature, with the U. S. using Fahrenheit and China using celsius, it is important for the learners to be aware of the difference.

Two systems of temperatures are

攝氏	shèshì	Celsius, centigrade
華氏	huáshì	Fahrenheit

2) There are three types of commonly used temperatures:

氣溫	qìwēn	atmospheric temperature, air temperature
體溫	tǐwēn	body temperature
室溫	shìwēn	indoor temperature, room temperature

3) Reading "below zero" in Chinese:

零上	língshàng	above zero (temperature)
零下	língxià	below zero (temperature)

In English, you say:　　　　30 below zero

                                        líng xià sānshí dù
In Chinese, we say：　　　　　零　下　30　度

你知道以下的常識嗎？ Did you know?

正常室温　zhèngcháng shìwēn　　normal indoor temperature（room tempera-
　　　　　　　　　　　　　　　　　　ture）

The normal/comfortable air temperature and room temperature is：

攝氏 20 到 22 度　　　　　　　20 to 22 degrees Celsius/centigrade

華氏 68 到 72 度　　　　　　　68 to 72 degrees Fahrenheit

正常體温　zhèngcháng tǐwēn　normal body temperature

The normal body temperature is：

攝氏 36.6 度　　　　　　　　36.6 degrees Celsius/centigrade

華氏 96 度　　　　　　　　　96 degrees Fahrenheit

And at one point，－40 degrees，Fahrenheit and Celsius are the same.

攝氏零下 40 度　　　　　　　40 below zero degrees centigrade

華氏零下 40 度　　　　　　　40 below zero degrees Fahrenheit

24

健康/身體/看病

Health/Body/
See a Doctor

談到健康就難免涉及目前的狀況和過去的經歷。這節列出所需的句型和詞彙讓兩者順理成章，教學的重點以詞彙開始以便利與其他話題的靈活組合。

When speaking about health and sickness, we cannot avoid talking about the present situation and past experiences. This chapter aims to relate the present situation with the past by supplying sentence structures and vocabularies for health, the body and seeing a doctor. The content of teaching and learning begins with vocabulary easily combined with other possible thematic unit designs.

教 學 重 點　Content of Teaching and Learning

身體部位	Body Parts
症狀	Symptoms
去醫院	Going to Hospital
談經歷	Discussing Past Experience

教 學 難 點　Cruxes of Teaching and Learning

"過" vs. "了"	
動量詞 "次"	Measure Word for Action— "次"
看病	Seeing a Doctor
"大夫" vs. "醫生"	How to Refer to a Doctor?

詞 彙 表　Glossary

身體部位	Body Parts
與得病有關的說法	Expressions Related to Illness
常見病名表	Names of Common Illnesses
常見病症	Common Symptoms
看病相關用語	Expressions Related to Hospital

教學重點

Content of Teaching and Learning

身體部位　Body Parts

頭部	tóubù	head	
頭	tóu	head	
臉	liǎn	face，front（part）	
眼睛	yǎnjing	eye	
眉毛	méimao	eyebrow	
鼻子	bízi	nose	
耳朵	ěrduo	ear	
嘴	zuǐ	mouth	
牙	yá	tooth	
舌頭	shétou	tongue	
下巴	xiàba	chin，lower jaw	
鬍子	húzi	beard，goatee，moustache	
頭髮	tóufa	hair（on human head）	
脖子	bózi	neck	
嗓子	sǎngzi	throat，larynx	
喉嚨	hóulóng	throat	

肢體	zhītǐ	four limbs，body	
胸	xiōng	chest	
後背	hòubèi	back（of the body，etc.）	
肩（膀）	jiān（bǎng）	shoulder	
胳膊	gēbo	arm	
肘	zhǒu	elbow	

手	shǒu	hand
手腕	shǒuwàn	wrist（of the hand）
手掌	shǒuzhǎng	palm（of the hand）
手指	shǒuzhǐ	finger
腰	yāo	waist
屁股	pìgu	butt，behind
腿	tuǐ	leg
大腿	dàtuǐ	thigh
小腿	xiǎotuǐ	lower leg，shin，shank
膝蓋	xīgài	knee
脚	jiǎo	foot
脚腕（踝）	jiǎowàn（huái）	ankle
脚趾	jiǎozhǐ	toe

臟器　zàngqì　internal organs

心	xīn	heart
肺	fèi	lung
肝	gān	liver
胃	wèi	stomach
腎	shèn	kidney
脾	pí	spleen

症狀　Symptoms

相關詞彙　Expressions related to illness

病 bìng　　　ill，illness，sickness，disease

become ill：

有病(yǒu bìng)／生病(shēng bìng)／得病(dé bìng)

serious illness：

重病（zhòng bìng）／大病（dà bìng）

seriously ill：

病得重（zhòng）／病得屬害（lìhai）

minor illness：

小病（xiǎo bìng）

not seriously ill

病得輕（qīng）

see a doctor

看病　kàn bìng　see a doctor

去醫院看病/去大夫那兒看病

病名　Names of Illnesses

感冒	gǎnmào	cold, common cold, flu
心臟病	xīnzàngbìng	heart disease
肺炎	fèiyán	pneumonia
肝炎	gānyán	hepatitis
腎炎	shènyán	nephritis
過敏	guòmǐn	allergy, hypersensitive
高血壓	gāoxuèyā	high blood pressure, hypertension
低血壓	dīxuèyā	low blood pressure

病症　bìngzhèng　Symptoms of Illness

發燒	fāshāo	have a fever, run a temperature
咳嗽	késou	cough
流鼻涕	liú bítì	have a running nose
打噴嚏	dǎ pēntì	sneeze
拉肚子	lā dùzi	have diarrhoea
癢	yǎng	itch
難受	nánshòu	feel ill
不舒服	bù shūfu	uncomfortable, not feeling well, ill
疼	téng	ache, pain

頭疼	tóu téng	headache
牙疼	yá téng	toothache
腿疼	tuǐ téng	pain in the leg
腰疼	yāo téng	backache, lumbago
嗓子疼	sǎngzi téng	sour throat
肚子疼	dùzi téng	abdomen pain

去醫院　Going to Hospital

地點　Places

醫院	yīyuàn	hospital
診所	zhěnsuǒ	clinic
醫務室	yīwùshì	medical clinic
藥房	yàofáng	drugstore, pharmacy

醫務人員　Medical Personnel

大夫	dàifu	doctor, physican
醫生	yīshēng	doctor, physician
護士	hùshi	nurse（in a hospital）
藥劑師	yàojìshī	pharmacist

檢查　Physical Examination

檢查	jiǎnchá	inspect, check, examine
體檢	tǐjiǎn	physical examination
量	liáng	measure
體温	tǐwēn	body temperature
身高	shēngāo	height（of a person）
體重	tǐzhòng	body weight
血壓	xuèyā	blood pressure
化驗	huàyàn	laboratory test
大便	dàbiàn	stool, feces

	小便	xiǎobiàn	urine
	血	xiě	blood
照 X 光		zhào X-guāng	take an X-ray
透視		tòushì	have an X-ray taken

開藥　Prescribing Medicine

吃藥		chī yào	take medicine
	西藥	xīyào	Western medicine
	中藥	zhōngyào	traditional Chinese medicine
	藥片	yàopiàn	pill
	藥水	yàoshuǐ	liquid medicine
打針		dǎ zhēn	give or receive an injection
藥方		yàofāng	prescription

服藥　fúyào　Taking Medicine

飯前	fàn qián	before meals
飯後	fàn hòu	after meals
睡前	shuì qián	before sleep
服用	fúyòng	take（medicine）

用法　yòngfǎ　Way of Using，Usage

每天三次	three times per day，or
一天三次	three times per day
每次三片	three tablets per dose，or
一次一片	one tablet per dose

談經歷　Discussing Past Expereince

句型　Sentence Pattern：

Verb	過（動量補語）	Object

Wǒ   chī   guo liǎng cì   Zhōngguócài
我   吃   過   兩   次   中國菜   。

Wǒ céngjīng chī   guo liǎng cì   Zhōngguócài
我   曾經   吃   過   兩   次   中國菜   。

I have had Chinese food twice before.

功能　Function：

Discussing about past experience.　　談經歷。

提問　Questions：

Experience

Nǐ   chī   guo   Zhōngguócài ma
你   吃   過   中國菜   嗎?

Have you ever had Chinese food?

Frequency

Nǐ   chī   guo jǐ cì
你   吃   過 幾 次?

How many times have you had Chinese food?

Conditions

Nǐ shì shénme shíhou chī de
你 是 什麼 時候 吃 的?

When did you have it?

Nǐ shì zài shénme dìfang chī de
你 是 在 什麼 地方 吃 的?

Where did you have it?

Nǐ shì zěnme qù de
你 是 怎麼 去 的?

How did you go there?

(See 教學難點 for more detailed explanations)

教學難點

Cruxes of Teaching and Learning

難點一 "過" vs. "了"

"過" 和 "了" 所指不同。"過" 強調過去經歷，"了" 強調特定事件的一次性完成。

"過" and "了" both can be put after a verb. "過" emphasizes the action as a past experience, while "了" indicates the completeness of a one-time occurrence.

我去過中國城，我吃過中國菜。(as a past experience)
I have been to Chinatown and I have had Chinese Food.

昨天我去了芝加哥的中國城，我吃了中國菜。(as a one-time action)
Yesterday I went to Chicago's Chinatown and I had some Chinese food.

難點二 動量詞 "次" Measure Word for Action "次"

"次" 是最常用的動量詞。見以下動量詞表。

"次" is the most commonly used measure word for actions. There are others. See below to examine the subtle differences.

常用動量詞使用比較表 Commonly Used Measure Words for Actions

遍 biàn   emphasizes the process from beginning to end

這本書，我看了兩遍。
I have read this book twice.

請你一個字寫五遍。
Please write each character five times.

次 cì   emphasizes the number of occurrences

這本書我看了五次才看完一遍。
I started this book five times before I finished the whole thing.

請你一次寫五遍。
Every time you write, please write five times.

回 huí   similar to "次", but used informally

這個電影我看了五回。
I have seen this movie five times.

趟　tàng　　emphasizes back and forth（of a round trip）

昨天他去了一趟圖書館。
Yesterday, he went（took a trip）to the library.

下　xià　　emphasizes briefness of an action

請給她看一下。
Let her have a look.

Note

"一下" vs. Duplication of Verbs：

"一下" when suggesting briefness of action, is equivalent to duplication of verbs：

Have a look/had a look $\begin{cases} 看一下 & 看一看 & 看看 \\ 看了一下 & 看了一看 & 看了看 \end{cases}$

動量詞在句中的位置　Position in a Sentence

動量詞在句中的位置有點複雜。見下例。

Where to place a measure word for action in a sentence is a little complicated. If the object of the action is a place/person, the position is more flexible：

（Place）我們去過兩次北京。

　　　　　我們去過北京兩次。

（Person）我們見過兩次這個人。

　　　　　我們見過這個人兩次。

If the object of the action is a thing, it can only be put before the object：

（Thing）我們吃過兩次中國菜。

難點三　看病 seeing a Doctor

英文説"go to see a doctor"，中文説"看病"。意思是説讓醫生看看你有什麼病。

In English, we say "see a doctor".

In Chinese, we say "看病", meaning that one wants the doctor to examine the possible heacth problem one has.

去醫院看病／去大夫那兒看病

難點四　"大夫" vs. "醫生" How to Refer to a Doctor?

　　怎麼稱呼？叫"大夫"還是"醫生"？這不是學生的問題，是老師的個人選擇。

　　總的來說，北方人用"大夫"，南方人稱"醫生"。或說"大夫"是口語，"醫生"是正式稱呼。

　　"大夫"的發音是"dàifu a doctor"。

This is not a difficult point for learners. It is a teacher's preference.

Generally speaking, people from northern part of China call a doctor "大夫", while people from south China call a doctor "醫生". Since the Common Speech "普通話" that we teach is based on the pronunciation of northern dialects, we generalize that "大夫" is a colloquial expression and "醫生" is a formal title. Also, the pronunciation of "大夫" is "dàifu a doctor".

Index
索引

Phonetic Chart

漢語語音表
（與 bopomofo 對照）

Group One Finals

	a	o	e	er	-i	ai	an	ang	ao	ei	en	eng	ong
b	ba	bo				bai	ban	bang	bao	bei	ben	beng	
p	pa	po				pai	pan	pang	pao	pei	pen	peng	
m	ma		me			mai	man	mang	mao	mei	men	meng	
f	fa						fan	fang		fei	fen	feng	
d	da		de			dai	dan	dang	dao	dei		deng	dong
t	ta		te			tai	tan	tang	tao			teng	tong
n	na		ne			nai	nan	nang	nao	nei	nen	neng	nong
l	la		le			lai	lan	lang	lao	lei		leng	long
g	ga		ge			gai	gan	gang	gao	gei	gen	geng	gong
k	ka		ke			kai	kan	kang	kao		ken	keng	kong
h	ha		he			hai	han	hang	hao	hei	hen	heng	hong
j													
q													
x													
zh	zha				zhi	zhai	zhan	zhang	zhao	zhei	zhen	zheng	zhong
ch	cha				chi	chai	chan	chang	chao		chen	cheng	chong
sh	sha				shi	shai	shan	shang	shao	shei	shen	sheng	
r					ri		ran	rang	rao		ren	reng	rong
z	za				zi	zai	zan	zang	zao	zei	zen	zeng	zong
c	ca				ci	cai	can	cang	cao		cen	ceng	cong
s	sa				si	sai	san	sang	sao		sen	seng	song
	a	o	e	er		ai	an	ang	ao	ei	en	eng	ong

Group Two Finals："i" and "i" Sounds

	i	ia	ian	iang	iao	ie	in	ing	iong	iou
b	bi		bian		biao	bie	bin	bing		
p	pi		pian		piao		pin	ping		
m	mi		mian		miao		min	ming		
f										
d	di		dian							
t	ti		tian							
n	ni		nian							
l	li		lian							
g										
k										
h										
j	ji	jia	jian	jiang	jiao	jie	jin	jing	jiong	jiu
q	qi	qia	qian	qiang	qiao	qie	qin	qing	qiong	qiu
x	xi	xia	xian	xiang	xiao	xie	xin	xing	xiong	xiu
zh										
ch										
sh										
r										
z										
c										
s										
	yi	ya	yan	yang	yao	ye	yin	ying	yong	you

Group Three Finals："u" and "u" Sounds

	u	ua	uai	uan	uang	uei	uen	ueng	uo	uong
b	bu									

p	pu									
m	mu									
f	fu									
d	du			duan		dui	dun		duo	
t	tu			tuan		tui	tun		tuo	
n	nu			nuan					nuo	
l	lu			luan			lun		luo	
g	gu	gua	guai	guan	guang	gui	gun		guo	
k	ku	kua	kuai	kuan	kuang	kui	kun		kuo	
h	hu	hua	huai	huan	huang	hui	hun		huo	
j										
q										
x										
zh	zhu	zhua	zhuai	zhuan	zhuang	zhui	zhun		zhuo	
ch	chu		chuai	chuan	chuang	chui	chun		chuo	
sh	shu	shua	shuai	shuan	shuang	shui	shun		shuo	
r	ru			ruan		rui	run		ruo	
z	zu			zuan		zui	zun		zuo	
c	cu			chuan		cui	cun		cuo	
s	su			suan		sui	sun		suo	
	wu	wa	wai	wan	wang	wei	wen	weng	wo	wong

Group Four Finals："ü" and "ü" Sounds

		ü	üe	üan	üen
	b				
	p				
	m				
	f				

	d				
	t				
	n	nü	nüe		
	l	lü	lüe		
	g				
	k				
	h				
	j	ju	jue	juan	jun
	q	qu	que	quan	qun
	x	xu	xue	xuan	xun
	zh				
	ch				
	sh				
	r				
	z				
	c				
	s				
		yu	yue	yuan	yun

Reference
建議參考資料

This series focuses on concrete examples and practical tips for classroom teaching and learning. For teachers who are interested in current research, theoretical frameworks and further guidance and tools, we provide a topical list of references.

　　這套書主要是爲初高中學漢語課堂教與學提供操作實例和具體技巧。都是經驗之談。對相關教學研究、教學理論或綱要及工具有興趣的老師,可參閱下列書目和網址。參考資料也是按題目排列的。

Adolescent Psychology

Rice, F. Philip. *The Adolescent — Development, Relationships, and Culture.* Needham Height, MA: Allyn & Bacon, 1999.

Assessment and Rubric

Bachman, L. F. & A. S. Palmer. *Language Testing in Practice.* Oxford: Oxford University Press, 1996.

Pearson Education Development Group. *Authentic Assessment Overview.* Retrieved from http://teachervision. fen. com/teaching-methods/educational-testing/4911. html

Chicago Public Schools. *The Rubric Bank.* Retrieved from http://www. cps. k12. il. us

The Web Portal for Educators! At http://www. teach-nology. com

Oral Language Assessment — *Oral Proficiency Interview (OPI)* and Written Language Assessment — *Written Proficiency Test (WPT).* Retrieved from http://www. languagetesting. com

Hancock, Charles R. *Alternative Assessment and Second Language.* ERIC Clearinghouse on Languages and Linguistics Washington D. C. , 1994.

Baker, E. L. , O'Neill, H. F. , Jr. , & Linn, R. L. (1993). Policy and validity prospects for performance-based assessments. *American Psychologist, 48,* 1210 – 1218.

U. S. Congress, Office of Technology Assessment. (1992, February). *Testing in American schools: Asking the right questions.* (OTA-SET-519). Washington, D. C. : U. S. Government Printing Office.

Bloom's Taxonomy

Bloom, Benjamin S. *Taxonomy of Educational Objectives.* Boston MA: Allyn & Bacon, 1984.

Differentiated Instruction

Tomlinson, C. *How to Differentiate Instruction in Mixed-ability Classrooms.* Alexandria, VA: ASCD, 1995.

Tomlinson, C. *The Differentiated Classroom: Responding to the Needs of All Learners.* Alexandria, VA: ASCD, 1999.

Wiggins, G. & McTighe, J. *Understanding by Design.* Alexandria, VA: ASCD, 1998.

Chinese Grammar

黎錦熙,劉世儒.《漢語語法十八課》.北京:商務印書館,1964.
李德津,程美珍.《外國人實用漢語語法》.北京:華語教學出版社,1988.

Cooperative Learning

Silver , Strong, & Perini. *So Each May Learn, Alexandria.* VA: Association for Supervision and Curriculum Development, 2000.

David & Roger Johnson. *Learning Together and Alone.* NJ: Prentice Hall, 1999.

Foreign Language Teaching and Learning Standards

ACTFL Foreign Language Learning Standards. Retrieved from http://www.actfl.org

ACTFL Performance Guidelines for K-12 Learners. Yonkers, NY: The American Council on the Teaching of Foreign Languages, 1998.

Language Learning

Curtain, H. & Carol Ann Dahlberg. *Language and Children — Making the Match.* Boston: Pearson Education, Inc., 2004.

Learning

Sousa, David A. *How the Brain Learns.* NASSP, VA: Corwin Press, 2000.

Multiple Intelligences

Gardner, Howard. *Frames of Mind: The Theory of Multiple Intelligences.* New York: Basic, 1983.

Gardner, Howard. *Multiple Intelligences: The Theory in Practice.* New York: Basic, 1993.

Gardner, Howard. *Intelligence Reframed: Multiple Intelligences for the 21st Century.* New York: Basic, 2000

Armstrong, Thomas. *Multiple Intelligences in the Classroom.* Alexandria, VA: Association for Supervision and Curriculum Development, 1994.

Problem Solving

Stanovich, Keith E. *Progress in Understanding Reading: Scientific Foundations and New Frontiers.* New York: Gilford Press, 2000.

Woll, Stanley. *Everyday Thinking: Memory, Reasoning, and Judgment in the*

Real World. Mahwah NJ: Lawrence Erlbaum Associates, Inc. , 2001.

Reading

Koda, Keiko Koda. *Insights into Second Language Reading.* Cambridge: Cambridge University Press, 2005.

Alderson, C. *Assessing Reading.* New York: Cambridge University Press, 2000.

Day, R. R. & Bamford, J. *Extensive Reading in the Second Language Classroom.* New York: Cambridge University Press, 1998.

Grabe, W. & Stoller, F. *Teaching and Researching Reading: Applied Linguistics in Action.* New York: Longman, 2002.

Pressley, M. *Reading Instruction that Works.* New York: Guilford, 1998.

Reading Critically. Reading Guide. Retrieved from http:// writing. colostate. edu/guides/reading/critread/pop4b. cfm

Student-Centered Learning

Aaronsohn, Elizabeth. *Going Against the Grain: Supporting the Student-Centered Teacher.* Thousand Oaks: Corwin Press. 1996.

Benson, P. & Voller, P. *Autonomy and Independence in Language Learning.* London: Longman, 1996.

Tudor, I. *Learner-Centeredness as Language Education.* Cambridge: Cambridge University Press, 1996.

Task-based Learning

Krashen, S. D. *Principles and Practices in Second Language Acquisition.* New York: Prentice Hall, 1987.

Willis, J. A *Framework for Tasked-Based Learning.* London: Longman, 1996.

Thematic Instruction

Bruning, R. H. , Schraw, G. J. , & Ronning, R. R. *Cognitive Psychology and Instruction.* Englewood Cliffs, NJ: Merrill, 1999.

Vogt, M. (1997). *Cross-Curricular Thematic Instruction.* Retrieved from http://www. eduplace. com/rdg/res/vogt. html

National Standards in Foreign Language Education Project. (1996). Retrieved from http://www. actfl. org

TPR

Seely & Elizabeth Kuizenga Romijn. *TPR is More Than Commands — At All Levels.* Berkeley California, 1995.

US Department of Education — Teacher to Teacher Initiative Workshops on Chinese Language Teaching. (2006). Retrieved from http://www. t2tweb. us/ Workshops/Sessions. asp

Bibliography

参考书目

ACTFL Foreign Language Learning Standards. Retrieved from http://www. act-fl. org

Bachman, L. F. & A. S. Palmer. *Language Testing in Practice.* Oxford: Oxford University Press, 1996.

Bloom, Benjamin S. *Taxonomy of Educational Objectives.* Boston MA: Allyn & Bacon, 1984.

Chicago Public Schools. *The Rubric Bank.* Retrieved from http://www. cps. k12. il. us

Curtain, H. & Carol Ann Dahlberg. *Language and Children — Making the Match.* Boston: Pearson Education, Inc. , 2004.

Krashen, S. D. *Principles and Practices in Second Language Acquisition.* New York: Prentice Hall, 1987.

黎錦熙,劉世儒.《漢語語法十八課》.北京:商務印書館;1964.

Rice, F. Philip. *The Adolescent — Development, Relationships, and Culture.* Needham Height, MA: Allyn & Bacon, 1999.

Silver , Strong, & Perini. *So Each May Learn.* Alexandria, VA: Association for Supervision and Curriculum Development, 2000.

The Web Portal for Educators! At http://www. teach-nology. com

US Department of Education — Teacher to Teacher Initiative Workshops on Chinese Language Teaching. (2006). Retrieved from http://www. t2tweb. us/ Workshops/Sessions. asp